About the Authors

David Craig has worked for and competed against some of the world's best and worst management and IT systems consultancies over the past twenty years. He has sold consulting to almost 100 organizations in fifteen countries across Europe, Asia and the US, as well as the British public sector. He is the author of the controversial bestseller *Rip-Off! The Scandalous Inside Story of the Management Consulting Money Machine* and four other books about management and organizations. He has an MA from Cambridge and an MBA from Warwick Business School.

Richard Brooks was a tax inspector for 16 years before becoming a journalist. He writes for *Private Eye* on a range of topics including the Private Finance Initiative, financial services, tax dodging, consultants and public-sector issues such as health and education.

PLUNDERING
THE PUBLIC SECTOR

How New Labour are letting consultants
run off with £70 billion of our money

David Craig

with Richard Brooks of *Private Eye*

Constable
LONDON

Constable & Robinson Ltd
3 The Lanchesters
162 Fulham Palace Road
London W6 9ER
www.constablerobinson.com

First published in the UK by Constable,
an imprint of Constable & Robinson Ltd 2006

A copy of the British Library Cataloguing in
Publication Data is available from the British Library

ISBN-13: 978-1-84529-374-1
ISBN-10: 1-84529-374-6

Printed and bound in the EU

4 6 8 10 9 7 5 3

Why worry?

- Blair's and Brown's New Labour are spending about £70bn of our money on consultants as part of their grand plan to 'modernize' public services

- New Labour have sidelined the Old Labour Party and the Civil Service so that most policy is now made and implemented by cash-hungry consultants

- The results so far have been disastrous – billions taken out of front-line services to be wasted on worthless consulting and failing IT systems

- Already we see administrative chaos, massive increases in management costs and reduced help for the needy as public spending and taxes shoot ever upwards

- The worst effects are in the NHS, with hospitals closing wards, making redundancies, cancelling operations and denying patients life-saving medicine due to budget cuts

- Meanwhile, the government is paying around £30bn for a new NHS IT system that is already showing all the symptoms of becoming a catastrophic failure

- If the £30bn NHS system ends up like all the other New Labour consulting disasters, this will cripple patient care for years to come

- New Labour have betrayed the electorate by handing power to unelected profit-maximizing consultancies

- We need to act now to prevent this massive plundering of taxpayers' money and the decimation of our public services

Contents

CHAPTER 1

The Government Goes Consulting Crazy

The £70 Billion Spending Spree

British companies have always been keen consumers of consultancy. They spend over £25m every working day, £125m a week, over £6bn a year for management consultants' advice – much more than any of their European competitors. In addition, they pay many billions more for IT systems consulting. And now the government appears to have caught the consulting bug. The reason New Labour have been hiring so many consultants has ostensibly been to improve public services through the injection of competition and private-sector managerial skills, and through the use of modern IT systems. This policy stems from the 1999 Government White Paper 'Modernising Government' which 'placed IT at the centre of its programme for the renewal and reform of public services'.[1]

When the Labour Party were in opposition, they lambasted the ruling Conservative government for spending up to £500m a year on management and IT systems consultants. This was, they thundered, a disgraceful waste of taxpayers' money – money that should be spent on front-line services like hospitals and schools rather than being handed over to a few already wealthy consultants.

Now New Labour are in power, they seem to have changed their minds. Blair's and Brown's New Labour will not be spending a mere £500m a year on consultants – they have much more ambitious plans than that. The government have evidently become tired of those who do not share their blue-skies thinking vision for Britain. So, in their grand plan to modernize the delivery of public services, they seem to have sidelined the Labour Party and the Civil Service and have decided to both make their new policies and implement them using their favourite management and IT systems consultants. This is turning out to be an expensive exercise that will cost us, the taxpayers, well over £70bn – more than £20bn for management consultants and at least another £50bn for IT systems consultants.

The vast amounts of taxpayers' money being handed over to consultants could be seen as evidence of a dynamic, forward-looking government investing in modernizing their country. At least, it would be positive were these massive investments successful. However, experience to date is less than promising. Judging by what has happened over the last few years, New Labour's investments in management and systems consulting appear to have just been a series of unmitigated and shameful disasters. So bad was the situation, that in July 2004 an all-party committee of MPs criticized the British government for both wasting taxpayers' money and trying to cover up the truth about its financial mismanagement. The committee concluded that the British government's record on IT consulting projects was 'an appalling waste of public money which Whitehall was trying to conceal behind a cloak of commercial confidentiality'.[2]

In its first term in office, Tony Blair's New Labour tried hard, but apparently unsuccessfully, to reform public services. After several years of fighting the vested interests of powerful groups like teachers, doctors and civil servants, an exasperated Blair talked of the scars on his back from his efforts to reform the seemingly unreformable. In its second term in office, New Labour was so busy helping George Bush try to start the Third World War that it had little energy to either fight with public-sector workers or to push an apparently recalcitrant Civil Service into anything resembling action. So, with neither the time nor the patience to listen to the naysayers within the old Labour Party, the Civil Service and the public sector, the government increasingly moved towards developing and implementing its reform agenda by throwing many tens of billions of pounds of our money at management and IT systems consultants. In his party's third term in office, Blair has pledged to be more radical in reforming the delivery of public services and the amounts of taxpayers' money heading towards the consultants' pockets is going to be quite incredible. In a consultancy journal article published just before the 2005 General Election, a leading management consultant advised his fellow consultants to vote with their wallets and vote for Labour because 'in government Labour have been reasonably consultant-friendly, with spending on consultants having risen from £217m to £1.3bn since 1997.'[3] The writer also warned of the dangers to consultants if the opposition Conservative Party came to power as 'they plan to spend £500m less on consultancy.' Other consultants have written about the 'feast of work from Whitehall', the huge growth in their public-sector practices, a consultants' 'recruitment frenzy' and the mouthwatering increases in their billing levels and profitability. Many consultancies are now complaining that they have so much work from the public sector that they can't hire sufficient staff quickly enough to meet the explosion in demand. In Britain, there is a veritable consulting gold-rush and all the main consultancies are posting almost embarrassing increases in profits.

Due to the government's repeated refusal to disclose how much it is giving to consultants, it is difficult to accurately calculate the total amount. But the few figures that are available give some idea of the vast scale of New Labour's spending spree with our money. Just between 2003 and 2004 for example, public-sector spending on management consultants' advice increased massively – the Ministry of Defence (MoD) achieved an impressive 178 per cent rise from £83m to £148m. They were outclassed by the NHS's 340 per cent rise from £25m to £85m. But with a 460 per cent increase from £50m to £230m, local government seems be well in the lead.[4] The figures for 2005 are expected to show even greater increases and consultancies foresee 2006 as being one of their best years ever. Moreover, these figures only cover just over a half of the management consulting industry – many leading consultancies do not reveal how much they earn from government work. Between their election in 1997 and the end of 2005, New Labour will probably have spent over £10bn on management consultancy. If spending continues at the current rate, by the end of their third term in office, at least £10bn more should have gone the same way. New Labour's Private Finance Initiative (PFI) and Private–Public Partnership (PPP) programmes have also been good to consultants and should yield another £5bn to £10bn or so in consulting fees. In addition to the money spent by the public sector on management consultants' advice, they will spend at least £50bn on IT systems consulting. We've already had at least £15bn spent on new systems, though it may well be more as one report says that £12.4bn was spent in just one year 2003/4.[5] We've seen Benefits Cards (scrapped after about £698m was spent), magistrates' courts (more than £200m over budget and years behind schedule), GCHQ (£400m over the original £21m budget). In fact, there have been massive cost overruns and administrative chaos pretty much everywhere you look – the Immigration Service, Customs and Excise, the Passport Office, the Child Support Agency (CSA), the Department for Work and Pensions and the Inland Revenue. But this catastrophic squandering of our money has in no way diminished our government's appetite for throwing our cash at their consultants. In fact, if anything these hundreds of millions of pounds' cock-ups were merely a kind of hors d'oeuvre. The main course is just beginning and here the amounts of money are bordering on the mind-boggling. In addition to all the 'smaller' several-hundred-million-pound projects given by government departments to consultants, in 2003/4 the Inland Revenue signed a £4bn outsourcing deal with the French firm Capgemini and in 2004/5, the Ministry of Defence awarded a £4bn multi-year IT systems contract to Texan software giant EDS. Local councils are spending close to £3bn a year, the NHS may spend more than £30bn on the NPfIT (*National Programme for IT*) and the Identity Card system is expected to cost billions or even tens of billions – the latest figures suggest about £19bn.[6]

As British soldiers died in Iraq through lack of proper protective equipment, the Ministry of Defence has paid hundreds of millions to PricewaterhouseCoopers (PwC) and McKinsey for their words of wisdom about, among other things, how to improve the procurement and supply of military equipment. And while British patients suffer and die waiting for operations as hospitals reduce services due to budget constraints, just one tiny piece representing less than 1 per cent of the grand new IT system being implemented by the NHS ran more than £140m over its original £65m budget and still didn't work.

A Catalogue of Catastrophes

It seems as if every single government department has had at least one major (and more often several major) consulting disasters. Yet on the few occasions when the National Audit Office actually reports on a department's failures, the role of consultants is seldom, if ever, mentioned. Usually after each disaster, nobody is reprimanded and everybody nods their heads wisely and agrees that 'important lessons have been learnt'. Then the government and its civil servants are lured into paying tens of millions, or even hundreds of millions, for the next ambitious project which inevitably repeats all the mistakes of the past and ends up years late, hugely over budget, providing fewer services than were promised and vastly increasing administration and management costs. This pattern has repeated itself so often that here we'll just summarize three typical cases.

In 2000, as part of New Labour's e-government initiative, Customs and Excise launched a programme to provide e-services. By June 2004, the department had spent over £100m on its e-VAT service. According to the Public Accounts Committee (PAC), the introduction of an electronic VAT return in March 2000 was a failure because the new system was more complicated than the previous paper-based version. So, four years after its launch, less than 1 per cent of traders were using it – somewhat below the target of 50 per cent. The solution proposed by Customs and Excise was to force companies to complete the electronic form. However, the PAC suggested that the department would be more likely to hit its targets by offering a decent service that businesses wanted to use. The PAC also criticized the department for having failed to properly test e-services before roll-out. In addition, the Customs and Excise PFI with Fujitsu didn't seem to be totally under control as its costs almost doubled from £500m to £929m. The PAC also criticized Customs and Excise for its use of management consultants. The department apparently spent £28m on 300 consultants between November 2001 and March 2003, without any clearly identifiable results. Overall, the PAC didn't appear too impressed with Customs and Excise's managerial capabilities and apparent profligacy with our money as it slammed the department for spending 'huge sums of public money without being confident of the scale of the likely benefits'.[7]

Another highlight of the 'disaster spotting' season is the consulting bought mainly, I believe, from Deloitte and the system from EDS for the Child Support Agency (CSA). A top executive from EDS admitted that in the IT consulting business EDS had at times been affectionately known as running 'your mess for less'.[8] Though with the CSA, it seemed that EDS had excelled themselves and provided a much greater mess for an awful lot more. The £450m-plus system due to go live in October 2001 was finally switched on in March 2003. A year later, fewer than half the 320,000 applications received had been processed. Moreover, the Work and Pensions Secretary Andrew Smith admitted that the cost of processing applications was 20 per cent higher with the 'new improved' business processes and EDS IT system than it had been before.[9] As staff battled with the new system, the money continued to pour out. A report commissioned by the Department for Work and Pensions reported that staff 'described a system with many problems not suited to their job . . . Members of staff were very frustrated by the speed of the new system and felt embarrassed when callers were kept on hold while screens refreshed very slowly.'[10] Moreover, staff were having to use pocket calculators to work out what people were owed due to the failure of the system. A commentator wrote, 'the workflow system is not working in any of the Business Units. These problems and low morale meant every single day someone in their office would be crying (literally) through stress and frustration.'[11] Soon the desperate performance of the system had led to delays in setting up maintenance payments of twenty-two weeks, against an original target of six. 'Over half a million children from broken relationships continue to suffer. The woeful record of the CSA is a shameful indictment of the government's priorities,' lamented the chairman of a parliamentary committee that examined the agency.[12] Professor Steve Webb, Lib Dem shadow Work and Pensions spokesman said, 'it is scandalous that the government continues to fritter away huge sums of money trying to put the CSA's house in order. Under Labour the CSA has gone from bad to worse. We now have two different systems that don't work properly and thousands of lone parents missing out. Lone parents have been let down and left out of pocket. It is high time the CSA was scrapped.'[13] Although the CSA chief executive stood down, a leaked internal document from EDS showed where much of the responsibility lay when it described the IT system it had created as 'badly designed, badly delivered, badly tested and badly implemented'.[14]

There have been many other catastrophes – from tiddlers like a £30m system binned at just one Scottish hospital to some real monsters like the systems developed by Siemens for the Immigration and Nationality Department and the Passport Office which both came in extremely late and millions over budget. But one of the most noteworthy fiascos must be the system developed by EDS and now run by Capgemini for the Inland Revenue to pay tax credits to poor families. A policy that could not have been designed to be more administratively complex combined with inadequate software to produce unprecedented confusion and hardship for hundreds of thousands of the most vulnerable members of society. The policy itself, demanding repayments of tax credits in-year when claimants' incomes increase, was a recipe for disaster for people on relatively low incomes who tend to spend their money and have trouble meeting demands for repayments out of the blue. It was never going to be helped by a useless computer system.

The launch of tax credits in April 2003 was spectacular. The government had invited claims from millions of families with a catchy advertising campaign. 'It's money with your name on it,' beamed the commercials. Unfortunately, the scheme depended on an IT system which crashed repeatedly under the weight of claims that it should have been designed to withstand. Around six million families receive tax credits and of these it was estimated that there were serious mistakes in paying credits to approximately two million recipients. Hundreds of thousands went without credits that they had been receiving relatively painlessly under the previous system and which formed a crucial part of their incomes. Tax offices up and down the country were besieged by angry claimants, some of whom became threatening and one of whom, in desperation after three fruitless days on the phone, super-glued his hand to an Inland Revenue desk before getting his money.[15] In July 2003 a parliamentary committee report on the introduction of tax credits concluded that, 'as a result of delays, the Revenue have made nearly 200,000 emergency payments, but cannot at this stage say how many families these relate to. For over 400,000 applicants their first payment was on a later date than notified, and, in addition, hundreds of thousands of people received a payment before they received their award notice. According to the Revenue the main cause of the problems, which came as "a bolt out of the blue", is the IT system designed and implemented by EDS.'[16]

Although the idea of tax credits was to help Britain's poorest families, a badly designed policy and repeated systems failures led to hundreds of thousands of the already poor becoming even poorer. As a newspaper wrote, 'the charity Citizens Advice

Bureaux said poor administration and system failure had plunged many families into debt after recovery of overpaid tax credits left them with incomes as low as £56 a week.'[17] So bad was the situation that some families had to rely on charity food parcels. A report by the Parliamentary Ombudsman found that the system had caused 'considerable distress and hardship to many families' and 'the complaints coming to us reveal a wide variety of technical problems or "glitches" which, over the last two years, have affected a considerable number of customers. Indeed, it is difficult to do justice to the sheer range of problems which have affected customers' awards.'[18] *The Times* described the effect of this disaster on families: 'The human cost is terrible. The two reports tell of people who have been forced to stop work because they could not pay for their childcare, of people whose homes were repossessed because they could not meet their mortgage payments.'[19]

By the end of the first year of tax credits the wreckage was strewn everywhere: £2.2bn had been overpaid, much of it due to IT errors, while automated demands for millions of repayments caused misery. Some £123m was written off for the year with subsequent government accounts showing that nearer to a billion pounds would never be recovered.[20] The administrative overload that the various failures placed on the Revenue produced farcical results, such as the game of tax credit ping-pong played between many families and the Department. One family received an overpayment of £3,500 twice and twice they returned it. When the money came a third time even their honest patience reached its limit and they kept it. A few months later they received a demand for repayment of £4,900.[21]

The new tax credits fared little better in their second year. A further couple of billion was racked up in overpayments and the newly merged department responsible for the system, HM Revenue and Customs, was threatened with legal action by the Child Poverty Action Group for the manner in which it pursued them. Soon a dubious landmark was passed: 100 million calls to the tax credit helpline, more than half of which had gone unanswered.

The Prime Minister Tony Blair even had to apologize for the failure 'for those families caused hardship or distress'.[22] However, the sincerity of this unusual apology was rapidly undermined by the Inland Revenue's inflexible approach to recovery of overpayments. Moreover, the ministers responsible seemed disinclined to accept that they could possibly be at fault. A *Times* columnist wrote, 'The Chancellor has resisted repeated attempts by the Prime Minister to demote Ms Primarolo [then Paymaster General], who is clearly not up to her job. As well as being incompetent, she has also proved astonishingly complacent in the face of repeated complaints about the system.'[23] The newspaper also highlighted the fact that the failure of New Labour's consultancy projects can also have a moral dimension, 'If Mr. Brown is still shielding her from the sack, he should examine his conscience. Which does he care about most? The plight of the poor? Or the plight of a time-serving, over-promoted, inept ministerial supporter.'[24] Meanwhile, as thousands of families were plunged into awful financial difficulties, the government department responsible, the Inland Revenue, seemed completely oblivious to the chaos and suffering it was causing. A spokesman for the Revenue said, 'This is all historical. Capgemini is our supplier now and the system is up and running.'

By 2005, the system certainly was 'up and running' as the Inland Revenue claimed. This was much to the delight of fraudsters who took the government's advertisement 'it's money with your name on it' a tad too literally. Using the tax credits online service, groups of criminals obtained the details of up to 13,000 Jobcentre workers and up to 30,000 Network Rail staff and were able to claim and divert up to £100 per month per person usually by changing the number of children and the employment status of the person whose identity they had stolen. By the start of 2006, at least 80,000 cases of fraud had been identified, though this may only be a small proportion of those actually carried out. This led to the online service having to be closed down completely. At least £15m, but probably closer to £100m or maybe more, has been stolen in what may be one of the largest and easiest frauds ever perpetrated against the British tax system. With the introduction of tax credits, Chancellor Gordon Brown and his consultants had managed to come up with a policy and supporting computer system that expensively transformed what had been a relatively effective part of the tax system into an administrative Armageddon. As *The Times* reported, 'ID fraudsters plunge tax system into chaos', the Shadow Chancellor called this latest development 'a huge embarrassment for Gordon Brown' on 'the Chancellor's pet project'.[25]

It's a Moral not just a Managerial Issue

Management and IT systems consultancies are businesses. As businesses, their aim is profit maximization. This means they must try and sell as much of their product as they can at the highest price possible. Just like any other business – manufacturers of soft drinks, breakfast cereals, photocopiers, paperclips, cars, burgers, cigarettes or whatever. When you sell management or IT systems consulting to another commercial company like a bank, insurance company or an oil company, you are playing a commercial game, where you both know the rules. You try to get as much of their money as possible by thinking up all kinds of 'essential' services and new IT systems you can sell them and you charge them as much as you think you can get away with. They, on the other hand, try to buy a minimum amount of your services as cheaply as they can. As everybody knows, that's how business works. There is nothing immoral here. This is simply the nature of free market organizations. And anyway most banks, insurance companies and oil companies are hugely wasteful bureaucracies that have more money than they know what to do with. Hardly a year goes by without banks and oil companies putting their charges or prices up and claiming that they are operating in really tough competitive market conditions; yet when their results are announced at the end of the year, they have once again made record profits.[26] So relieving them of a few million, tens of millions or even hundreds of millions really causes nobody any great distress or hardship. In fact, when selling pleasurably expensive management and systems consultancy to them, you're just taking from the incredibly rich to give to the even richer – as a sort of modern day, free market Robin Hood. Moreover, if you also pad out your earnings by things like overcharging a little on your consultants' daily rates, billing for non-existent administration costs, making clients pay for internal consultancy activities and retaining kickbacks on your consultants' travel expenses, are you being dishonest or is it fair to say that you are just playing by the normal rules of business and that your clients should have had the brains to audit your invoices more closely? Also, if you lure a client into paying millions for implementing a fashionable, if unnecessary, new organization structure or if you manage to convince a client to spend a couple of hundred million on a shiny new computer system, when you know perfectly well that they could have got the same result by spending just a couple of million simply upgrading their existing system – is that dishonesty or good salesmanship? Here it is predator against predator, and the victims (who are invariably clients who have more money than sense) deserve neither sympathy nor mercy. Though, of course, the many tens of thousands who lose their jobs each year as a result of consultants' recommendations may not see it all as a game.

However, having spent over twenty years selling consulting and IT systems to many companies and government departments, I believe there are a number of important moral issues that arise when a profit-maximizing company like a consultancy sells its services to public-sector organizations. In the public sector, every hundred million that is channelled into management and IT systems consultancies' pockets means a hundred million less that can be spent on providing essential services in areas like health, defence, schools, social services and police. So the government has a moral, as well as a managerial, duty to ensure that money given to consultants provides value for taxpayers and for the people who rely on public services. If the government allows a management consultancy to sell a project where it places fifty to sixty inexperienced consultants in some government department or other, when two or three experienced consultants could have done the project more quickly and much more cheaply, then the government has squandered several million pounds that should have been spent on front-line services. Similarly, if an IT systems consultancy manages to convince a government department that it should spend say £400m on building a completely new IT system, when an existing system could have easily been upgraded for less than £40m – there's £360m that the government will have to take out of public services because of its civil servants' failure to exercise proper control over their consultants. If consultancies also systematically manage to overcharge the government for their consultants' time, bill for fictitious administration, charge the government the full cost of travel expenses while retaining kickbacks from travel companies and make the government pay for time consultants and their managers spend on internal consultancy activities – the question arises, shouldn't the government and its employees have been a little more circumspect in managing the consultants they have been so keen to use on public-sector work?

There is another moral dimension to how our government spends our money on consultants. If a consultancy or systems provider fails to achieve the promised results for a private-sector company, so that a supermarket runs out of stock, a breakfast cereal manufacturer delivers everything to the wrong places, an oil company has no idea which customers have had shipments or a bank is unable to extract money from its customers, nobody really gets hurt. In fact, sometimes a system failure can seem to have an amusingly positive effect – for example, the hapless British supermarket chain Sainsbury's reportedly had to recruit 3,000 shelf-stackers to manually fix the damage caused by the disastrous new logistics system it implemented as part of its multi-billion-pound Transformation project helped by Accenture.[27] But what if inexperienced junior consultants set meaningless targets for the health service which lead to ward closures and fewer patients being treated or what if consultancies produce IT systems fiascos for government departments that prevent people from travelling due to them not having passports, that leave over 176,000 immigrants stuck in limbo for months because their applications cannot be processed, that prevent courts prosecuting criminals, that cause families to lose their homes or that impoverish hundreds of thousands of low income households, we have to ask why our government, which has promised repeatedly to improve public services, has allowed the string of expensive disasters that we have seen in almost every single government department since New Labour came to power. Consultancies are only doing what they have always done – maximizing their own profits – it is up to government to ensure those who elected them get value for all the billions being given to consultants.

However, seeing what is happening in the British public sector, even some consultants are starting to get concerned. In a recent book about the consultancy industry, the Director-General of the massive NHS IT project is reported as saying, 'the consulting industry is lost. It needs a new blueprint. It lacks a sense of its role at a societal level and has become very self-serving as a result'. Then, apparently referring to how the bonus structures of many consultancies encouraged their consultants to sell whatever they could even if they were providing no value to their clients, he went on to say 'they will do everything in their power to keep the meter running – and they're doing the industry an enormous disservice'.[28] Others quoted in the same book seemed to express similar concerns about the lack of professional standards of many consultants, for example 'unlike doctors and lawyers, anyone can call themselves a consultant' and 'professional codes do not always protect against incompetence or greed'.[29] And commenting on the consulting industry in general, the blurb for the book admitted, '$200 billion a year is spent on business consulting, much of it ineffectively'.[30]

The fact that money being spent on things like consultants means less money for front-line services was made clear in a press release from the Treasury in 2004 explaining that they were launching an efficiency programme, no doubt helped by expensive consultants, in order to release taxpayers' money for front-line services. Under the headline *Releasing Resources to the Front Line*, the Treasury wrote: 'Stretching efficiency programmes will deliver gains of over £20 billion a year by 2007–08, increasing resources available for front-line priorities, Chancellor Gordon Brown announced today, following the publication of the Independent Review of Public Sector Efficiency led by Sir Peter Gershon.'[31]

Gordon Brown himself confirmed his dedication to ensuring our money was not wasted and went to the front line, when he said: 'I am grateful for the thorough and detailed work that Sir Peter and his team have conducted. Alongside the spending allocations announced today, this announcement reaffirms the Government's commitment to providing excellent services to the public, with more resources directed to the front line, while ensuring value for money for the taxpayer. My Cabinet colleagues and I shall be working closely to deliver this important agenda.'[32]

In the light of this promise that our money should go to front-line services, it should be interesting and informative to examine the tens of billions that our Chancellor is giving to consultants and what value we are getting for this money.

Value or Cost?

One big question about the flood of consultants into the public sector is whether they can effectively apply their mainly private-sector management practices to the provision of services like schools, hospitals, the Armed Forces and the police. There are, of course, many features of private-sector management that can give benefits to public-sector organizations – establishing clear responsibilities, setting performance targets, rapid decision-making and accountability. And in my experience of working with public-sector management, these skills and practices are too often sorely lacking. But running a school, hospital or army is more complex than making breakfast cereal, managing a supermarket or producing cars – there are more stakeholders involved, more conflicting interests that have to be balanced and it is more difficult to define the right performance levels and criteria for success.

Too often, consultants with little or no public-sector experience have caused chaos by unthinkingly trying to transpose private-sector methods into public services. Typically, consultants impose targets and measurements that are too simplistic and lead to behaviours and practices that are counter-productive and often the direct opposite of what was intended. Any consultant knows that 'what you measure is what you get.' So you have to be very careful that the measurement parameters you use will lead to the behaviours and results you want. Even the most junior consultant knows that if you wish to measure, for example, customer satisfaction with delivery performance, you would quantify what percentage of customers received their products on the date they requested. You would obviously not measure something like 'what percentage of deliveries were received within 48 hours of receipt of order', as many customers may not even want their deliveries sent so quickly. Yet when setting targets for doctors' surgeries, consultants decreed that a certain percentage of patients should be seen within 48 hours – whether the patient wanted to be seen within 48 hours or not. This led to something approaching chaos at many surgeries as they tried to hit the new target. For example, many surgeries refused to let patients book appointments more than two days ahead. Data from the National Patient Survey, the government's annual public appraisal of the NHS revealed, 'that a high number of practices are preventing patients from making advance bookings in an effort to comply with Whitehall targets.'[33] This made it difficult for people to plan ahead to schedule time off work the following week to see their doctor, as they were not allowed to book an appointment so far ahead. Yet if they waited till the next week to contact their surgery, they could not know until it was often too late whether the doctor would have time to see them or not.

Similarly, the incompetent way certain targets and budgets were set for hospitals led to some being penalized for being 'too efficient' and treating 'too many'[34] patients. In one reported case, a nine-year-old boy died when his operation was cancelled because his hospital had been 'too efficient'[35] and had achieved what was called 'over-performance'.[36] As a result, the hospital was forced by the local health authority to shut down 100 beds and slow down the rate at which it handled its patients. One committee investigating the New Labour government's use of management consultants concluded that targets set by consultants 'got in the way of healthcare delivery'.

There is growing evidence that the introduction of so-called 'competitive markets' into public-sector organizations has merely led to an explosion in administration costs as cooperation between departments is replaced by everybody trying to invoice each other for their services. While other private-sector consultancy-driven ideas like 'outsourcing' and 'privatization' may also have had negative effects. For example, the decision to contract out hospital catering and cleaning, especially cleaning, can clearly be linked to Britain having one of the highest rates of hospital transmitted infections like MRSA in Europe – forty to fifty times higher than Britain's close neighbours like Denmark and Holland. It is estimated that every year over 600,000 people in Britain acquire infections in hospitals and of these around 5,000 die. And the privatization of British Rail seems to have both wasted over £6bn of our money and given Britain one of the least modern, most expensive and most dangerous railway systems in Europe – though many managers, accountants, consultants and lawyers became multi-millionaires in the process.

NIHS at the NHS

The British NHS seems to have been struck down by one of the most severe cases of the NIH Syndrome ever recorded. NIHS – Not Invented Here Syndrome – is a condition whereby senior managers are persuaded by their consultants to spend vast amounts of an organization's money expensively reinventing something that already exists, in the usually mistaken belief that nothing produced anywhere else by anybody else can possibly be as wonderful as their own work and that they personally have nothing at all that they can learn from anybody else's experiences. The NIH Syndrome is incredibly profitable for consultants as it provides them with huge amounts of (unnecessary but well-paid) work, but it can be serious and even fatal to an organization, those it employs and those it serves.

The NHS NPfIT (*National Programme for IT*), the largest civil computer project in history, now sexily renamed *Connecting for Health*, is in full swing. More than £6.5bn of contracts to develop new systems have been handed out to an extremely small group of management and IT systems consulting firms. Many thousands of management and systems consultants are hard at work. And the first showpiece of the great project has been proudly revealed – the *Choose and Book* system, enabling doctors to book hospital appointments for their patients at a choice of hospitals. *Choose and Book* was reportedly budgeted at £65m, has so far cost over £200m and in 2004 managed to make all of 63 appointments against a target for the year of 205,000. A specialist magazine seemed unimpressed with *Connecting for Health*'s extremely expensive lack of progress in developing the new booking system: 'this is bog standard business technology. This is simple stuff, but they just can't get it to work.'[37] By the end of 2005, following the government's offer of 'incentives' of £100,000 in cash to any GP practice using the system, about 60,000 appointments, equivalent to 0.7 per cent of hospital appointments, were supposedly made using *Choose and Book* against a government plan of 9 million appointments for the year – though there are indications that most of these 60,000 were actually made by phone without involving the system at all.

When a bank or an oil company needs a new IT system, it is probably justified in paying to develop its own new system. Its competitors would not let it copy their systems and it would anyway want a better one to maintain competitive advantage. But a public service organization like the NHS is in a completely different position. It does not have competitors. In fact, health services in other countries would be only too pleased to let the NHS copy or use any good systems they had developed – especially if they could earn a few million in licensing fees from sharing their technology and experience. There are probably about a billion people in the developed world being served by about twenty-five national health services and around 70,000 hospitals. Health services, hospitals and doctors tend to do the same sorts of things regardless of where they are – GPs see patients and refer them to hospitals if necessary, hospitals treat them and have to do things like maintaining patient records, providing medicine, financial budgeting, managing their staff and so on. Wherever you are in the developed world, although there will be differences in how they are organized and funded, you will probably not find enormous differences in the activities carried out by different health services. Somewhere in these twenty-five health services and 70,000 hospitals, there must already exist some smart computer systems that could be adapted for the British NHS, particularly as numerous case studies have already been written detailing how hospitals abroad have implemented precisely the same sorts of systems that *Connecting for Health* will eventually and expensively give us. There are massive advantages in adapting or upgrading existing systems rather than building new ones – it costs ten to a hundred times more to build a new system than it does to improve an existing system. Also, an adaptation of an already working system is more likely to be up and running in less than a third of the time and with fewer technical problems than a completely new system.

So you would have thought that, before they generously started handing out all these juicy contracts for great big new systems to their consultants, the masters of *Connecting for Health* would have done a swift survey (or even a very detailed survey) to see if there were any existing systems working somewhere in the world that could be adapted reasonably rapidly and relatively cheaply for the British NHS. Not only do the worthies at *Connecting for Health* and their consultants appear not to have done this, they also seem to have disregarded systems, that were already in use in Britain. Displaying the classic symptoms of a severe attack of NIHS, they seem intent on ignoring experience, common sense and the protests of the people who will use the systems, and so, rather than trying to re-use what already exists, they have launched off into building their own completely new systems. Yet in 2003, the head of the NHS had already assured a parliamentary committee that all the systems needed were already in place somewhere within the NHS so that the programme was merely a matter of extending their use throughout the NHS: 'we have introduced somewhere in the NHS everything that we want to install, but we have never done it on a scale that is implied as necessary and correct in order to support the National Health Service.'[38] Moreover, the NHS's consultants are developing these huge new systems using almost exactly the same approach and processes that have already led to a long string of catastrophically expensive IT systems consulting failures both in the NHS and in most other government departments. This decision to comprehensively reinvent the wheel, using methods which have repeatedly been shown to be inappropriate, may end up costing close to £30bn of other people's, namely we the taxpayers', money. In addition, it may come up with something that is more square than round, as the programme already shows clear signs of being yet another totally predictable technical and financial disaster.

If the NHS were a private-sector organization, this expensive and risky decision would just be an issue of questionable management – a possible waste of billions of shareholders' money. But when the money is being diverted from patient care, the decision to unnecessarily build new computer systems rather than adapting existing ones could be seen as a moral and not just a managerial issue. Waiting times for MRI scans can be more than a year, 50,000 people a year have to go abroad for operations and budget restrictions prevent patients getting the medicine they need. In the year 2004/5 it was reported that the NHS would have a deficit of £140m and this was forecast to rise to £630m in 2005/6. Because of this deficit, health authorities were making serious cutbacks in the provision of healthcare. One newspaper reported, 'frantic cost-cutting measures had led to closed wards, cancelled operations, reduced staff numbers and angry creditors.'[39] Yet the 2004/5 £140m deficit is insignificant in comparison to the billions that could be wasted by the NHS on these new computer systems. In fact, this £140m deficit, which has already led to reductions in patient care, is less than the cost overrun on just the tiny *Choose and Book* system – £140m so far and rising. (When questioned, a spokesperson on the NHS IT project denied that *Choose and Book* was over budget and claimed that the cost had always been £200m even though previous press releases had quoted £65m.[40])

The tendency for the NHS top brass to disdainfully ignore anything done by anybody else and to refuse to learn anything from their own previous mistakes has been seen many times before. For example, the NHS wasted £32m on an unsuccessful attempt to produce its own version of a medical coding system which already functioned perfectly well in the US. Eventually, they had to abandon their own efforts and use the US version. Moreover, while the NHS executive claimed they had learnt 'useful lessons' from their own IT systems failures, the Public Accounts Committee (PAC) were surprised that the NHS waited four years before evaluating a key failed project and expressed disappointment and concern at the repeated and continued inability of the NHS to learn anything at all from its past experiences. The severity of the case of NIHS at the NHS was summed up well by one of the MPs on the PAC when reporting on the explosion of MRSA cases in hospitals. 'You just do not listen, you do not take advice, you just go your own way.'[41]

In January 2006, a survey of hospitals revealed that three quarters of them were having to reduce patient care due to budget constraints and up to 4,000 medical jobs were at risk.[42] Unless a cure for the severe attack of NIHS at the NHS is found quickly, we can expect to see a whole series of IT systems catastrophes over the coming months and years, while tens of thousands of patients cannot be treated, staff levels are further reduced and essential drugs cannot be supplied due to budget constraints.

'The People at the Treasury Are Not Stupid'

At a dinner recently, I was sitting next to a gentleman who shall remain nameless. He had an impressive blue-blood pedigree and at various times had been a professor at a leading business school, a director of the Bank of England, a former member of the Cabinet Office Central Policy Review Staff (the 'Think Tank'), a director of the Treasury and a director of a major bank. He also had a knighthood and was no doubt in line for several other honours. I started talking to him about my concerns regarding the amount of taxpayers' money being handed over to consultants and the series of catastrophes that had ensued. I then suggested that the government was allowing itself to be taken for a very expensive ride by its consultants. The gentleman looked down his long aquiline nose at me and said dismissively in his highly educated upper-class accent, 'I find your arguments fallacious and lacking in intellectual rigour – the people at the Treasury and the Bank of England are not stupid.'

Having seen so much consultancy bought by so many government departments yielding so little in the way of results, I think it's time to reveal what really happens when management and IT systems consultants are encouraged by the government to bring their magic into public-sector organizations. Then readers can make up their own minds about the gumption or otherwise of the people at the Bank of England, the Treasury and all the other government departments who have contributed so generously to the welfare of already wealthy management and IT systems consultants by giving them almost unbelievable quantities of taxpayers' cash.

This is the story of how huge amounts of our money are being spent. I hope you enjoy it.

CHAPTER 2

The Takeover

The Andersens Move in

New Labour's enthusiasm for consultants can be traced back to the party's transformation in the mid-1990s. With John Major's Tory government riven by infighting and sinking in a vat of sleaze, an inspiring young opposition leader called Tony Blair promised a brighter future. As it transformed itself into an electable party, New Labour started to prepare in earnest for power – and that meant acquiring a more businesslike image.

With the party's 'Clause Four' commitment to public ownership safely ditched, New Labour could begin wooing the City as it sought to shake off once and for all its anti-business reputation. Out went such old-fashioned policies as a commitment to re-nationalize the railways and utilities, and in came a consultancy firm already well-connected with some of the more commercially minded members of New Labour's top brass.

The name Arthur Andersen had long been mud in government circles. Banned in the 1980s from any public contracts because of its role in the £77m DeLorean Cars fraud scandal in Belfast, the firm was still being sued by the Tory government when Labour were elected in 1997. Its sister firm Andersen Consulting had, however, been far shrewder and was already inveigling itself with New Labour. Five years earlier, in 1992, it had offered its services for free to the Social Justice Commission under the then Labour leader John Smith. Not long afterwards the revolving door between New Labour and the consultants took its first spin as deputy chairman of the Commission and long-time Labour activist Patricia Hewitt took up the position of Andersen Consulting's director of research.[1]

It wasn't long before the Andersen–New Labour relationship began to bear fruit as Arthur Andersen became the party's prime consultant on economic policy, courtesy of shadow Chancellor Gordon Brown's backer and Coventry MP Geoffrey Robinson. The man who was to become Brown's first Paymaster General (PMG) paid the fees as the firm's Stephen Hailey, Chris Wales, Chris Sanger and Chris Osborne met in Robinson's flat to help develop the next government's early radical fiscal policies.[2] All three Chris's were to bolster their impressive CVs by securing jobs as government special advisers after the 1997 election.

But perhaps Andersen Consulting's most telling contribution to New Labour's ascent to power took place amid Oxford's dreaming spires. In the summer of 1996, 100 top Labour MPs enjoyed a series of seminars on grooming themselves for government, or 'training in public affairs'.[3] A leading figure at these sessions was a 26-year-old Andersen consultant called Liam Byrne, who soon took up a position as an adviser to the Prime Minister. (Later, following New Labour's historic third election victory, just eighteen months after becoming an MP in a by-election, Byrne became a health minister under his old Andersen colleague Patricia Hewitt.) Former Labour cabinet minister Lord Healey was apparently unimpressed by the event as he said, 'these management consultants are just making money out of suckers'.[4] And even one shadow cabinet member questioned Andersen Consulting's motives for helping the opposition Labour Party, confessing that 'a lot of people are sucking up to us at the moment'.[5]

Labour came to power with an instinctive suspicion of civil servants they believed to have been politicized by eighteen years of Tory rule. Encouraged by the way consultants' help had contributed to their election victory, New Labour started to see advisers, rather than civil servants, as their natural partners in government. So it wasn't surprising that the balance of influence on the new government in May 1997 moved away from the mandarins and came to be dominated by a growing army of special advisers. At any one time over eighty of this breed were to be found stalking the corridors of power, compared to fewer than forty under the Tories.[6] This was far fewer than the number of senior civil servants, but the advisers had huge influence over ministers and an increasingly powerful remit to command the work of key government departments.

Arthur Andersen appeared to be richly rewarded for its faith in the New Labour project. When in opposition Labour had insisted that the Tory government had a 'public duty' to continue the DeLorean action in order to recover hundreds of millions in pounds in damages from Arthur Andersen.[7] But shortly after Labour's 1997 landslide election victory the action over the DeLorean scandal was dropped for a paltry £18m (compared to a loss in today's money of over £200m). One journalist wrote, 'a lingering suspicion remains, however, that close links between the Labour party in opposition and Andersens have borne fruit for the accountancy firm.'[8]

No sooner had the firm escaped from the DeLorean debacle, than it was allowed to bid for government contracts again. Millions in consultancy fees flowed from the New Labour government, including for recommending the Private Finance Initiative that would see the firm's and its fellow consultants' earnings rocket (see Chapter 7). Meanwhile in 2000, sister company Andersen Consulting was similarly let off the hook after an unfortunate attempt to implement the National Insurance Recording IT system (called NIRS2). It had won the contract in 1995, but a series of problems with the system led to delays in pension payments, costs that were £165m over budget and compensation to long-suffering pensioners of £100m.[9] Cementing the bond between government and the consultants, Robinson's successor as PMG, Dawn Primarolo, generously declined to recover any of the wasted taxpayers' money from the firm as 'taking action against Andersen Consulting would prejudice the partnership relationship now established between it and the Inland Revenue.'[10] Four years on, the relationship became closer still when Ian Watmore, a managing director from Andersen Consulting, was appointed to run the Cabinet Office's e-government unit, which became a driver of many expensive new IT initiatives. However, the firm, by now known as Accenture, really scooped the jackpot under the government's multi-billion-pound initiative for health service IT, when it was awarded virtual monopoly status as IT services provider to the NHS for almost half of England.

The Bonanza Begins

Since New Labour opened the doors of government departments to its new confidants, government spending on consultancy has gone through the roof. In 1996 the Management Consultancies Association (MCA) reported that its members, who only account for around half the industry, earned £196m from the public sector; by 2004 that had increased by 850 per cent to £1,865m, excluding the costs of developing IT systems.[11] Even the traditionally austere Treasury under the supposedly prudent Gordon Brown generously spent 500 per cent more in 2004 than it did in 1996. Between 2002 and 2005, the Treasury shared out these spoils among a staggering 350 different individual consultants or firms.[12]

Despite the Civil Service's history as the original independent consultancy to government ministers, and its 3,000 mandarin-grade officials, not to mention tens of thousands more at professional grades, schooled over their careers in providing policy advice, Whitehall departments increasingly turned to consultants and by 2004 accounted for 55 per cent of the public-sector spending on them.[13] How times had changed from 1994, when the then shadow Health Spokesman Alan Milburn told Parliament, 'we have more financial directors, more pieces of paper, more trading in health care, and more PR specialists and management consultants, and they are all looking to make a killing in the new environment.'[14] If they were making a killing then, New Labour has allowed them to become mass-murderers.

While a government that increasingly sees the role of its officials as being to 'deliver' and maintains that bringing in armies of consultants is an effective way of importing the kind of skills its programme of 'modernizing public services' demands, those on the ground are far from convinced. Jonathan Baume, the general secretary of the top Civil Servants' union the FDA, pointed out that 'there's no coherent overview of consultant use. Quite frankly, monitoring and accountability could be better. Then we could better ascertain if we were getting value for money.'[15] When in July 2004 the Chancellor announced the results of the Gershon 'efficiency review' that would see over 80,000 public sector jobs axed, Baume voiced the concerns of many when he predicted that the cuts would 'inevitably lead to an increased reliance on external consultants and contractors which we know from experience end up costing the taxpayer more in the long run'.[16] When yet higher spending on consultants was announced the following year, Mark Serwotka, General Secretary of the Civil Service rank and file union, the Public and Commercial Services Union, was even more forthright: 'it is sheer lunacy and represents little value to the taxpayer, especially when you have consultants sitting opposite civil servants doing the same work but being paid up to ten times more.'[17]

Big Four, Big Bucks

Arthur Andersen weren't the only accountancy firm to shake off their staid image in the roaring 1990s by turning themselves into 'one stop shops' that, along with checking the books, could also tell companies how to run their businesses. All the then 'Big Five' firms – Arthur Andersen, Pricewaterhouse Coopers (PwC), Ernst & Young, KPMG and Deloitte – had

a go with varying degrees of success. However, scandals such
as Enron, audited by Arthur Andersen as it simultaneously
made tens of millions from selling financial engineering and
tax-avoidance advice, exposed the conflict between acting as
consultants and as supposedly impartial auditors who more
often than not ended up checking their own work. One
commentator described Arthur Andersen's conflict of interest
at Enron: 'in effect, the firm was working on the accounting
systems and controls with one hand and attesting to the
numbers they produced with the other.'[18] This lucrative expansion of the accountants' activities hit a snag when the
Securities and Exchange Commission (SEC) in the US took
action against the obvious conflicts of interest by pressuring
the accountants to sell their consultancy arms in the early
2000s. Ernst and Young (E&Y) sold its 10,000-strong
consultancy division to Capgemini of France for $11bn
($3bn cash and the rest in shares), while KPMG similarly sold
its consultancy practices around the world to the highest
bidders, and PwC's 30,000 consultants were snaffled by IT
giant IBM for just $3bn. Only Deloitte carried on with its dual
role, seemingly cocking a snook at the SEC's concerns.

The separation was, however, largely illusory as the by now
'Big Four' accountancy firms (Andersens having sunk following the fatal Enron blow) stopped acting as consultants in
favour of providing 'advisory' and 'professional' services.

Meanwhile, regulators on this side of the Atlantic happily
allowed the conflicts of interest to persist. Indeed, the New
Labour government gave the arrangements the most ringing
official endorsement of all: yet millions more of taxpayers'
money for consultancy (professional services) from the same
firms.

New Labour, New Opportunities

Privileged access to government for the big accountancy partnerships didn't start with New Labour; indeed the typical high-
powered bean counter was more traditionally a Tory creature.

But as New Labour set out its stall in the late 1990s for an explosion of private-sector involvement in public investment and services, a new and immensely profitable dawn broke for the major firms. Over the previous decade their core audit work had become more important for the opportunities it provided to sell consultancy services to clients on matters ranging from internal controls to management, tax planning and IT systems, than for the audit fees themselves.[19] Even the most unprepossessing bean counter was schooled in sales techniques and offered bonuses on the professional services they managed to cross-sell to their audit clients. Auditors, who traditionally saw going through the books as a crucial safeguard on the operations of companies with complex affairs and limited liability, now performed their work with one eye on 'the books' and the other firmly and profitably fixed on the 'cross-selling' opportunities auditing afforded.

Unsurprisingly, the same firms quickly set about ensuring they were able to cash in on New Labour's expansion of private-sector involvement in 'modernizing' public services, presenting their professional advisory services as the natural gatekeeper in the arrangement. Key to their success in achieving this was to join forces with the parts of government that were driving the policy of opening up the public sector to private companies and with the innumerable panels, taskforces and quangos that sprang up to promote these reforms.

Secondments became an increasingly favoured method of gaining influence, particularly into the part of government setting industrial policy, the Department of Trade and Industry, which routinely houses at least half a dozen staff from the Big Four firms at any one time. Most active provider of expertise was probably E&Y, which by 2004 had five of its staff ensconced at assistant director level or higher in government departments, including an adviser at the Treasury on tax policy – despite the firm's well-documented tax-avoidance activities and its reputation in Whitehall as 'probably the most aggressive, creative, abusive provider of schemes and arrangements among the major accountancy firms'.[20] Whereas in the 1980s the Tories had banned Arthur Andersen for its failures in the

DeLorean affair, by the end of the 1990s firms that were acknowledged by the Treasury to be costing the exchequer billions by selling tax-avoidance schemes were not only handed valuable contracts but were welcomed into the heart of government without any questions.[21] The idea of threatening to withhold public-sector consultancy work as a means of getting the bean-counters-cum-consultants to stop their tax-avoidance work seems not to have crossed New Labour ministers' minds. Public concerns about the forgiving nature of the relationship between the New Labour government and the Big Four cannot have been diminished when senior officials from some government departments moved across to well rewarded positions with the Big Four. Following the obligatory three-month wait after his retirement, in 2004 career civil servant Sir Nicholas Montagu joined the advisory board of PwC. Montagu's final public-sector position had been as Inland Revenue chairman while PwC was busy corralling multinational companies into challenging British tax rules on the grounds that they breached European law, at a likely cost to the taxpayer of several billion pounds. PwC had also lobbied against a tax-avoidance clampdown, for which they had been condemned by the Treasury as 'tax-avoidance advisers'.[22] Not long afterwards, Sir Steve Robson, the managing director at the Treasury until resigning in 2001, added to his portfolio of private-sector positions by becoming an adviser to KPMG.

Within weeks of New Labour's first election victory a host of quangos had appeared – 'the PFI Taskforce', 'Commission on Public Private Finance' and 'Public Service Productivity Panels', for example – all stuffed with consultants from the big accountancy firms. Other pro-privatization think tanks partly funded by the then Big Five firms and supported by the government included the New Local Government Network and the New Health Network, while all the firms could be found sponsoring and hosting countless conference speeches and government freebies. Meanwhile, contracts with central and local government flooded in. By the end of Labour's first term just one firm, KPMG, was earning around £300m in fees for work derived from public-sector initiatives.[23]

The accountancy firms' commitment to the New Labour cause, and the government's increasing dependence on them, had also seen them rewarded with the gift of being allowed to trade as limited liability partnerships, restricting the extent to which they could be sued for the dodgy audits that (as experience around the world suggested) became more common as the firms moved increasingly into more lucrative consultancy work.[24]

Much of the Big Five's work came from the Private Finance Initiative (PFI), where they simultaneously managed to promote the policy through taskforces and secondments to key government positions, and advise both public-sector purchasers of the schemes and the companies supplying them. But this wasn't the only area in which the New Labour government was more than happy to take the advice of accountants whose interests, and whose clients' interests, were often diametrically opposed to the government's.

The Foreign Office's review of financial regulation in Britain's overseas dependent territories came to epitomize this conflict. KPMG were appointed in 1999 to conduct this review. After a long inquiry (during which the fees racked up), followed by a further period in which to implement some mild recommendations, in December 2001 the islands were given a relatively clean bill of health. They could thus continue to provide their financial services to the world's tax avoiders and evaders.[25] Meanwhile, KPMG's lucrative operations in all the territories apparently remained undiminished. Soon afterwards KPMG was exposed by a Senate Finance Committee inquiry in the US for selling $2.5bn worth of tax-avoidance schemes using some of the same tax havens, in what the Justice Department characterized as 'the largest criminal tax fraud in history'.[26]

For sheer nerve, however, Deloitte must take the prize. When the Inland Revenue and Customs & Excise sought to sell off their properties to raise some cash following the government's 1998 spending review, the firm famous for tax avoidance was appointed financial adviser. Such was the trust placed in the hands of the team running the project and

their consultants that the top brass at the Revenue were not
even aware of the plan to sell the estate to a company based
in Bermuda so that the purchaser could avoid tax. When the
dreadful truth emerged some time later, the best excuse that
the Revenue could offer was that Deloitte had considered
the set-up 'entirely a normal arrangement'.[27] The Treasury
wasn't the only public body to shell out to Deloitte for work
in areas where its reputation was less than spotless. In 2005
the firm was asked by the Financial Services Authority (FSA)
to review the cost of compliance with financial regulation,
something in which its significant interest had been demonstrated just the previous year when the FSA fined Deloitte's
'wealth management' arm £750,000 for 'serious compliance
failings'.[28] In another recent review of regulation handed
over to the Big Four, PwC similarly added a survey of the
costs to business of dealing with all red tape to their
burgeoning portfolio of government consultancy work.
PwC specialises in examining knotty policy issues in which
it has a tremendous interest, and has for example been
employed by the FSA as an adviser on the regulation of
hedge funds, an industry whose participants it also targets
for consultancy fees as a 'proven leader in serving the hedge
funds industry'.[29]

Another nice little consultancy earner for PwC was the
London Underground Public–Private Partnership (PPP). This
was eventually signed off in March 2003, by which time
bankers', lawyers' and consultants' fees came to an amazing
£455m. PwC earned £21m[30] and KPMG, E&Y and Arthur
Andersen (before its collapse) also cashed in to varying degrees. In total the bidders' and London Underground's advisers' fees came to £455m. All these riches came on the strength
of a PwC report five years earlier for the Treasury recommending just what the government – but not what Londoners –
wanted: a PPP. The result was vastly greater expense to
Transport for London (TfL) as it had to borrow at interest
rates charged to the private sector rather than those available
to public-sector bodies with copper-bottomed government
guarantees, even though, as a parliamentary committee in

March 2005 found, TfL retained 95 per cent of the risk while the deal's private-sector backers carried hardly any.[31] Two years into the deal, the maintenance and improvements that had been handed over to the private sector were well behind schedule while the consortia responsible – Tubelines and Metronet – were heavily criticized by Transport for London. But they were already coining handsome profits even as passengers on the tube suffered from rapidly increasing fares and numerous problems including a 43 per cent rise in disruptive signal failures and seemingly endless line closures for routine maintenance.

Outside the Private Finance Initiative, PwC's steadiest and most profitable consultancy activity is probably in defence, where the firm earns tens of millions of pounds every year for helping set up financial-management systems and for procuring equipment. In 2001/2 alone, PwC was reported to have pocketed over £100m from the MoD.[32] Every couple of years the Ministry of Defence's performance in both financial reporting and procurement are roundly condemned by the Public Accounts Committee, most recently when cost overruns in 2003/4 and 2004/5 of around £5bn rising to £6bn were reported.[33] The consultancy arrangement nevertheless seems to continue undisturbed and unquestioned.

Public money continues to find its way into the Big Four's pockets, including spending on the most iconic project of all: the 2012 Olympics. By the end of 2005 PwC had already earned hundreds of thousands for 'cost and benefit analysis' while KPMG pocketed similar sums for its 'Olympic Games Validation' work.[34] The Games, already generously underwritten against any financial loss by the Treasury, look set to channel many millions more to the Big Four.

At Your Service

The big accountancies weren't the only ones to spot the openings in the more nebulous world of management consultancy, where failure is neither admitted nor penalized and projects almost never come under the scrutiny of the National Audit Office (NAO) or get served up to an unforgiving Public Accounts Committee (PAC), parliament's public spending watchdog. From the opposite end of the spectrum to the accountancy firms came the 'service providers', firms that specialized in taking labour-intensive support functions off businesses' hands on the promise of cutting costs and improving service levels. These companies soon found that with New Labour's rush to open up the public sector to private operators, it was just a few short steps from emptying the bins, via running back-office administration, to setting boardroom strategies and running major operations.

Capita punishment

One of the principal beneficiaries of this trend was a service provider called Capita, formed from a management buy-out of the Chartered Institute of Public Finance's small consultancy arm in 1987, which went on to take advantage of the Conservative government's enthusiasm for 'outsourcing' support operations. Building its business from local government, it was soon taking on major central-government contracts such as Civil Service recruitment and running the teachers' pensions agency as well as all of the Metropolitan Police's payroll and pensions service.

The Tories had been happy for firms like Capita to take over non-core elements of public service, bringing terms such as 'contracting out' and 'market testing' into the public-sector lexicon, in spite of vociferous Labour opposition. But it was only under New Labour that these companies started to earn some serious taxpayers' money by taking on crucial public services wholesale. And while Capita's record in local-government services was far from spotless, with several local authorities having suffered as they handed work such as benefits administration to the firm, it soon became the company of choice to run many of New Labour's pet projects. As with other consultants that found their way into government affections, it relied heavily on lobbying to do so, in its case employing the services of LLM, the initials of three men who had been advisers to Tony Blair, Gordon Brown and Jack Straw. The firm was famously exposed by *Observer* journalist Greg Palast in 1998 when, posing as a businessman, he was told by one of the Ls in LLM that the firm could 'reach anyone . . . we can go to Gordon Brown if we have to.'[35] Capita duly enjoyed enormous success over two New Labour terms – while its staff numbers went up around six and a half times from 3,500 to 23,000, its turnover rose tenfold from £112m in 1996 to £1.28bn in 2004 and profits ballooned by over 1,000 per cent.

Along the road to these riches, however, were littered some public service fiascos to rival the great consulting disasters at the Child Support Agency and the Inland Revenue's tax credits. Perhaps the most infamous of these was the launch of the Criminal Records Bureau (CRB) under a contract awarded to Capita in 2000. The idea was to streamline the process of checking applications for jobs in sensitive areas, especially working with children, for any criminal past. But what ought to have been capable of being organized fairly straightforwardly with a bit of competent management was left to the mercy of the market through a Public–Private Partnership between the Home Office and the lucky winning bidder. Capita secured the contract by submitting a bid that accepted the civil servants' prediction that 75 per cent of approaches to the agency would come over the phone. Rival bidders sensibly questioned the bureaucrats' assumptions and came in with higher-priced bids. In the event, as might have been predicted, organizations looking for important safe-guards on potential employees wanted to put everything in writing, and large employers preferred to submit bulk applica-tions to match the way they recruited. When the Capita-designed system was switched on in March 2002, seven months late, it simply couldn't cope and soon a backlog of 300,000 applications had built up. Thousands of teachers weren't cleared in time for the new term in September, causing pupils to be shoehorned into other classes and several schools to delay opening that year as Capita failed to meet promises to

clear the backlog. Education Secretary Estelle Morris unsurprisingly declared herself 'a very dissatisfied customer' –
though, unlike most customers, she could not take her business
elsewhere. The cost to the taxpayer shot up from Capita's
£250m bid to £395m, much more than what the other bidders
had quoted. In spite of the huge rise in cost, two years later a
parliamentary committee found, 'the Bureau is not yet providing the standard or range of service originally envisaged.'[36]

Despite the delays and extra costs, the CRB did at least
survive, which is more than can be said for another big
initiative handed over to Capita: the Individual Learning
Accounts programme that the government wanted to take
over from the old Training and Enterprise Councils. The idea
was a perfect marriage of New Labour initiative-itis and
consultantese: people would buy 'learning episodes' off a
variety of providers in return for credits from their virtual
personal accounts, with the aim of enrolling a million 'individual learners'. But not only was it naïve to believe this would
ever inspire the masses to educate themselves in their millions,
it was also a recipe for fraud, as various hucksters pretended to
have trained people who had never come near to a 'learning
episode'. When the scheme was closed down in October 2001,
just a year after opening, over £122m of taxpayers' money had
vanished. At least £67m had been lost to fraud and another
£55m had been paid to Capita. And that's without the ongoing
costs of many police investigations.

The smooth move of firms like Capita from outsourcing into
management consultancy has taken them closer to the centre of
government policy-making. Capita has won contracts from
most Whitehall departments, including the Foreign Office,
Cabinet Office and Department for Education and Skills,
which in October 2004 handed over the national primary
and Key Stage Three (up to age 14) education strategies to the
firm under a five-year £177m contract.

Meanwhile, the language Capita uses to describe its work
shows just how well the company has adjusted to the world of
management consultancy. Reporting how it had applied some
communications spin to Railtrack's safety work, the company

boasted: 'In a facilitated workshop with senior management, Capita first identified communications objectives to underpin Sentinel's [the safety system's] newly defined vision and values, identified and analysed key stakeholder audiences and outlined and secured agreement for desired messages. The next step was to establish and agree a programme of research to capture the "big picture", ensuring all relevant stakeholder views were sought. Research methods included survey, one-to-one interviews and focus groups, together with desk research.'[37]

By the late 1990s, even companies with long histories in established professions apparently unrelated to providing consultancy services to the public sector had twigged that this was a lucrative act to get in on. Engineering companies glided from their traditional specialism, via engineering consultancy, to management consultancy. Typical of them was Serco, originally the UK arm of the Radio Corporation of America, which moved into defence maintenance work before a management buy-out in 1987, swiftly followed by flotation the following year. From there the firm moved into other areas such as transport and was ideally placed to cash in on the Private Finance Initiative as it took off in the late 1990s. It was then only a short step to consultancy, in which Serco now boasts of expertise in health, finance, justice and transport, to name but four sectors. In education Serco took over running schools from some local education authorities, not always successfully. In Yorkshire its subsidiary Education Bradford had to negotiate lower performance targets after it missed 47 of the 52 original ones, despite promising improvements. Naturally it also asked for, and received, more money too.[38]

In criminal justice, the firm's Premier subsidiary has been plagued by controversy. In March 2005, the BBC exposed how cost-cutting and staff shortages at a prison run by Premier in Scotland led to abuse of offenders and basic suicide checks on at-risk prisoners being skipped.[39] Shortly before that the young offenders' institution run by Premier under a £30m PFI deal had been named the most violent prison in Britain, with much of the problem caused by pay rates for officers that

were significantly below those in publicly run prisons, leading
to shortages of trained staff.[40] A year on things hadn't improved as Premier's electronic tagging service failed to report
several breaches of a probation licence by an offender, including removal of his tag, shortly before he went on to commit
murder. The company was severely criticized and fined by the
probation inspectorate but, more importantly, lost none of its
valuable public-sector contracts.[41]

Despite this less-than-enviable record in running operations,
Serco's public-sector consultancy work grew by 250 per cent in
the two years to 2005 according to a director of Serco Consulting.[42] The firm is now welcome in the heart of Whitehall,
where among its more politically sensitive projects was one for
the Department of Constitutional Affairs on the costs of postal
voting. Though the results of this work haven't been published,
the government continues to favour postal voting despite
several well-publicized voting-fraud scandals, which became
so widespread that they gave Robert Mugabe the opportunity
to mock British democracy. When asked what special ability
Serco brought to the issue, the firm admitted it didn't have any
but considered such work to be merely 'bread and butter
consulting'.[43] The firm showed a similarly cavalier approach
to the conflicts of interest that arise when a service provider
starts to advise an organization on strategy, with the obvious
incentive it would have to advise outsourcing as much as
possible. Explaining the attractions of management consultancy, Serco's director told *Consulting Times*: 'It's how the
accountants originally sold consulting – they already had an
audit relationship, we already have a service relationship.'[44]
Perhaps someone should have told him that the dual auditor–
consultant role he was so keen to mimic was exactly the one
played by Arthur Andersen for Enron.

IT's a Wonderful World

While the management consultants earn billions determining
swathes of government policy, earnings from this business are

put in the shade by those of their IT consultancy counterparts. A typical government IT systems project will be budgeted at £200m to £300m and will actually cost at least twice as much. Most systems projects will last for several years – a couple of years to develop the system and then a couple more to try and sort out the mess when it is found that the system doesn't work as expected and that the services provided fall way short of those that were promised. And, as the consultants are the only people with a clue how the system is constructed and often hold the intellectual property rights over the software, they are assured of many tens of millions more for many more years in maintenance and 'upgrading' work.

Estimates in the first chapter suggested that well over £15bn has already been spent on IT systems consultants, £8bn more has been committed by the MoD and the Inland Revenue, another £6.5bn has been awarded in contracts by the NHS and another £30bn to £40bn has still to be allocated to other New Labour public-sector modernization initiatives. And most of these billions will be given to just eleven massive companies. For these lucky winners, IT's a wonderful world.

Department for Work and Pensions (for Consultants)

Perhaps one of the government departments that has seen the greatest invasion by consultants in recent years is the Department for Work and Pensions (DWP), whose expenditure on 152 different consultancy firms and individuals in the three years to March 2005[45] might lead a cynic to suggest that 'for consultants' should be appended to its name. Not that the 30,000 staff earmarked to lose their jobs as part of government cost-saving measures are likely to find their employer's profligacy amusing.

The Department's generosity peaked in 2003/4 when it spent a total of £412.5m on outside advice, £306.7m of it for management and IT consultancy on 'modernizing our legacy IT infrastructure, integrating business processes inherited from our predecessor organizations and modernizing service delivery, including the introduction of pension credits'.[46] Despite this outlay, or maybe because of it, in November 2004 the Department experienced the worst IT crash in government history, as 80,000 computer screens went blank and tens of thousands of benefits claims couldn't be processed for about a week.[47] The technology was run under an outsourcing contract with Texan software giant EDS, who blamed 'human error' for the problem. Just nine months later, the Department handed EDS a renewed five-year contract worth £2.6bn.[48]

Establishing exactly what some of the DWP's consultants do is a job in itself. A request under the Freedom of Information Act elicited the revelation that American outfit Booz Allen Hamilton are engaged on a 'Pensions Transformation Programme' that will cost £21.7m between April 2004 and March 2006. Asked what this meant in practice, the Department explained that 'they translate high-level business strategies into workable business solutions.'[49] Further pressing elicited this illumination: 'the Pensions Transformation Programme will totally transform the way the business of the Pension Service is delivered. It aims to achieve three key objectives: improved customer service; more efficient & cost effective service delivery; increased take-up of social security benefits for pensioners. The transformation requires new operating processes and structures, supporting IT and cultural change for staff. It is a major undertaking over a number of years, which will provide significant investment return in relation to the three objectives above.'[50]

Not to be outdone, in the eighteen months up to the end of 2005 Capgemini earned almost £30m on 'interim management/support solution' and 'human resource change programme' contracts. Such extravagance can always be justified by claiming untestable savings from the work, as in the DWP's explanation of Capgemini's role: 'DWP is currently half way through one of the biggest staff reductions and modernization programmes ever seen in government. In total staffing has already fallen by over 14,000 since March 2004 and the total reduction will reach 30,000 net with annual savings of nearly £1 billion by

March 2008. The contract with Capgemini gives the Department access to the skills needed to carry through this Programme, particularly as regards the delivery of the IT systems the Department needs to deliver its efficiency commitments.'[51] Thus the cross-Whitehall efficiency programme launched in 2004 following the Gershon review paradoxically provides a consultancy bonanza – next to billion-pound savings from slashing jobs, even consultancy fees look like small beer.

In total, in the three years to March 2005, the DWP spent £270m on management consultancy (i.e. excluding IT work) of this nebulous variety.[52] Despite the staggering levels of public money channelled through the department into the consultants' pockets, the effectiveness of its spending remains almost unmeasured. Beyond its look at the Department's annual reports, qualified for fifteen consecutive years because of the extent of benefit fraud and errors in payments, the National Audit Office has barely considered whether any improvements have been achieved. Its only 'value for money' report to go beyond narrow individual social security policies came in November 2005 when it reported on 'dealing with the complexity of the benefits system'. The report outlined the problems of a byzantine welfare system and concluded that the organization needed a 'systematic and strategic approach focusing on the system as a whole', something that clearly the 152 separate consultancy firms employed over the three years to March 2005 with their relentless quests for 'transformation' had completely failed to deliver. Equally alarmingly, despite the staggering sums involved, the DWP admitted that 'the Department has kept detailed statistics on consultancy and finance/accountancy expenditure only since April 2004.'

Vote McKinsey?

New Labour's programme to modernize the delivery of public services has provided unimaginable wealth to a host of consulting services companies. But one has also gained unprecedented power over the lives of British citizens.

McKinsey is the original American management consultancy describing itself as being 'the United Nations of business consulting with one crucial difference: it works'. Its consultants bring a self-confidence built on intellect, reputation and powerful connections that can easily intimidate many a nervous executive into implementing their expensive strategies. McKinsey operates a collegiate but demanding system for its staff, in which assessments of companies become 'studies'. Its strict 'up or out' policy ensures that nobody loses their zeal, while those who go out do so with a near evangelical faith in the McKinsey methods and create a network of alumni at the top of the world's most important companies and, more recently, governments.

The firm came into its own in Britain in the 1980s and early 1990s as Thatcherite economics dictated that almost any service could, and should, be commercialized. McKinsey consultants who expertly espoused the philosophy naturally became Tory favourites and the firm's alumni seamlessly acquired public power: one of the bright graduates the firm nurtured in the early 1980s, William Hague, rose to the dizzying heights of Conservative party leader. Other McKinsey alumni to prosper around the same time included Howard (now Sir Howard) Davies, whose skills have since been deployed at the Audit Commission, the Bank of England, the Confederation of British Industry (CBI) and the Financial Services Authority.

But New Labour's re-election in May 2001 on a promise of accelerated public-sector reform through the introduction of competition and private-sector managerial practices soon brought the industry leader McKinsey closer to the centre of power than it had ever been when the Tories were in government. Frustrated at the sluggishness of reform in his first term, Blair shifted the balance of power from government departments into the centre, as he strengthened his own policy unit and set up a 'delivery unit' under his control in the Cabinet Office. Both quickly became home to scores of committed 'third way' policy wonks and their kindred spirits – management consultants.

Leading industrialist – and no enemy of commercial principles in the exercise of government – the late Lord Hanson, was probably one of the first people to raise the alarm over the ever-expanding influence of consultants in the corridors of power. In 2002, he expressed his concern over what he called 'ministerial infatuation with consultants'. He gave a prescient glimpse into the emerging methods of the New Labour government: 'It is in central government that management consultants are probably most over-used. What is the Civil Service for if the Ministers feel they have to employ a vast range of so-called outside experts? Why are vast departments like The Cabinet Office crawling with consultants when they have armies of their own researchers, policy advisers and analysts? In my experience top-level civil servants are highly intelligent, far-seeing and independent. It is scandalous that, when it comes to advice, they should be so ruthlessly sidelined.'[53]

Much of the concern about consultants' influence at the heart of government centred on the role played by Lord Birt. Lord Hanson had criticized Birt's performance as Director-General of the BBC: 'the BBC is a classic example of a public body which, under the laughable Lord Birt, was in the thrall of management gurus, who only succeeded in vastly expanding the bureaucracy while programme quality declined.' Under Birt's attempts to create an Internal Market at the BBC, money was taken away from making programmes to pay for increased administration costs of around £140m while the overall numbers of employees decreased. Management consultants, mainly McKinsey, were paid around £20m a year for achieving this disaster. Following his time at the BBC, Birt joined McKinsey – to whom the BBC had just given so many tens of millions of pounds of our money.

In late 2001 Birt was drafted into Downing Street as the Prime Minister's 'blue-skies thinker' with an extraordinarily broad remit: transport, education, crime, drugs and Civil Service reform. He was allowed to keep his £100,000 a year retainer as a McKinsey adviser provided he took care to 'avoid using information acquired during the course of your work to further your private interests'.[54] This secrecy surrounding Birt's work for the Prime Minister was at a level normally reserved for matters of national security. Scores of questions in Parliament, notably from Lib Dem MP Norman Baker and Tory peer Lord Hanningfield, were stonewalled, while the Prime Minister steadfastly refused to allow Birt to appear before Parliament's Public Administration Committee in the way that other special advisers routinely had done.

Birt was given his own office at No.10 Downing Street and had easy access to the Prime Minister. Some observers saw this as yet another worrying sign of how civil servants and elected politicians have been excluded from the policy-making process by advisers and consultants. One remarked that, 'Blair is far more drastic in his contempt for parliament, the cabinet and, above all, the institution of civil service independence, a concept Blair appears not to understand. Departmental papers to cabinet are all but discontinued. Cabinet no longer discusses policy, but is merely a ministerial briefing room. Whitehall is a "delivery mechanism" for targets conjured out of thin air by consultants and spin-doctors. Civil servants must be on message or leave the tent.'[55]

Politicians were concerned at how they had been sidelined. A member of Labour's National Executive Committee, Mark Seddon, wrote: 'I told Tony that many Labour Party members no longer thought they could make policy . . . I already knew the perennially useful John Birt had come up with a "Command and Control" diagram for New Labour similar to the one he foisted on the poor old BBC. This was euphemistically titled "Partnership in Power" and it marked the death of the Labour Party conference and much else beside.'[56]

Seddon also criticized the way government meetings were now run when he talked of 'blue-sky thinking, roll-out and all the other meaningless management consultancy drivel that has kept some of us entertained and horrified at the same time during interminable meetings'. His concern at the role of consultants was echoed by another member of the Labour Party, the MP Jim Cousins: 'This is part of a wider problem in which the Government is increasingly run by people who do not understand the political impact of what they propose. These private-sector consultants seem to be impatient with the views of the party and they alienate the civil servants who have an ethos and commitment to public service.'[57]

Lord Birt's influence seemed to increase even further as Tony Blair planned to reduce the power of both the Treasury and the Civil Service during his third term in office. One newspaper reported that 'The Prime Minister has asked his adviser, the former BBC Director-General Lord Birt, to consider plans for the abolition of the Cabinet Office . . . Lord Birt is also looking at the idea of removing key responsibilities from the Treasury as part of a renewed effort to break the political and administrative resistance to the kind of radical reforms Blair feels have been diluted or delayed in his first two terms.'[58] In addition, a former senior executive with McKinsey, David Bennett, was appointed to run a 'policy directorate' in Downing Street and drive through New Labour's reforms.[59] The government contemptuously dismissed the notion that Bennett's appointment to the heart of government might be of public interest. 'No press release is being issued, and MPs will have to table questions if they want to ask about his salary or job,' No.10 told an inquisitive journalist.[60]

One MP, Liberal Democrat Norman Baker, called for Lord Birt to be investigated for potential conflicts of interest because 'in addition to his unpaid work for the Prime Minister Lord Birt is a paid adviser to management consultants McKinsey'. Baker described Lord Birt's role in government as 'entirely improper', prompting Cabinet Office minister John Hutton to dismiss Baker as 'president of the obsessive conspiracy theorists' club'.[61] In 2005, Birt left McKinsey – a move that, in the firm's words, 'reflected a desire on both sides to avoid any potential misunderstanding about Lord Birt's role with Global Media Practice and McKinsey's work in the public sector – though in fact no conflict ever arose'. This message was helpfully reinforced in a statement by Lord Birt: 'I wish to make it clear as McKinsey has done that no conflict of interest ever arose between my consultancy role with McKinsey's Global Media Practice and the firm's UK public-sector work.'[62]

Just like Andersen/Accenture, the firm it seemed to have supplanted as pet government consultant, McKinsey's strategy of close alignment with those in power has brought untold riches as public-sector contracts have been showered on the firm. Defence has proved a particularly rich seam, providing McKinsey with fifteen contracts worth £53m since January 2000, the largest being the £23m ongoing deal to 'transform' the MoD's logistics systems.[63] Of these huge contracts, three were awarded without any competition and seven 'on a single source basis, since they related to work that had already been placed with the company following competitive tender'.[64]

At the end of 2005, ex-Accenture consultant Ian Watmore was appointed head of the Prime Minister's Delivery Unit at top Civil Service level of permanent secretary. With a senior ex-McKinsey partner, David Bennett, running the Policy Unit and Watmore, running the Delivery Unit, the consultants' takeover of No. 10 seems almost complete.[65] As our government oversaw the flow of billions of pounds from taxpayers' pockets into those of the major management and IT systems consultants, voters could be forgiven for wondering who they elected on 5 May 2005 – the Labour Party or an elite of unelected advisers and consultants who are now becoming even wealthier as, under the guise of modernizing public services, New Labour gives them free rein to plunder the public sector.

CHAPTER 3

Defending the Indefensible

Under New Labour, the Ministry of Defence (MoD) is just one among many government departments that have become avid consumers of consulting. However, as a reasonable amount of information is available in the public domain regarding the MoD's use of consultants and the results of the hundreds of millions of pounds the MoD has paid them, it makes an interesting case study on the value that we taxpayers get, or more often fail to get, from our government's enthusiastic use of consultancy support.

You can see the influence of consultants in the MoD's Annual Report. This is presented in the style of what is called a 'Balanced Scorecard' – a reasonably profitable consulting fad of the late 1990s. The Balanced Scorecard has now become a bit outmoded for private companies. But it still sells well to public-sector departments in Britain and to companies in the Third World, as both groups tend to lag about five years behind large Western companies in their rate of expensively picking up (and then abandoning) the latest consulting fashion. You can also sense the presence of consultants in the liberal use of 'consultantese' in the MoD's report: 'The Defence Balanced Scorecard encapsulates the Defence Management Board's key objectives and priorities over the whole range of MoD business. In the Report, these objectives are grouped into the four perspectives of: Outputs and Deliverables, Resource Management, Enabling Processes and Building for the Future. Within these perspectives, the main section headings correspond to high-level Scorecard objectives.'

In spite of MoD claims that the people making the key decisions in the Defence Management Board, 'come from the front-line, go back to the front-line,' it seems somewhat unlikely that the above piece was written by a battle-hardened squaddie just returned from the heat, dust and danger of fighting in Iraq or Afghanistan. Moreover, the fact that the MoD seems to be referring to itself as a 'business' should set the alarm bells ringing. It is not a 'business'. It never has been a 'business'. It never should be a 'business'. It is there to protect us against our enemies. And, as we will see, most of the efforts to make MoD employees think and act like business people have been misguided and destructive and some appear to have put the lives of our soldiers at risk.

The MoD has spent many hundreds of millions on a series of consultancies. This includes several hundred million pounds given to PwC to improve procurement, logistics and accounting systems and at least another £53m paid to McKinsey for assistance in several areas especially procurement and logistics.[1] On its website, PwC advertises its extensive experience of working with the MoD. 'The MoD has been a major client of PricewaterhouseCoopers for over 20 years. As a result, we employ a large number of advisers with an excellent understanding of the MoD and the wider defence industry.' PwC also writes about its skill in 'getting military platforms and equipment procurement right, at the right price'.[2] On their website McKinsey are much more discreet about who they work for and what they do for their clients. They merely say, 'McKinsey is a management consulting firm that helps leading organizations improve their performance.'[3]

Certainly as you read the MoD's Annual Report for 2003/4, you cannot help but be impressed by the claimed achievements of the Department and its obviously highly accomplished consultants: 'The MoD makes the best possible use of available resources and provides the UK armed forces with the capabilities they need for operations today and in the future. The

Defence Procurement Agency (DPA) delivered equipment valued at over £3.6bn during the year . . . This represented 97%
of the asset value planned for delivery in-year and exceeded a
Departmental target of less than 15% variance between
planned and actual asset delivery value.'

Not only does the MoD appear to have provided virtually all
the equipment planned, it also states that it has exceeded its
own targets. Moreover, in the Report the Department goes on
to reassure us with the fact that most of its major projects are
running pretty close to schedule and to budget: 'the average in-
year programme slippage for major projects was 2.4 months
overall for newer projects and 2.8 months for older projects.
The average in-year cost increase was 2.7% measured against
approval levels and 3.1% compared to estimated project costs
at the beginning of the year.'[4] This is certainly an extraordinary achievement considering the size, technological challenges
and complexity of some major defence projects – there are
many private companies that would be more than delighted if
they were able to match this exemplary level of performance.

McKinsey were responsible among other things for the
introduction into the MoD of *Smart Acquisition* in 1999.
Smart Acquisition, as the name suggests, was a programme
designed to dramatically improve the way that the MoD
project-manages the purchase of weapons and equipment.
The *Smart Acquisition* programme was then 'reinvigorated'
in April 2004 to further raise the MoD's already remarkable
level of success. An interesting issue arises with regard to the
multi-million pound *Smart Acquisition* way of running defence
equipment procurement projects. At about the same time as
McKinsey were implementing *Smart Acquisition* in the MoD,
the Office of Government Commerce (OGC) were also spending millions on consultants to help design and implement their
Gateway Review process for managing large complex projects.
When asked by the Public Accounts Committee (PAC) whether
the MoD should be using *Smart Acquisition* or the *Gateway*
process, the grandly titled Permanent Under-Secretary of State
at the MoD explained: 'As a result of the Strategic Defence
Review we had a specific McKinsey review of defence procure-

ment. They gave us a model for this process which we are using. It is not exactly the same as the OGC one, but we are aligning it, we are part of their process. We do benchmarking exercises and peer reviews of each other's programmes and that sort of thing. It is not a significant difference.'

Later he said, 'the differences are probably more of form than of substance.' Then when describing how one key project would be managed, he said, 'it will go through the analogous process we have, but this is semantics: it is broadly the same.'[5] The main difference in these two approaches to managing complex procurement development projects seems to be that the main review points in *Smart Acquisition* are called 'Gates' while in the *Gateway* process they are called 'Gateways'. An ordinary taxpayer, unversed in the apparently subtle semantic differences between the MoD's *Smart Acquisition* project management process and the OGC's *Gateway Review* project management process, might well be forgiven for thinking that two government departments had just given away many millions each to different consultants to come up with almost exactly the same thing.

Where is Reality?

While the MoD's Annual Report for 2003/4 paints a picture of efficiency and effectiveness that would put most private-sector companies to shame and amply justify the huge sums of money paid for consultants' help over so many years, the report by the PAC portrays a different version of reality for the same 2003/4 period. 'Although the Department has introduced some measures to improve performance, the cost overruns in 2003 and 2004 are worse than at any time in the last decade.'[6] The PAC seemed almost upset as they concluded, 'This report once again records the woeful performance of the Department in procuring defence equipment, and its inability even to follow its own, broadly sensible, procurement rules. To all appearances, however, no-one is ever held responsible for these failures, and the careers of those involved remain unaffected.'[7]

According to the National Audit Office (NAO) report used by the PAC,[8] the budget for the MoD's twenty largest projects had gone up in just one year from £44.1bn to £50bn – a £5.9bn increase – more than 10 per cent and certainly more than the couple of per cent which the MoD's own Report admitted. In addition, during just the previous 24 months, these twenty projects had further delays of 206 months to their expected delivery dates – an extra ten months per project – somewhat higher than the more modest figures of two to three months claimed in the MoD's Annual Report. Moreover, in spite of all its consulting help from PwC, McKinsey and others, the MoD was unable to give a firm undertaking to the PAC as to when it expected to show consistent year-on-year improvements on the cost and time performance of the twenty major projects. As it surveyed this apparent shambles, the PAC was concerned about the effect the cost and time overruns would have on the safety of front-line troops: 'the Armed Forces will not be getting the most effective capability at the right time. There will be further cuts or cancellations in equipment and the Armed Forces will have to operate older, less capable, less efficient equipment for longer.'

In the face of this attack on its competence, the MoD defended its record by highlighting its improving performance: '*Smart Acquisition* programmes currently have less slippage and fewer cost overruns compared to legacy programmes.'[9] No doubt this success was a cause for celebration at the MoD and McKinsey. However, the PAC seem less impressed: 'six years since the introduction of *Smart Acquisition*, there is still little evidence of the Department having improved its performance in delivering projects to cost and to time. *Smart Acquisition* is at risk of becoming the latest in a long line of failed attempts to improve defence procurement.'[10] The PAC also highlighted the lost opportunity of getting an awful lot of useful extra equipment for its budget had the MoD not overspent on its major projects by close to £6bn. As examples, the PAC reported that for less than the £6bn overspend during just the previous year, the MoD could have also bought six Type 45 destroyers or eighteen Nimrod Maritime Patrol and Attack

aircraft or three Astute Class submarines – all these representing perhaps a better use of the money.

Another worry expressed by the PAC was a possible tendency of MoD procurement to 'gold plate' its equipment – this
means that the MoD was specifying material that had much
higher performance characteristics and therefore was much
more expensive than was necessary. 'There has been a lack of
willingness to trade off capability, time and cost to manage
cost increases and to ensure more timely delivery of an effective
level of capability.'[11] As an example of this, the PAC cited
Global Positioning Systems (GPS). For the invasion of Iraq, the
MoD needed 10,000 GPS. As only 2,000 military specification
ones were available, 8,000 civilian specification GPS were
bought 'off the shelf'. The military specification GPS cost
£4,000 each while the civilian ones cost £400 each, giving a
saving of almost £29m just on this one small item. Now, of
course the civilian GPS were less accurate and less robust than
the military specification products, but it was discovered that
most soldiers only needed the accuracy of the civilian ones.
Also, with technology changing so rapidly, there was a risk of
the more robust military GPS, like so much other material
bought by the MoD, becoming obsolete long before the end of
their working lives.

Despite claiming that *Smart Acquisition* had delivered truly
world-class results, the MoD had apparently recognized some
performance problems in its procurement and had already
launched yet another new programme, *DPA Forward*, to
improve the results of the *Smart Acquisition* programme.
The PAC reported, 'the Defence Procurement Agency's programme of reform to reinvigorate *Smart Acquisition, DPA
Forward*, has been rolling out since April 2004. The Chief of
Defence Procurement acknowledged that none of the principles of *Smart Acquisition* were intellectually difficult, but it
was a question of leadership and consistency across a very
wide community.' As part of the new *DPA Forward* programme, which is probably also being supported by McKinsey,
the DPA would engage in a number of activities often found in
management consultancy projects:

- Frame the Key Targets in a way to challenge and motivate project teams to improve and force continued improvement
- Change the culture and behaviour of the Department
- Create good working relationships with internal and external stakeholders

But in spite of hundreds of millions spent on consultants and this new initiative, the MoD could not confirm when it would actually start to improve its performance. The Chief of Defence Procurement explained: 'We are already showing considerable improvement this year, over the last three years on a like for like basis. So there is cause to believe that we are beginning to move in the right direction; but one swallow does not make a summer, there are a lot of uncertainties out there and I will continue to push on in this direction and wait another year before I can give you any form of authoritative estimate of how long it is going to take.'

At least one member of the PAC questioned the MoD bigwig's latest slightly poetic clarification: 'Sir Peter [Spencer], every review seems to bring a new gimmick, but with it it also brings the regular spring swallow, which you have just referred to, and you have seen the swallow but you are not sure you are going to see the summer. That swallow has circled this room every one of the 15 years that I have been a member of this committee. When is the damn thing going to deliver?'[12]

Swallow Delayed

We cannot predict what will happen during the next NAO report into the MoD's progress on procurement nor how the PAC will react. However, already the signs are not good for any twitchers hoping to see swallows triumphantly heralding the summer that both the MoD and the PAC have apparently been waiting for. A Defence Committee (DC) report produced in December 2005 examined two of the MoD's largest and most important projects – the Future Carrier (CVF) and the related Joint Combat Aircraft (JCA). The plan is reasonably straightforward. The MoD plans to replace the Royal Navy's three aircraft carriers with two larger, more versatile carriers capable of carrying a more powerful force. The JCA will replace the Harrier and will be flown from the two ships. Incidentally, a recent book suggests that we probably shouldn't be buying these pieces of expensive hardware in the first place.[13]

The two huge carriers are being built using the McKinsey *Smart Acquisition* approach that the PAC's 2004 Ministry of Defence Report found had so demonstrably failed to perform on so many of the MoD's other major projects. At the end of 2005, a key decision Gate on the ships was already two years late and now the MoD had no target date regarding when the decision would be taken. The DC found this situation quite worrying, 'given that the original target date for Main Gate approval on the CVF programme was two years ago, it seems to us extraordinary that there is now no target date at all.' The DC was also concerned that although the key decision would probably end up being taken at least three years late, the MoD had not made any changes to the expected in-service dates of the ships of 2012 and 2015. The DC found it difficult to believe that the ships would be built on time when they were already around three years late, particularly in view of the fact that nothing seemed to have happened since the previous review twelve months earlier: 'Progress on finalizing the Alliance Agreement does not appear to have progressed substantially since this issue was examined by the previous Defence Committee. In May 2004, Sir Peter Spencer, Chief of Defence Procurement (CDP), told our predecessors that "there is agreement on the large majority of the detail, there are one or two loose ends which we are tidying up". However, CDP told us, some eighteen months later, that those loose ends turned out to be much more fundamental than I had understood them to be at the time.'

In November 2004, the DC was told that 'we have 60% design definition now, which is higher than any other project.' A year later, the MoD admitted, 'if it was 60% then, my judgement is that it is not a great deal further on.' When questioned about the final likely cost of the two carriers, the MoD refused to answer, claiming that the information was 'commercially sensitive'. When questioned about the likely in-service dates of the carriers, the MoD refused to answer, again claiming that the information was 'commercially sensitive'.

The plane (JCA) wasn't looking too chirpy either. Originally, its in-service date was planned as 2012, sensibly coinciding with the date of the first of the two carriers. But by the end of 2005, this date seemed to have slipped two years to 2014. Then there was another not totally minor problem – the aircraft was probably too heavy to use on the carrier. Additionally, the Americans, who were developing the plane, had not yet agreed to hand over the technology to the British even though the deal had apparently been agreed and £2bn already paid over. The DC were concerned about the British having a plane without knowing how it worked: 'there is a risk that the UK could find itself in a position where it had one of the most advanced military aircraft but could not operate it independently of the US.' The MoD claimed it was actively negotiating for the handover of the vital technological know-how. However, a year earlier, the former chairman of BAe Systems had highlighted what most of us would probably have thought was a 'no-brainer' when he warned the DC that negotiation was somewhat difficult after you had signed a contract: 'it is no good when you have signed up and paid your cheque over then to go back to negotiate the release of technology.'

The DC had numerous other misgivings with these two critical programmes. One was that any delays in either project could entail major extra expenditure as the service life of existing carriers and/or aircraft would have to be extended. But perhaps the most significant issue was that 'the UK could be left with new carriers without new aircraft to operate from them, or new aircraft with no carriers to operate from.'[14]

Judging from the MoD's apparently continued inability to achieve anything with its *Smart Acquisition* programme, swallows may well have become extinct long before the MoD shows any improvement in its project management results.

The next NAO report and PAC review should make interesting reading.

Measuring Smoke and Mirrors

Another key area where the MoD had used a considerable amount of help from consultants – PwC in this case – was in improving its accounting, financial control and measurement processes. As *Management Consultancy* magazine reported in 1999, 'in 1996 an accounting system integrator (ASI) was appointed, a consortium led by PwC MCS, to design and implement the systems, redesign the financial processes and train staff. The task is huge and complex. For example, the processing of accounting transactions is devolved to over one hundred entities, each with its own suite of accounting ledgers.' Fortunately, PwC appeared to show great motivation and dedication to complete this Herculean task successfully. As the ASI project director at PwC said, 'we are incentivised to help them work it. We get lump sums by demonstrating that they are able to operate the system – we are paid to care whether the system works. Our staff are burning the midnight oil to make sure it does.'[15]

Unfortunately, the claimed achievements of the MoD and its consultants in supercharging their financial and measurement systems just weren't fully appreciated by the members of the PAC. For a start, the MoD had difficulty in confirming whether their cost overruns in 2003/4 were £4bn or £6bn. When asked how much the MoD's overspend was in real cash terms, the Chief of Defence Procurement replied, 'We do have a figure and I will find it for you. The total amount of cost growth this year . . . I think is £4bn, but I need to make sure that those are the correct figures . . . May I correct the figure I just gave you as £4bn, it should be £6bn.'[16]

However, using a quite original interpretation of its figures, the MoD explained to the PAC that the £4bn or £6bn was not really what could be called 'overspend' at all: 'This is not money which we have overspent on this. It is a reflection of the lack of realism in the original estimates against the budget and that is an important point to reflect in this discussion because the whole approach that the tools are bringing to us is to get greater realism from the outset. So what you are seeing is a level of disappointment.'[17]

Thus, almost ten years after launching a major programme supported by PwC consultants to improve its financial budgeting and control, the MoD is saying that we shouldn't take seriously any of the budgets for equipment, which were the basis for the purchases being approved in the first place. The MoD, according to the MoD, apparently does not overspend. So when, due to woeful project management, it squanders billions more than planned, it blandly claims that this is purely because the original plans were too optimistic. In a world of bureaucratic smoke and mirrors, there is apparently no such thing as overspend, just a £6bn 'level of disappointment'. One suspects that soldiers in places like Afghanistan and Iraq, who cannot get sufficient body armour or properly armour-plated vehicles due to MoD budget constraints, and the families of soldiers killed due to this lack of equipment, might feel more than 'a level of disappointment'.

To stay on the subject of measurements, the MoD has a pretty interesting way of measuring its performance. You or I, when employing a builder or a plumber, would expect to agree a price and then expect the work to be done at that price. Not so the MoD. The MoD sets at least two budgets for each equipment programme. There is the 'expected cost' and the 'highest acceptable cost'. For example, the expected or budgeted cost for a major piece of equipment is what it is planned to cost and should cost – this might be £1bn. However, if lots of problems were encountered, the cost would rise and so the MoD also sets a 'highest acceptable cost' – if things do go pear-shaped, this is the upper cost limit at which the equipment purchase would still be worthwhile – which might be £1.5bn. However, as soon as the project starts, the MoD seems to forget the original budgeted cost of £1bn and so measures its progress, not against the budgeted 'expected cost' but against

the 'highest acceptable cost' of £1.5bn. As the MoD explained
to the PAC, 'practice was to measure performance against the
approved level; in other words, the highest acceptable level of
cost.'[18] The problem this presented, of course, was that if
everybody was only trying to achieve the highest acceptable
cost, then there was no way the overall procurement programme could possibly come in on its real original budget.
That means if a series of projects is planned to cost say £20bn,
all those involved might set out to meet a 'highest acceptable
cost' of £30bn. Meanwhile, the Defence Management Board
are still expecting the projects to cost only the original £20bn
target. As the MoD explained to the PAC, 'when you add all
this up across the whole programme that gives you a major
problem. The Defence Management Board had been hoping
things would come out at their expected value.'[19] A member of
the PAC was somewhat surprised that it had taken the MoD
about ten years to discover that if everyone planned to overspend by billions, then it was somewhat unlikely that the
overall defence budget would be met. 'I congratulate you on
identifying this issue, but when you identified it, did it not
strike you as blindingly obvious and almost incredible that it
had not been identified before?'[20]

In spite of these problems, the MoD was so satisfied with its
own performance measurement processes, that it saw itself as a
source of expertise and best practice that could be passed on to
other, less professional organizations. In its Annual Report, the
MoD wrote, 'MoD performance management expertise has
been used to help other Government Departments, local
authorities and other nations' Defence forces, including the
U.S. Department of Defence, develop their own performance
management regimes.'[21] In fact, so wonderful was the MoD's
Balanced Scorecard performance measurement that the MoD
seemed to be considering going into the management consulting business: 'we are also considering its potential for selling
into wider markets as a commercially available performance
management tool.'[22] One could be forgiven for thinking that
the MoD top brass were overdosing on consultancy and thus
getting slightly confused about their department's role in life.

Unfortunately, in spite of managing to convince itself that it apparently had enviable world class performance management, the MoD was unable to convince anybody else. Embarrassingly, the MoD could not confirm to the PAC whether the millions spent on *Smart Acquisition* had given a measurable result as 'data to support *Smart Acquisition* savings proved to be unreliable.'[23] All in all, the uninitiated might wonder what value PwC and others had provided when, after so many years and so many hundreds of millions of pounds of consulting, the MoD's performance measurement systems were still apparently inconsistent, unreliable and seemingly owing more to fiction than to fact.

Light at the End of the Tunnel?

But all is not gloom and doom in the world of MoD weapons procurement. In addition to its normal purchasing programme, which is probably about £5.9bn overspent and in which some items are up to six years late, the MoD runs an Urgent Operational Requirements (UORs) process. This is a process for rapidly getting hold of essential equipment and weapons should the British Armed Forces ever be sent into military action. Compared to the overall defence procurement budget of around £6bn a year, the items in the UORs are relatively small – for the Afghanistan conflict the UORs were only £148m and for Iraq they cost £811m. The MoD was commended by the PAC for its success in pushing through the UORs so rapidly and efficiently when supplying British troops in Afghanistan and Iraq: 'I should like straightaway at the start of the hearing to pay tribute to the ingenuity and hard work of all your staff, Sir Kevin, in backing up our armed forces in Iraq and often moving very quickly indeed when necessary.'

However, as with so many aspects of the performance of the MoD bureaucracy, what appears to be satisfactory at first glance loses a bit of its shine on closer inspection.

For a start, just over a third of the equipment hurriedly acquired under UORs should actually have been in stock anyway as it was part of the regular purchasing programme. But it wasn't in stock because the huge budget overruns at the MoD meant there wasn't enough money to buy these essential items. Secondly, around a third of the equipment bought under UORs for the Iraq invasion wasn't actually available for the start of the conflict. As a member of the PAC said, 'it is highly regrettable that only two thirds of UORs were fully delivered for the start of warfighting in Iraq.' And, thirdly, because much of the equipment arrived just before the start of hostilities – the Minimi machine gun and the One Shot Mine Disposal System, for example – there was insufficient time to train the troops in its use.

The PAC was also concerned that there was no separate process and there were no special staff for handling UORs in the event of a potential conflict. As a management consultant, I find this surprising as in any commercial organization you would have separate and differing processes for managing something that takes seven years to acquire compared to something that takes just seven weeks. But the consultants being paid by the MoD appear not to have noticed any difference in these two types of equipment purchase and so people working on other procurement projects just had to struggle through with the extra workload.

What seemed most puzzling to the PAC was why the MoD's performance on equipment supply was so dismal year after year, when in the event of a war it had shown it could react so rapidly: 'Many of the UORs to support operations in Iraq were successfully deployed and introduced into service in very short time-scales. Much of the Department's regular procurement is to deliver items of similar cost and complexity, yet takes much longer. The Department should examine what lessons it can learn from its flexible approach to UORs . . . Under the pressure of conflict, the Department and its industrial partners have shown considerable resourcefulness in coming up with good solutions to address urgent shortfalls in capability. These successes contrast with the recurring interminable time and cost problems reported regularly in the Major Projects Report.'[24]

So, once again, questions can be asked about what value PwC, McKinsey and others had been providing when the processes which they had ostensibly been improving actually performed so badly.

To Be Lean Is to Be Liberated

In the MoD, as in most government departments, it can be difficult to find out precisely how many millions have been given to which consultants and for what. I have been told, but have not seen documentation to support it, that one of the projects run by consultants was to implement in our military services the kind of stock management practices used in private industry by companies like car and photocopier manufacturers to keep down their stock levels and costs of inventory. These 'Just-in-Time' stock and logistics policies are great for reducing the costs of making cars, photocopiers or whatever, where market demand levels can largely be forecast. But one might be justified in questioning whether they are quite so suitable for the military who may quickly have to go from a peacetime situation into armed conflict and so will rapidly need weapons and other basic equipment.

Near the Iraqi city of Basra in 2003 Sergeant Steven Roberts was shot in the chest after being asked to hand in his body armour because it was in short supply.[25] It appears that this incident led to a change of policy on levels of stock. Replying to questions put by the Public Accounts Committee about reports of troops lacking basic equipment following the death of Sergeant Steven Roberts, the Permanent Under-Secretary said, 'we had a lively exchange in the Committee as to whether these were exaggerated or accurate. To some extent there was validity in the point; I think it had been overdone, but nevertheless we were stretched. As a result of that, we now keep slightly higher levels of stock of those equipments.'[26]

This would seem to suggest that the MoD had allowed stock levels of essential equipment to go below sensible levels. However, without better inside information, it would be difficult to draw a link between the consultants' work and the death of at least one soldier.

We also know that McKinsey received generous amounts of our money to implement the *Smart Acquisition* process to reduce cost and time overruns on military equipment purchasing, that the MoD have had difficulty proving any positive results from this and that the MoD's £6bn overspend on its main projects appears to have led to budget cuts and seems to be preventing the purchase of vital equipment for front-line soldiers. As a recent book asked: 'What on earth is going on? Whatever can be so important, and so expensive, that we are actually cutting back on our splendid, useful, hard-bought infantrymen, rather than sorting out their problems – given that it would cost us almost nothing to do so?'[27]

In October 2005, Sergeant Christian Hickey was killed when his vehicle was blown up by a roadside bomb. He was in a Land-Rover protected by composite fibreglass designed to stop rifle fire but useless against bombs. The MoD claimed that the decision not to supply troops with armour-protected Land-Rovers had nothing to do with budget restrictions but was purely because they were not suitable for use off-road.[28] Sergeant Hickey's commanding officer was reported to have been furious over the death and to have 'resigned after failing to obtain armoured Land-Rovers for his patrols'.[29] The MoD naturally insisted that there was no connection between the officer's resignation and the armoured Land-Rovers issue. Meanwhile, an armoured car was provided at home for the Prime Minister's wife. Some commentators have questioned the government's priorities[30] and speculated that driving on patrol through the streets of Basra was possibly more dangerous than driving to work, the gym, the hairdresser or a therapist through the streets of London. One wrote, 'Cherie travels in an armoured car while British squaddies in Iraq are denied any such protection'.[31] He then went on to ask, 'I wonder how Cherie Blair would justify her four-ton Omega to the family of, say, Sergeant Christian Hickey killed 10 days ago when his unarmoured Land-Rover was blown up by a roadside bomb while on patrol in Basra.'[32]

In addition, we know that despite PwC working in logistics for many years, McKinsey were also commissioned to work in the same area. The MoD has announced in its Annual Report that, supported by McKinsey, it expects to reduce its head-count in logistics by 3,000. In November 2005, the Armed Forces Minister Adam Ingram announced 2,000 job losses in defence repairs as the MoD closed aviation and land vehicle repair depots as part of its programme to 'modernize logistical support'. Union leaders characterized the job cuts as 'an absolute disgrace' which could jeopardize the safety of the Armed Forces.[33]

Looking at these and similar incidents in the MoD and other government departments, one could be forgiven for suspecting that management consultants are inappropriately applying practices from private-sector companies to public-sector orga-nizations – and the results are not pretty. There is a McKinsey maxim, 'to be lean is to be liberated'. While McKinsey and other consultancies may profitably apply this philosophy to their clients in the private sector, causing many thousands of job losses in the process, it is not so obvious that reducing stocks and support staff to the minimum is quite as suitable for our armed forces when we send them into dangerous situations where their lives are dependent on their having the right equipment and support. Let us hope that at the time of Britain's next military adventure, we do not once again find that our soldiers lose their lives because logistics have been 'modernized' even closer to the bone, and so we lack essential equipment and the facilities to keep that essential equipment in working order.

The Magic Disappearing Trick

Another area where McKinsey have been supporting the MoD has been on a programme to reduce stocks. The 1998 Strategic Defence Review concluded that there was scope for significant reductions in stocks following the end of the Cold War. At the time, the MoD held stocks valued at £19bn. A target of £2.2bn of stock reductions was set. The rationale was that the savings in logistics could be used to fund the required increases in military capability to support joint expeditionary forces. Certainly, studies done by the MoD and McKinsey showed major potential stock reductions. For example, the MoD held 1,775 long distance refuelling tanks. With an annual demand for four, this meant there was sufficient stock for 440 years. On many other items there were up to 60 years' stock available. And there were about three times as many helicopter engines as there were helicopters to put them in.

By 2003, the MoD could be congratulated for overachieving against its stock reduction target of £2.2bn with claimed stock reductions of £2.8bn. Once again, however, closer investigation revealed that there might be a more than significant gap between what the MoD and their consultants claimed and what happened in reality. At least half of the supposed stock reduction was achieved by clerical changes such as writing down the value of many older items of stock. The air force, for example, managed to notch up £755m of 'stock savings'. But around £400m of this came just from changing the book value of items in stock with no change in the actual volumes of physical stock held. Huge 'stock savings' were also claimed when they were simply due to correcting previous clerical errors. There were 1,175 brass nuts worth £0.01p each. Although the whole lot were only worth £1.17, their value had previously been incorrectly listed as £83m. So making this correction achieved an impressive 'stock saving' of £82,999,998.83. Not bad for two minutes' work. Likewise an item with an apparent stock value of £192m turned out to be worth £1.9m – giving an instant 'stock saving' of £190.1m. These are just two of many examples where the mere wave of a bureaucratic magic wand made hundreds of millions of pounds of unwanted stock mysteriously disappear, providing, no doubt, a great sense of achievement for the MoD and their consultants.

PwC, who had worked on the financial systems at the MoD, claim that they had 'enhanced performance in planning, objective setting, management reporting, record keeping and reviews of performance following the introduction of Resource Accounting and Budgeting'.[34] However, their efforts do not seem to have resulted in particularly robust systems and information. Due to problems of missing and inaccurate data, the National Audit Office was unable to find out whether the 'successful' stock reduction programme had reduced stock or not; if it had reduced stock, nobody was really sure by how much: 'Despite the evidence provided by the Department that it had indeed disposed of a large amount of stock, the National Audit Office was unable to validate whether or not the stock reduction target had been achieved. Three factors stood in the way of the validation. The original baseline was not reliable. The basis of measurement was not consistent between the services. And the reporting of achievement was not accurate.'[35]

These findings that the MoD's figures were effectively useless could lead one to question the efficacy of PwC's marvellous 'enhanced' financial reporting systems.

Lions, Tigers, Donkeys and Asses

It should be hoped that no British soldier ever takes the time to study the verbal evidence given by the top brass of the MoD to inquiries like the PAC's. If they were to read it, they would probably give up all hope, pack their kit bags and go home. As you read through page after page of stonewalling, circumlocution, apparently deliberate opacity and consultantese, you get the impression of an organization whose leaders have disappeared up their own rear ends into a fantasy world of consultants and management-speak and have lost touch with their original aims and purpose – protecting us from those who would harm our interests.

Stonewalling In answer to a series of questions about the possibility of BAe withdrawing from the project to build a new naval carrier, the MoD representative says, 'I cannot speak on behalf of BAe,' and 'You asked me three questions, which one would you like me to answer first?' As well as, 'I am not prepared to answer speculative comments in the newspaper' and 'I am not prepared to answer in open session'.[36]

Circumlocution A member of the PAC stated that 2004 has been 'another disappointing year'[37] following 2003 'which of course was a very bad year'. The MoD worthy replies, 'performance next year will show a continued improvement in the right direction' – an answer that doesn't correspond whatsoever to comments by the PAC about the MoD's ever worsening performance.

Opacity Asked if the cost overruns would affect the capability of the Armed Forces, an MoD grandee replied, 'clearly there is not a one-to-one relationship between the change in one programme and the effect because there is a range of impacts that it will have.'[38]

Consultantese A member of the PAC asked, 'do you feel that the reaction in the department is sufficiently focused for you to sit there and tell us with confidence that next year will be better?'[39] The reply would have warmed the heart of anyone who likes playing the game one should always play when listening to a management consultant – Buzzword Bingo: 'I am not yet content with the level of focus at all levels in such a large number of projects with such a large number of people, and anybody who has led a major improvement programme will tell you that it takes time to tackle the cultural and behavioural issues. What we have done in the immediate term is to considerably tighten up our processes so that we now have project reviews, assurance processes, key supplier processes and a greater emphasis on engaging with the military customer on managing time and cost overruns, to show that we can demonstrate a movement in the right direction.'[40]

In the First World War, the British Armed Forces reputedly consisted of lions led by donkeys. In the Second World War, they were probably more like lions led by tigers. Now we seem to have lions led by tigers supported by donkeys – or should we say 'asses'?

CHAPTER 4

Is Anybody Responsible?

The Bureaucratic Maze

As over £70bn of our money will have to come out of the budgets of front-line public services such as hospitals, social services, the police, fire brigades and so on to be handed over to consultants, it is probably worth while taking a little time to try and find out who exactly in Parliament or in the Civil Service is responsible for ensuring that this money is being well spent.

We can start with the government. As Britain does not have a constitution, there cannot be any constitutional duty on the government to spend our money wisely. So, as a group, the government have no 'duty of care' with our cash.

The way the British system of government has developed it is, in theory, the Crown that decides how our money is spent. The Crown does this through its ministers, principally the Cabinet. As the government website explains: 'The Crown is charged with the management of all the revenue of the State and with all payments for the public service. So, acting with the advice of its ministers, it presents to the House of Commons its requirements for the financing of public services. In return the Commons authorises expenditure (through granting Supply) and provides the ways and means to meet that expenditure, through taxes and other sources of revenue.'

The House of Lords has a rather peripheral and largely ceremonial role in the control of expenditure: 'The role of the House of Lords is confined to assenting to those financial provisions of the Commons which require statutory authorization. Since the withholding of the Lords' assent to a money bill is effective only for a month and would in any event be treated by the Commons as a serious breach of its privileges, it is, in effect, the lower House which exercises Parliament's financial control.'

Moreover, the functions of the House of Commons are also restricted. The Commons can only approve or reject expenditure proposals coming from the Crown: 'The principle of the Crown's sole responsibility for expenditure, which is embodied in parliamentary procedure (Standing Orders 48 and 49) has a number of practical implications for the financial procedure of the House of Commons. In particular, Parliament does not vote money unless required by the Crown; Parliament does not impose or increase taxes at its own initiative; and private members or the opposition are unable to propose increases to charges on public funds (i.e. public expenditure).'

So it is clear that all decisions about how much to tax us and how to use our money must come from the Cabinet. If we look at how the Cabinet can spend our cash, the only restrictions on them are that their decisions must be legal and approved by the House of Commons: 'Generally speaking, ministers may do anything which they are not precluded from doing by statute, but they will only be able to finance their activities if Parliament provides the resources.' However, though ministers have the ability to spend what they want however they want, there is no duty on them to ensure value for money. They have the authority to spend billions of pounds without the responsibility for overseeing that those billions are well spent. That's an enviable position to be in.

But, if ministers are not responsible for proper management of our money, presumably someone else is. At first sight this would appear to be the Treasury: 'In addition to parliamentary control, expenditure is also subject to administrative control exercised by the Treasury. While public expenditure pro-grammes are the responsibility of the departments which administer them, the Treasury has primary responsibility on policy for the financing of expenditure and controlling public expenditure within agreed totals. In addition, by convention no expenditure can be incurred without Treasury approval.'

The government website then lists some of the Treasury's key tasks in more detail:

- Managing comprehensive reviews
- Coordinating the presentation of estimates by departments
- Monitoring expenditure and ensuring that agreed plans are delivered
- Improving financial management and value for money

If the Treasury is responsible for 'improving value for money' then it could be interpreted as being responsible for ensuring that our money is well spent. But the Treasury seems to avoid this responsibility by delegating it to the departments that spend the money: 'Treasury approval is required for all resources and expenditure, but in practice the Treasury dele-gates to departments the authority to spend within specific criteria and financial limits.' It seems that although the Treas-ury can limit the overall amount spent, it cannot or will not intervene in how the money is used. Instead it sees itself as a 'focal point' that can be 'consulted'. The reason for this delegation of authority from the Treasury to departments is to achieve 'the right balance between the Treasury's need for control in order to fulfil its responsibilities to Parliament and the department's freedom to manage within the agreed limits laid down by the government'.

Thus the responsibility for achieving value for money for the consultants' £70bn must rest with the heads of the spending departments. At first sight this does appear sensible. However, the way this responsibility is assigned to department heads looks slightly odd to anyone with experience of how organiza-tions actually function. When an individual is appointed head of a department they are also given the title of Accounting

Officer ('When the permanent head of a department is appointed, he or she is separately appointed by the Treasury as Accounting Officer for that department'). The responsibilities of the accounting officers are very clear. They must ensure that:

- The resources available to their department are organised to deliver departmental objectives in the most economic, efficient and effective way, with full regard to regularity and propriety
- A sound system of internal control is maintained that supports the achievement of the department's policies, aims and objectives
- Proper financial procedures are followed and suitable accounting records are maintained
- The public funds for which they are individually responsible are properly managed and safeguarded

So it is the accounting officers, namely the heads of department, who are responsible for ensuring that our money is well spent. This means that, in addition to spending our money, the heads of department are responsible for ensuring that they spend our money wisely. This dual role could cause difficulties. It's a bit like telling a criminal that you would rather he didn't do anything naughty, however, should he feel the urge to carry out some illegal acts, and because he is also appointed an honorary member of the police, he is responsible for policing his own behaviour. It's probable you will find many criminals who will happily fulfil the first part of the role – go out and commit some crimes – but not many who will be minded to fulfil the second part – be so helpful as to tell the police what they've been up to. Likewise, you will find most Civil Service department heads are quite enthusiastic about spending all the money they get from us, but somewhat less than eager to tell anybody like the Treasury if they, the departments heads, have inadvertently wasted a few hundred million or even a few billion on a consultancy or IT systems fiasco. In fact, as we shall see a little later, this dual role of robber and cop leads to some quite entertaining exchanges in public hearings as one head of department after another tries to weasel-word their way out of accusations of having taken incompetence and profligacy to heights of which most of us could only dream.

Who Catches the Baddies?

However, all is not lost. The Treasury has put in place what it would probably claim is a mechanism to ensure that heads of department both spend our cash wisely and also fulfil their role as controllers of their own behaviour. There is a person with the rather grand title 'Comptroller General of the Receipt and Issue of Her Majesty's Exchequer and Auditor General of Public Accounts', usually abbreviated to 'Comptroller and Auditor General' (C&AG). This individual is absolutely key in ensuring our money is used with the greatest of care. The C&AG has a whole lot of bean counting to do: 'As Auditor General, the statutory duties are to certify the accounts of all government departments and a wide range of other public-sector bodies; to examine revenue accounts; and to report the results of these examinations to Parliament.' However, in addition to being head bean counter, the C&AG also seems to be the local sheriff and can go out wherever he or she sees fit in search of anyone they feel might be up to no good. 'The C&AG also has wide statutory powers to carry out, and report to Parliament on, examinations of economy, efficiency and effectiveness in the use of resources by those bodies audited or to which the C&AG has rights of access. These are generally referred to as value-for-money studies.' Some people might find this an unusual combination of roles – it is not obvious that the person who is best at counting the beans is also the person you would send out to bring wrongdoers to account. One might be tempted to think that the two roles actually required slightly different skill sets. But apparently this contradiction inherent in the C&AG's dual functions has not occurred to the powers that be.

The whole process for appointing and paying the C&AG seems rather splendid. 'By statute, the Comptroller and Auditor General enjoys a high degree of independence. The individual is appointed by the Queen by Letters Patent on an address from the House of Commons moved by the Prime Minister after agreement with the Chairman of Public Accounts. The C&AG can be removed from office only by the Queen on an address from both Houses of Parliament. His or her salary is paid directly from the Consolidated Fund without requiring the annual approval of the Executive or of Parliament.'

So it's the head honcho bean counter who decides where and when to go out and get the baddies: 'the C&AG alone decides on the extent and conduct of the audit and other examinations which are carried out and the content of reports which are made to Parliament.' However, it's not always obvious that the C&AG has the balls to go after the real baddies. For example in the 2005/6 session, the C&AG launched investigations into some issues that may not quite seem critical – Northern Ireland's waste management strategy, the Royal Parks and the Princess Diana Memorial Fountain. Moreover, in spite of the fact that the NHS *Connecting for Health* programme could cost over £30bn, for more than three years the C&AG appears to have felt no need to assess the overall plans and progress of the largest civil consulting and IT systems project in world history.

The Sheriff and the Posse

The way that the C&AG ensures our money is well spent is through the work of the National Audit Office (NAO), which works directly for the C&AG. 'The National Audit Office, created by the National Audit Act 1983, replaces the Exchequer and Audit Department. The C&AG, as head of the NAO, has power to appoint staff considered necessary to enable the C&AG to carry out the office's functions.' Just like its top man, the C&AG, the NAO has two main functions. As its name suggests, it must carry out annual audits on the accounts of government departments to assess 'whether the financial statements of the organization give a true and fair view, and that they do not contain material errors or are presented in a way which might mislead a person relying on the accounts.' But it is also responsible for overseeing that our cash is well spent. 'The National Audit Act 1983 provides a statutory basis for the C&AG's value-for-money studies. Under section 6 of the 1983 Act, the C&AG may, under discretion, carry out examinations of the economy, efficiency and effectiveness with which any body to which this section applies has used its resources in discharging its functions.'

Again one might be tempted to wonder whether the kind of people who are really tremendous at ensuring that all the 'i's are dotted and all the 't's are crossed and that all the figures have been added up correctly really are those best endowed to uncover all the devious tricks used by heads of department to cover up any financial profligacy and mismanagement. In a private company, for example, you wouldn't normally put the accounts clerks in charge of taking on your toughest customer. But it appears that in the public sector nobody sees a logical inconsistency in this rather odd combination of responsibilities.

It also seems as if the approach taken by the NAO is quite civilized and gentlemanly and designed not to ruffle any important feathers. In its terms of reference, the NAO is instructed to work hand in hand with those whom it is meant to be objectively auditing: 'The contents of all reports are always discussed with the audited bodies before publication to ensure that the facts are complete and fairly presented. When considering draft reports, departments should ensure that not only the facts and how they are presented but also all comments and opinions are agreed. Any comments or opinions which the department does not accept should be clearly attributed to the NAO and the department's differing view should also be stated. This applies to the conclusions and recommendations as well as to the main body of the report.'

Some people might see this agreement between the parties as necessary to ensure the accuracy of the NAO reports. Those of a more cynical disposition, however, could view the above requirements as a licence to cover up and whitewash – an opportunity for both sides to get together and ensure that nobody rocks the boat in which they are all comfortably cruising – at our expense.

The C&AG and his staff, the NAO, are not allowed to question the merits or otherwise of the policy objectives of any department. They can only assess whether departments are delivering value for money.

The way that the NAO feeds back what it discovers is through reports to Parliament, though these are normally first examined by the Public Accounts Committee (PAC). Of all the groups involved in ensuring value for money, the PAC could be seen to be one of the most impressive. It is nominated by the House of Commons and consists of up to fifteen members, with four making up a quorum, and is drawn from all the parliamentary parties. What gives the PAC some teeth is that the chairperson is traditionally from the Opposition and there-fore less likely to display the supine obedience to the govern-ment that one could expect from a member of the governing party. Although comprised only of politicians, the PAC is assumed to be non-partisan and non-political. 'The PAC adopts a non-party attitude in its work and seeks to reach dispassionate findings and recommendations whichever party is in government.' Great in theory, dubious in practice.

There appear to be at least two important weaknesses in the PAC process. Firstly, the PAC has no authority to instruct the C&AG as to where NAO audits should be should carried out. Secondly, the PAC does not have the power to demand action. It can only make recommendations: 'It is a duty of departments to consider the Committee's reports which relate to them and to provide answers to the House of Commons in consultation with the Treasury.' Assuming any real criticisms of department heads actually make it through the gentlemanly process of agreeing the findings with the NAO bean counters, depart-ments are pretty much free to ignore any recommendations if they so choose – and that appears to be the most frequent response. On almost all occasions when the NAO has con-ducted follow-up audits on departments audited several years previously, it is found that few to none of the PAC's recommendations have been actioned. Moreover, as the NAO tends to report on problems months and even years after massive amounts of money have already been wasted, all everybody ever seems to do is to nod sagely, say that 'important lessons have been learnt' and carry on as before with the next even more costly disaster. This worry that the C&AG and the NAO do much too little much too late was expressed well by one member of the PAC. Their comments about the massive NHS *Connecting for Health* programme show that they felt the tardy action of the C&AG severely limited the ability of the PAC to hold errant officials to account: 'Well, I think we are going to have a report from the National Audit Office next year on it, which again highlights the fact that the programme has been going for two and a half years already and it will be three and a half years before we in this Committee look at it for the first time and it suggests that the method of departmental accountability through this Committee to Parliament is not necessarily as strong as it should be.'[1]

The NAO have announced that they are reviewing *Connecting for Health*: 'The study examines the procurement processes used for placing the contracts; whether the contracts are likely to deliver good value for money; how the Department is implementing the programme; and the progress made by the programme so far.'[2]

Unfortunately, the NAO report is proving to be as difficult to locate as the MoD's notoriously elusive swallow. The NAO review was first due in August 2005. This was then put back to November 2005. Then it was put back again to February or March 2006. Then it was announced that it would appear in the summer of 2006 at the earliest. One commentator expressed concerns at these continual delays on this important report, 'the later the report is published, the more difficult it is likely to be to apply any lessons from the report or take any remedial actions recommended to the ten-year NHS IT programme.'[3]

Moreover, you cannot really have any form of accountability unless there are sanctions in place to deal with those who don't perform. As to the question – does anybody in the Civil Service ever get fired for utter ineptitude? – the answer is invariably 'no'. As a member of the PAC stated, 'I know when we have been asked about how many members of staff have been sacked or replaced for what has amounted to total incompetence and mismanagement of schemes, the answer has been once again "none". And in a PAC hearing on the disastrous results of the MoD's weapons procurement programme, a senior official at the MoD said that it would be unfair to "blight someone's career" if they were "incompetent", because they would only have been "carrying out their duties".

Theatre of the Absurd

In summary, it appears that the only people who are really responsible for ensuring the wise use of the £70bn or so of our money that New Labour are giving to management and IT systems consultants are the strange two-headed creatures who run the spending departments. Now, a person with two heads may have worked well in *Hitchhiker's Guide to the Galaxy*, but in real life it is not obviously the most effective way of ensuring our £70bn is put to the best use. Lest anybody is naïve enough to think that this arrangement – department supremos policing their own spending – actually can work, it might be worthwhile to give some examples of the verbal acrobatics and logical contortions used by the responsible individuals on the few joyous occasions that the NAO has actually dared criticize them and the PAC has had sufficient nous to try and hold these worthies to account.

In PAC hearings, the accounting officers and their various stand-ins and side-kicks seem to use a variety of creative tactics to avoid even the slightest suggestion of accountability for their waste and mismanagement of our money. A good blocking move is to hear the exact opposite of what has just been said. As we have seen, when criticized year after year for their ever worsening performance in terms of budget and cost overruns on weapons procurement, the MoD bosses time and again maintain that the MoD is continuing to improve its performance. Another favourite is outright denial of reality. After a discussion which featured more than £1bn wasted in IT systems catastrophes at National Air Traffic Services, the Child Support Agency, the Criminal Records Bureau and Inland Revenue tax credits, the top gun from the Office of Government Commerce was asked if his department was finally addressing 'the disasters that we have had to look at over the years on IT projects'.[4] The gentleman blithely replied, 'I think there have been some very misleading reports, if I may say so.'[5] Unfounded and vague metaphorical optimism is likewise quite useful in deflecting criticism. Under pressure for the department's inability to do its job properly, the OGC boss said, 'there have been very significant forward movements. So we are on a journey and I think we are making progress on that journey.'[6] Talking tough can also work a treat in dealing with awkward issues. 'There is no hiding place now,' said the accounting officer at the OGC as 87 per cent of Civil Service projects successfully avoided scrutiny as to whether they had ever achieved any results.[7]

The individuals responsible for the Government Communication Headquarters' (GCHQ) new accommodation programme also showed great resourcefulness when they appeared before the PAC. They had to explain away why their IT systems costs were originally budgeted at £41m, then put into the project plan at a mere £21m and actually ended up costing over £450m. There was forgetfulness: 'I am searching my memory because a lot has happened since those days.'[8] There was an argument that is often used: although we were incompetent, actually there was an excellent reason for what we did: 'I do not attempt to excuse what happened; it clearly should not have done, but I think there was a rational explanation to where we were. We were in a period of transition.'[9] Of course, there was the old favourite about lessons learnt: 'I am sure there are a lot of valuable lessons we should have learnt.' And there was putting a brave face on it and defying the questioner: 'it was a very large sum of money, but it does represent real value.' Then when all else fails, there was bluff it out by heaping huge amounts of praise on your staff: 'the new Programme Director is a very experienced director of large programmes. He works on the basis of a very rigorous approach.'[10] However 'rigorous' this person may or may not have actually been, this still doesn't quite explain how a budgeted £21m of taxpayers' money so quickly became £450m.

Those implicated in the Criminal Records Bureau *Delivering Safer Recruitment* project – a programme setting up an organization to do background checks on people applying to work with vulnerable groups such as children and the elderly – put on a similarly world class show. They had to justify why the expected cost was £250m, the actual cost will be over £400m, the project came in late and the service will probably be ineffective as key identity checks and other services have been quietly dropped. Various dramatic poses were struck by those being interrogated by the PAC. There was – it was a noble cause – 'in the end my priority was the protection of children and the protection of the vulnerable.'[11] This was a fine answer, but it didn't explain the disappearance of over £150m of our money, nor the fact that the service will be all but useless at preventing dangerous individuals getting near the vulnerable. There was also – we battled bravely against almost impossible odds – 'as soon as we realised that there was a difficulty to be overcome, we worked very hard and everyone put their shoulders to the wheel in terms of putting it right.'[12] Again, stirring stuff. But given that the 'difficulty' referred to was entirely due to the incompetence of those involved, the answer falls a little short of total clarity. And then when things got a bit tough, they just refused to answer the questions.

Many of the above are potentially Oscar-winning performances. However, the Golden Smokescreen Award, the much sought-after award which goes to that government department which most successfully manages to deny its glaringly obvious inaction, ineptitude, profligacy and incompetence, must surely go to the grandees from the Department of Health. In 2000, the NAO wrote a damning study on the level of hospital-acquired infections. Another report in 2004 showed that infections had risen dramatically and that little to nothing had been done about its recommendations. Moreover, the Department of Health had no way of knowing whether the real level of such infections was 300,000 a year or 600,000 a year or even much higher – the Department's most recent figures were from a ten-year-old study done in American hospitals and extrapolated to Britain. No similar study had ever been done in Britain. So although they hadn't a clue about the overall incidence of infections, but did know that on just one type of infection, MRSA, Britain's rates were 70 times higher than Denmark's and 40 times higher than Holland's or Sweden's, the Department still maintained, 'to be absolutely clear, their levels of hospital infection are not that dissimilar to ours.'[13] When asked why rates of MRSA were still rising and why nothing appeared to have happened since the assurances of imminent action given following the report four years earlier, the worthies from the Department replied, 'I think the assurances were that we would put in place the mechanism to make the changes to improve our control of infection arrangements to ensure that we get the better position to tackle this.'[14] A rough translation into plain English probably means they'd been asleep for the last four years and hadn't actually done anything. And when questioned as to why many hospitals had not released figures of deaths from hospital-acquired infections, the Department said that they didn't want people like journalists contacting the patients concerned: 'it is possible that someone – a journalist or someone else – might be able to find out who that individual is and approach them.' The Department grandee then added, to show his concern for maintaining high ethical standards, 'those are some of the rules in handling statistics.'[15] Helpfully, one of the PAC MPs asked whether, as the patients concerned had already departed this life, helped on their way by the infections they acquired in hospital, a journalist or anyone else would really be interested in approaching them: 'I am sorry. I do not understand that: they are dead, are they not?'[16]

At the time, the *Sun* had described the head of the NHS as

'arrogant', 'smug' and 'complacent'[17] and one MP on the PAC appeared unimpressed with the Department's performance when he said, 'frankly, the answers you have given this afternoon I am amazed at. I do not see it substantiates what the *Sun* said about you but, by gum, it is not far off to be quite honest.'[18] It will probably be some years before any government department puts in such a splendid performance.

The PAC hearings are great entertainment and probably briefly uncomfortable for the over-promoted, inept officials and dazzlingly wealthy and successful suppliers forced to attend. But in terms of being an effective mechanism for preventing the waste of our money on a truly historic scale, they are about as useful as a chocolate teapot. The hearings are equivalent to trying to shut the stable door two or three years after the horse has bolted. Meanwhile, the person responsible for looking after the stable door has already been given a knighthood, a few gongs, a couple of company directorships and a massive pension, for which we taxpayers will also have to pay.

OGC: We're Just Here to Help

As we continue to search for someone who might actually be effective in ensuring our money is well spent, there is one more body we need to look at – the Office of Government Commerce (OGC). The OGC, which has a budget of around £30m a year, was established in April 2000 to promote best value for money on major government programmes by providing advice and promulgating good practice with the aim of improving success rates. More recently, following the 2004 Gershon Review of efficiency in public spending, the OGC have also been tasked with supporting the delivery of the public sector's £21.5bn annual efficiency gains by 2007/8 and making a £3bn saving in central-government procurement also by 2007/8.

The first main service developed by the OGC to improve value for money was the *Gateway* process. As described earlier, this was aimed at providing a process for managing large complex projects. I have been told that the OGC developed *Gateway* with the help of management consultants. *Gateway* gave a systematic series of project reviews that spending departments were encouraged to use on their major initiatives. As the OGC website informs us: 'The OGC Gateway Process examines a programme or project at critical stages in its lifecycle to provide assurance that it can progress successfully to the next stage; the process is based on well-proven techniques that lead to more effective delivery of benefits together with more predictable costs and outcomes.'

The OGC appear quite proud of their *Gateway* process: 'OGC's Gateway process has been heralded as key in supporting the Government's value for money gains.'[19] So, theoretically, all that departments need to do is to apply the *Gateway* process and we will no longer be faced with the unedifying spectacle of increasingly costly disasters. Of course, life is not quite that simple. Firstly, many departments seem to be avoiding *Gateway* like the plague for fear of what using it might reveal about the unsightly things going on in their pet projects. The PAC reports, 'there is evidence, however, that Gateway is still not taken seriously enough by departments'.[20] The result seems to be a boringly predictable repetition of errors by government departments, 'with the same issues and shortcomings repeatedly highlighted by reviews'. The OGC's ability to ensure that the taxpayer gets value for money is limited by the fact that it does not have any executive authority; it can only act as a consultant to departments interested in using its services. 'The OGC has no authority to direct departments but encourages them to secure value for money.'

When *Gateway* is actually used by departments, the results are less than encouraging. Of the projects reviewed under *Gateway*, only 22 per cent were on target. And, of the 78 per cent that were in trouble, well over half had showed no improvement or even got worse at the next *Gateway Review*. Furthermore, a key part of *Gateway*, in ensuring we get value for the billions that government departments spend, is the final review – *Gateway Review 5*. This assesses whether expected benefits are being delivered and what is being done to pursue continued improvements. So lacking in confidence were spending departments that their projects had achieved any of their goals, that a mere 13 per cent of projects were put through *Gateway Review 5*. The other 87 per cent just seemed to magically disappear from the process. One suspects that had these 87 per cent actually achieved anything at all, their sponsors would be noisily shoving them through *Gateway Review 5* and loudly advertising their successful completion.

Questions could also be asked about the effectiveness of *Gateway*. For example, the hopelessly managed consultancy projects for the Child Support Agency, Inland Revenue tax credits and Criminal Records Bureau all passed through the *Gateway* process with flying colours and the tax credits project was even singled out and praised by the OGC as being an example of excellent project management. One member of the PAC expressed his concern at the apparent inability of the OGC's *Gateway* process to spot lame ducks, white elephants and other kinds of hideously deformed excuses for a project: 'The National IT programme of the Health Service is going through green lights, yet we know that there is a huge problem with management engagement. The clinicians are not engaged in that process, sometimes they feel ignored, they feel unconsulted and the same criticism is being levelled with the Criminal Records Bureau and we are now facing the possibility of GPs boycotting the booking system because they do not think it is going to work.'[21]

With the credibility of *Gateway* under attack by the PAC, the OGC worthies seemed to do a lot of back-pedalling. Initially, they had vaunted the great achievements of *Gateway* in helping departments successfully manage their projects. But when the PAC pointed out the gaps exhibited by the OGC's process as it rubber-stamped so many fiascos, the OGC Accounting Officer seemingly was quick to deny any responsibility for anything: 'you misunderstand the nature of the *Gateway* process. The *Gateway* process assesses what the *Gateway* process covers. No one is saying that the *Gateway* process is a substitute for proper, sound management.'

The repeated failure of *Gateway* to prevent a series of

consultancy project meltdowns led to the OGC designing a new suite of services aimed at helping spending departments improve their programme management performance. As the Accounting Officer explained to the PAC, 'it is extremely important that we push forward with the skills agenda to reinforce the work that departments are doing. That is the whole point of having a range of products and services available to a department.' These products and services developed by the OGC and their consultants include the *Successful Delivery Toolkit*, the *Successful Delivery Skills Programme*, the *Programme and Project Management Specialism* and the promotion of *Centres of Excellence*.

In April 2002, the OGC introduced the *Successful Delivery Toolkit*. This was intended to assemble best practice for buying and running projects. However, less than half of government departments used this service as it was found to be 'confusing, contradictory and difficult for inexperienced users to access'.[22] Yet the people who should derive the most benefit from the toolkit would normally be those with the least experience. Moreover, the Home Office and the Department for Work and Pensions actively discouraged their staff from accessing OGC guidance directly.

Then in September 2002, the OGC established the *Successful Delivery Skills Programme* to try and deal with lack of good project management skills in government departments. This seems to have had more success with over a thousand civil servants going on the course. What result it will actually have on departments' projects remains to be seen. But the lateness and cost overruns of programmes like the NHS *Choose and Book* suggest that those involved are managing to live down to the abysmal levels of performance so consistently achieved before the introduction of the OGC training programme. Also the PAC was unimpressed with the way the OGC went about imparting its knowledge and wisdom: 'The OGC has not yet provided departments with a single clear point of engagement for accessing its expertise, and has not yet realised its aim of getting good practice embedded in departments. Departments themselves are not always aware of the relevant guidance and advice available to them, and the products offered by the OGC in some cases duplicate actions already being taken.'

As for the OGC's *Centres of Excellence*, they were only set up in a few departments and of those that were set up only a quarter were found to have had any impact on the way projects were being run.

The OGC also claims it has been very active in working with the IT industry to ensure close cooperation between the industry and government departments. Yet once more the PAC was underwhelmed by the OGC's success: 'The OGC has worked closely with industry – particularly with Intellect, the IT industry's trade organization – to develop a mutually beneficial relationship. This work has included drawing up frameworks and codes of practice but these have yet to have an impact within departments or project teams.'[23]

OGC – Overly Generous to Consultants

Given its important role in supporting the achievement of the Gershon Review savings, the OGC clearly should be ensuring that the services of consultants are procured at a reasonable cost. But when it comes to consultancy services, there is no mention by the OGC of what might often be the greater saving of not employing them in the first place. Indeed the set-up of the agency and several of its initiatives seem to invite extra spending on consultants. Along with its S-Cat consultancy catalogue service, the OGC will help with approaches to consultants, with whom it has excellent relations through its Professional Services Forum, chaired jointly by the OGC's chief executive and his counterpart from the Management Consultancies Association and including representatives of fifteen of the big consultancy firms. One of the forum's several sub-groups, snappily entitled 'Articulating the Value', works on tasks such as drawing up case studies showing 'where the public sector and the professional services industry have pro-duced demonstrable benefits'. These 'will be referred to as part of round robin guidance for answering PQs [parliamentary questions]'.[24] In other words, the consultancy industry and the arm of the Treasury responsible for pushing through the massive Gershon Review savings have come together to put a positive spin on consultancy in the public sector.

The consultants and the OGC have also united to issue a statement of best practice for dealings with each other, from the engagement of a consultant to the end of the contract. But along with 'best practice', it also encourages among occasionally unworldly civil servants a touching faith in consultants, when history suggests hard-nosed scepticism might be more appropriate. The code tells civil servants, 'do not be afraid of providing too much information' and helpfully (for the consultants) reminds civil servants to 'ensure payment of invoices'. The code's instruction number two to public bodies brings to mind the big bad wolf dressed up as Grandma when Little Red Riding Hood visits: 'Do not be defensive. The consultants are there to assist your organization.' Making as much money as possible is clearly the furthest thing from their minds.

Mind the Accountability Gap

No measurement of the effectiveness of consultancy in the public sector has ever even been attempted and there have been no audits in which the results of the consultants' work were analysed. Without detailed investigations, only the highest level questions can be asked. For example, have the extra tens of billions spent on consultants over eight years of New Labour correspondingly improved public services? To the extent that there have been improvements in public services, can any be attributed directly to the consultants' interventions? A quick glance at the performance of departments where most has been spent – in the Department of Health on IT, in the Inland Revenue on tax credits, on 'transforming' the Department for Work and Pensions, on the Child Support Agency, on procurement for the Ministry of Defence, for example – suggests not.

Despite the many public-sector consultancy balls-ups on record, only rarely does anyone other than the taxpayer, or the hard-pressed user of the blighted service, pay. For its part in the tax credits fiasco, EDS was eventually forced to put its hand in its pocket, enabling HM Revenue and Custom's chairman David Varney to comment on the 'unusual, if not unique'[25] incidence of the taxpayer actually getting some money back – albeit peanuts next to the damage caused.

To date only large-scale IT projects have been scrutinized by the National Audit Office and parliamentary committees. Even then criticism of the most incompetent consultancy efforts is generally tempered with the reassurance that government and consultant are working to put things right in 'partnership'. Never has the possibility been raised of a consultancy company being dropped or suspended from public-sector contracts.

Pure management consultancy, more slippery and less visible than its IT cousin, doesn't even meet with that much scrutiny. No public audits of the vast expenditure on transformation programmes can be traced; nor has Parliament questioned these intangible but expensive and often open-ended projects. Tens of millions of pounds in consultancy fees slip through public bodies' accounts unannounced and unnoticed – as the FDA, the union representing the senior civil servants working most closely with the consultants, testified: 'Nobody knows how much money is spent, it often doesn't appear in department running costs, and it is just spiralling out of control.'[26]

When things go wrong, like any manager, the public-sector managers buying consultancy services find themselves with conflicting interests: they are both dissatisfied customers and potentially embarrassed custodians of other people's money. Seeking redress is likely to expose as much about their organization's inability to handle the project and the consultant properly as the consultant's failures. And, worst of all, disputes will bring attention to deals of dubious value in the first place which would otherwise be unlikely to be known about by anyone other than those working on them. Best all round to keep quiet and hope nobody notices. Hence there are examples of departments choosing to continue paying for computer systems that don't work and that they have no intention of ever implementing, rather than admitting there is a problem. As a consequence, despite their often questionable track records, consultants are able to claim something close to perfection, or as PA Consulting put it in its entry in the government's S-Cat catalogue: 'We have successfully delivered over 500 S-CAT projects since April 1998. Not one complaint has been raised about PA service in that time.' In that time PA Consulting was brought in by the Home Office to look at Capita's bid for the Criminal Records Bureau. Despite noting that the system wasn't fully functional, PA recommended that the deal go ahead, with calamitous results. No doubt none of the bureaucrats involved complained about that very expensive piece of help, which a member of the PAC described as 'duff advice'.[27]

Occasionally the light of democratic accountability is shone on some of the government's more management consultancy-intensive functions, but even when these are found wanting the role of the consultants escapes censure. For decades the Ministry of Defence's enormous procurement programme has relied on consultants, notably PwC, Serco, McKinsey and WS Atkins (who were handed wholesale the task of procuring the £6bn 'future rapid effect system' in 2004). The MoD incredibly can't say how much it hands to each consultancy firm, it merely annually reports payments to individual companies in very broad bands.[28] The scale can be appreciated, however, by the statistic that members of the Management Consultancies Association, which doesn't include Serco or McKinsey, received £144m just from the MoD in 2004.[29] It was therefore striking when, in October 2005, the Public Accounts Committee reported on cost overruns on major defence procurement to the tune of £5bn in just two years, and savaged Civil Service managers – 'Doubtless . . . they proceed serenely on in their careers without censure' – but had not one bad word for the consultants.[30] While a government department's performance is theoretically the responsibility of ministers and their officials, yet again an opportunity to consider their reliance on the consultancy industry went begging.

With precious little democratic scrutiny of the flow of money from taxpayers' wallets to consultants' bank accounts via the generous giving hands of our government, it might be hoped that there would be some constraints on the advisers' behaviour. But there is no such thing as regulation of the consultancy 'profession': no entry requirements, no inspections, no supervision and no auditing of the consultants' work. Even the Institute of Management Consultancy, established to give the business a veneer of respectability, describes it as a 'largely unregulated profession' (for 'largely' read 'completely'). When consultants were almost exclusively fleecing rich businesses who could afford their fees, government may not have had great cause for concern (even if the thousands who lost their jobs as a result of the consultants' boiler-plate cost-cutting strategies might not have agreed). But with billions of pounds of public money now at stake, the case for some sort of control is strengthening. Luckily for them, however, de-regulation – euphemistically called 'self-regulation' – looks set to remain the policy fashion for many years to come.

Changes in British case law over the last ten years or so put legal obligations on consultancies to deliver what they promise. But the New Labour government never seems to exercise its legal rights and consultancies are always paid for their services, however abysmal their performance. The exemption of consultancy from the constraints that generally accompany access to huge amounts of other people's money (regulation) and power over public services (parliamentary scrutiny) add up to a democratic deficit. Accountability disappears when the only obligations that the consultants are under are contracts that are deemed by the government to be 'commercially confidential', as anyone impertinent enough to have asked to see one will have discovered. The public, the media and even Parliament can whistle if they want to find out how the consultants are performing on what they're paid for, and what consequences they face when they don't, while the New

Labour government remains only too ready to spare their blushes. On one of the rare occasions that a consultant appeared before Parliament's Public Accounts Committee to explain himself, EDS's then UK managing director was asked whether his firm would be paying compensation for its part in the tax credits debacle. The Inland Revenue chairman moved in to demand a 'degree of protection' from such intrusive questioning on a commercially sensitive issue. Asked by Frank Field MP why it was sensitive, the Revenue grandee trotted out the line that the all-important discussions 'are covered by the normal terms of commercial confidentiality that extend to negotiations between partners'. That was enough for the normally mild-mannered Field, who spoke for the millions who had suffered at the consultants' hands and might have expected their Parliament's questions to the perpetrator at least to be answered, as he gave a simple but elegant response: 'I think that is just crap.'[31]

So, Is Anybody Responsible?

From all this one could get the impression that here we have a lot of highly paid, highly respected people with generous index-linked pensions, knighthoods, KCBs, CBs and many other honours playing an elaborate game of musical chairs, in which they all successfully manage to avoid ever placing their well-padded derrières on the chair marked 'Responsible'. No doubt this is an entertaining and rewarding game for those involved, but it doesn't really seem to answer the legitimate claims of taxpayers that their cash should be spent wisely. All these grandees seem to participate in the process of handing out our money to management and IT systems consultancies and many of them will later take up extremely lucrative advisory positions with the selfsame consultancies. But none of them actually seems to believe that he or she is in any way responsible for ensuring that our many billions might achieve something that looks or smells like value for money.

In most of my dealings with civil servants, I find this

tendency to prioritize their own well-being over their duty of care with our money. For example, I recently had a meeting with a manager in a major Whitehall government department. I was working with a small group of experts who specialized in reducing the costs of IT projects and bringing runaway projects back on schedule. We asked if there were projects in his department that could use our service. He said that he could think of a few that were real disasters and so needed the kind of help we could supply. 'However,' he added, 'if I were to get you involved, I would be stepping on the toes of some very senior civil servants. That would not be a wise career move.'

CHAPTER 5

The Money Machine

A Licence to Print Money

Management and IT systems consulting is one of the most profitable businesses in Britain today. We can take somebody straight off the street, teach them a few simple tricks in a couple of hours and easily charge them out to our clients for more than £7,000 per week, while we probably pay them around £700 per week. If a new consultant has any kind of reasonable education, yet no business or working experience whatsoever, they'll fetch at least £8,000 per week. And if they have also worked for a few years in what we call 'a proper job' before becoming a consultant, anywhere from £10,000 to £25,000 per week is normal. Surprisingly, very few clients do the simple mathematics and ask why they should be paying over £300,000 a year for an inexperienced junior consultant who is being paid just over a tenth of that.

When selling large projects to government departments, some consultancies will work at lower fee rates than they would charge at a bank or oil company, but the profit margins are still bordering on the obscene. PA Consulting, whose fees tend to be lower than firms like McKinsey or Capgemini, were reportedly getting over £5,000 per week for each of the consultants they had working on the Identity Cards project.[1] The rates they were charging a few years ago on the Criminal

Records Bureau (CRB) project ranged from £3,500 per week for a junior to £8,500 for a more experienced person. Using the very low rates charged at the CRB project, if we assume that consultants are able to bill their time for 75 per cent of the year (39 weeks) a junior consultant would earn a firm like PA £136,500 a year while being paid about £35,000, while a more senior person would bring in £331,500 per year while being paid around £80,000. Since then the weekly billing rates for consultants have increased by at least 20–30 per cent as there has been a growing shortage of people to do all the work New Labour is giving to consultancies.

Now, of course, the difference between billing and salaries is not all profit. There are also overhead costs to be paid – pension contributions, offices, training, support staff and sales expenses. But these tend to be much less for consultants than for any other white-collar employee. Very few consultants have their own offices or even desks – they spend most of their time working on clients' premises. Likewise they don't have secretaries, canteens and so on. The client supplies almost everything – even their stationery.

Typically, on a pure management consultancy project, profit margins, after all costs and expenses are deducted, are around 70 per cent when working in the private sector and nearer 60 per cent when working for government. For an IT systems project, margins might be 65 per cent with a business client and around 55 per cent on a public-sector engagement. So, to put it simply, if you sold a £100m systems programme to a government department, £45m would go towards paying the real costs and £55m would go straight into the consultancy partners' pockets as profit. And when the New Labour government ends up giving £70bn of taxpayers' hard-earned cash to a variety of management and IT systems consultants, less than £31bn will be the actual cost of the services and more than £39bn will be profit for the consultancy partners and directors. New Labour have often vaunted their intention to use the tax system to achieve a 'redistribution of wealth'. It is not obvious that some Old Labour MPs would consider that taking £39bn of taxpayers' funds out of front-line public services and donating this massive amount of money to the already wealthy was the policy on which they were originally elected.

Consultancies, of course, will vigorously deny that their profit margins are anything like as high as I claim. Moreover, as consultancy margins are normally closely guarded secrets, it could be difficult to prove they are being more economical with the truth than they are with our money. However, it has been revealed that on year two of the £76m National Insurance Recording System project, Accenture were found to have made what the PAC described as 'super profits' of 54 per cent.[2] In 20 years in the business, I have never seen a consultancy project that made less than a 55 per cent profit margin – even after a huge amount of creative accounting to hide our true profits from over-inquisitive clients and tax authorities.

Five to ten years as a partner in a management consultancy pulling this kind of loot is not the worst way to spend one's working life. Directors of consultancies are very, very rich people. This is perhaps one reason why there has been almost a stampede of public-sector employees into management and IT systems consultancies and why many senior civil servants are also crossing over to where the grass is an awful lot greener – having seen the amount of the taxpayers' money being donated by the government to us consultants, they realize they've been in the wrong game for most of their lives. For example, one consultancy specializing in public-sector work grew from three employees in 1999 to around 2,000 by 2006, with more than 1,200 of its staff coming to it directly from the public sector and doubtless significantly increasing their salaries in the process.[3]

Some Consulting Profit-Boosters

Unfortunately, consultancy bosses are not only very, very rich, they also have an insatiable appetite for money and are always looking for new, ingenious ways to squeeze more out of their unsuspecting clients. Below are just seven of the most widespread techniques my various employers have used when working in the British public sector.

Profit-Booster 1 – Travel Rebates

I have seen this practice going on for about twenty years, but it only started to surface publicly towards the end of 2003. In December 2003, the US division of PwC agreed (without admission of liability) to pay a former client $54.5m as compensation, when it, KPMG and E&Y were sued for 'unjustly enriching themselves at the expense of their clients'. The allegation was that for a decade the three firms worked with outside suppliers such as airline firms and travel agencies to obtain rebates of up to 40 per cent on airfare and other costs that were not passed along to clients.[4]

The reason why PwC decided to refund $54.5m to its client had, it claimed, absolutely nothing to do with it being caught red-handed with its fingers in the till. It was, the firm maintained in the court records, 'to permit the operation of PwC's business without further expensive litigation and the distraction and diversion of PwC's personnel with respect to the matters in this action.'

Moreover, at about the same time, the *Wall Street Journal* wrote that the US Justice Department was accusing a number of consultancies of 'fraudulently padding the travel-related expenses they billed to clients by hundreds of millions of dollars'. The Justice Department had started an investigation 'focusing on whether they have submitted false claims to the Government because they have failed to credit Government contracts with amounts they have received as rebates from travel providers'.[5]

Following this, PwC agreed to repay the US government (again without admission of liability) $41.9m allegedly defrauded from the Defense, Education and Justice departments and the Environmental Protection Agency using the profit-boosting travel expense rebates method. KPMG, Ernst & Young and Booz Allen Hamilton also all agreed to pay millions of dollars back to the Department of Justice (again without admission of liability) for allegedly using the same method.[6]

Consultants tend to travel a lot for work and stay much of the time in hotels near clients' sites. A typical consultant might be spending £10,000 to £20,000 a year on travel, accommodation and food. So a firm with say ten thousand employees would be spending over £100m a year on travel. Naturally, this huge buying power can be used to negotiate sizeable discounts with hotels, airlines and car hire firms. A consultancy could choose to agree 'spot discounts' with travel suppliers – immediate reductions on prices paid. But then the consultancy client would get the benefit as they would have lower travel costs to reimburse. To avoid clients getting this money, most consultancies set up deals with travel management companies (TMCs) or else directly with hotel chains and the main airlines for end-of-year rebates. All consultants are instructed to use the consultancies' TMCs, the 'partner' hotel chains and the chosen airline(s) whenever possible. The consultancy invoices the client for the full travel and accommodation costs, which the client contractually must pay. Sometimes the consultancy even adds on an administration charge. At the end of the year, the consultancy receives a large rebate from the TMC, hotels and the airlines. *None* of this rebate is ever passed back to the clients who have paid for all the travel and accommodation in the first place.

Embarrassingly for one of the defendants, documents already provided to the court showed that there were 'complaints by some partners that the practice was unethical'[7] and in an email, the head of the ethics department 'described the firm's practices as "a bit greedy"'.[8]

Using a most curious form of logic, the accused admitted to the allegations, but denied any liability claiming that they had done nothing wrong: 'The defendants have acknowledged retaining rebates on various travel expenses, for which they had billed clients at their pre-rebate amounts. However, they deny that their conduct was fraudulent, saying that the proceeds offset amounts that would otherwise have been billed to clients. They say they have discontinued this practice.'[9]

However, after this I worked for one of the companies involved, a company doing billions of pounds of work for the British government, and they had certainly not 'discontinued this practice'. As a colleague in that company wrote in an email, 'Here's how we do it every time. We state in our contract that we will bill for "actual" expenses. Then we bill them for your air travel expense. Then we get a kickback on your air ticket. But we don't give the client back the kickback.'[10]

One consultant who contacted me after the publication of my book *Rip-off!* estimated that his employer had stolen over £20m from just one British government department using the travel expenses end-of-year kickback. 'The firm had splendid discount rates on hotels and flights – about 66% reduction on rack rates, but they charged the client the rack rate plus admin costs (and remember that there were HUNDREDS of staff in hotels for up to 2 years).'[11] In an international consultancy, which also works extensively in the British public sector, an American court found that the travel expenses fraud was more profitable than the firm's largest client.

Assuming that the travel expense kickback fraud is still as widespread as it seems to be, huge sums of money that could have been used to build scores of hospitals and schools or to pay for thousands of doctors, nurses and teachers are instead being poured by our government into the pockets of multi-millionaire consultancy partners and directors.

Profit-Booster 2 – Relocating Staff

Many management consultancies are international. One advantage of this is that they can move staff to where the business is. For example, if there is a temporary downturn in the USA and growth in Europe or the Far East, these consultancies can shift experienced staff from the USA to countries where there is more work. Conversely, if European business dips, they can fly out an army of eager staff to projects in the States. Most consultants would rather spend a few well-paid months on another continent than be fired every time there's a downturn in activity, so there's normally no lack of volunteers for temporary relocation.

Now you might think that consultancies would absorb the costs of relocating their staff. After all, being able to move staff to where they have projects suits the interests of the management consultancies. Clients would be best served if consultancies had sufficient numbers of experienced staff based locally. Why should a client have to pay intercontinental and international flights, relocation costs, school fees, accommodation and so on for consultants and their families, just because the consultancy has not been able to recruit and train someone locally to do the job?

To illustrate this, I'll take a real-life example from a tiny £2.3m project I helped sell in Britain to a regional health authority for a well known firm of international consultants. The practices employed by this particular consultancy were so inventive that, unusually, the project was later subject to a number of official investigations and some quite colourful articles in the press. (I say 'unusually' because, as noted before, consultancy screw-ups are typically swept quickly and efficiently under the carpet and life goes on. Consultancies know this and exploit it shamelessly).

At the time, this particular consultancy, which was based in the US, was just building up its British operations. We were growing more rapidly than we could hire new people and when the project was sold to the health authority, there were not enough UK-based consultants available to staff the assignment. So two Americans were put on the six-person team. The Americans did not have any special skills that could not be found in the UK. Nor was their background or experience particularly relevant to the assignment – in fact, neither of them had ever worked on a public-sector project before. The consultancy simply had not recruited sufficient UK staff at that point, and there was insufficient work for all the American staff in the US.

Nevertheless, the health authority paid through the nose for these consultants, using money that might have been better spent looking after patients. Firstly, there was the equivalent of £8,000 per week fees for each consultant. Then there was about £300 per week for each consultant's hotel costs, also at least another £300 per week for each consultant's meals, plus a bit more for laundry, dry cleaning, phone bills and entertainment.

Then there were the consultants' families. They had no desire to live in the unfashionable provincial town where the assignment was based. They wanted to live in London – and not only in London, but in the better parts of London. So there were a few other not inconsiderable items to which the regional health authority made a generous financial contribution. For example, there was up to £200 per week for each consultant to travel to London every weekend to see their families. There was a bucket of money paid out per week for each family's comfortable flat – one in an exclusive mews in Kensington and the other in Hampstead; a few hundred pounds a week for each family's food and entertainment; the fees for the children's private schools; the taxis used when the bored wives went shopping and, of course, the shopping trips themselves. There were the many afternoon teas taken by the bored wives at the Ritz and the Savoy and the occasional £70 taxi fare when the wives decided it was less trouble to make a taxi wait than go to the effort of finding another when they had finished shopping or drinking tea. Nevertheless, the client seemed to swallow all this abuse with good grace. It was only when the project manager hired a private plane to return from a long weekend break to attend a meeting that the auditors finally got wind of what was going on and the press also started poking around.

All in all, the regional health authority ended up paying a couple of thousand pounds a week extra for each of these American consultants, purely because the consultancy did not have enough people available in the UK at that time. This was confirmed in an internal memo from our CEO: 'The project took place at a time when we were still heavily supported by US expats. Naturally we accommodated them and their families and a proportion of these costs were charged to the client.'[12]

When the press began to get a little too nosy, our management tried numerous ways of avoiding adverse publicity. At the time, we had just been acquired by a large IT systems consultancy and changed our name. When the bad press started to appear, our CEO issued an internal memo that contained the immortal lines: 'You will have noticed in the press recently that ABC Consultants [our previous name] has once again been mentioned in connection with the West Midlands Regional Health Authority. The connection between ABC Consultants and XYZ Consulting [our new name] has now been made despite our efforts – successful until very recently – to avoid this.'

The gentleman had clearly been hoping that the change of name would enable the previous consultancy to miraculously disappear for ever and for us to re-emerge whiter than white. The memo also mentioned and tried to describe as normal business practice things like 'the hire of a private plane, provision of expensive accommodation for executives and their wives, and lavish entertainment with fine wines'. It also, with an unusual degree of honesty, admitted that although around £40m in financial benefits were promised to this client, little was achieved during the project and once the project was completed 'it is probable that no further benefits emerged.'

The magazine *Health Service Journal* was not complimentary about our contribution to the health of the British taxpayer and accused the health authority of financial profligacy: 'The crisis came to a head last September when the District General Managers (DGMs) were asked to topslice £4.3 million from their budgets for the rest of the year to pay for the reorganization of regional supplies. Included in the £4.3 million cost, say DGMs, was a bill of £2.3 million from ABC Consultants to help manage the reorganization, which Regional Health Authority (RHA) officials first claimed would save the region £40 million over the next four years. The RHA has consistently denied ABC Consultants' cost was £2.3 million, but has refused to say what the figure is. The way the ABC Consultants' contract was awarded is at the heart of what one DGM describes as a "financial fiasco". The claim is that the RHA exercised a lack of financial and management control – a claim backed by the Carver report.'[13]

I understand from someone working inside *Connecting for Health* that large numbers of consultants have been shipped in from other European countries where there is perhaps not enough work for them and where daily fee rates are lower than in the UK. No doubt more operations will be cancelled and fewer patients will be treated as funds are diverted from looking after patients to paying the travel and accommodation costs for these consultants. But there should be no surprise here; the NHS has always been one of the world's most fertile feeding grounds for many species of hungry management and IT systems consultants.

Profit-Booster 3 – Partner Billing

Most consultancies have a rule that partners must bill some or even all of their time to clients. To quote an email I received from someone who read *Rip-Off!*, 'I am a secretary to a Tax Partner in a Big Four firm. My boss has to deliver 40 charged hours per week as minimum. A large part of my function is to administer his costs and charges. Whether he is working, on the golf course or on holiday, his clients are charged 40 hours. This is normal practice, no doubt fraudulent, in the firm.'[14]

One of the directors of a firm where I worked continually boasted to his subordinates about the amount of time he spent getting special services in some of the most exclusive brothels in the world. As he used to say, when explaining why he made such frequent visits to expensive whorehouses, 'good sex means inflicting pain and you wouldn't want to do that to someone you love.'

So you find that consultancy partners or directors divide their time up among their various clients and allocate a certain number of days each month to each client – even when this time is actually not spent working for that client – even if it is, in fact, spent selling to the next bunch of clients, on the golf course or even in a high class brothel. As each partner is probably charging his or her time at up to £20,000 per week, this is very profitable.

In addition, you often find ordinary consultants being told

to charge clients for time spent on internal consultancy business. To quote a consultant from another massive consulting firm, 'I was at an internal meeting with more than 100 other consultants. Partner told us to charge the day to the project so we could bill it to the client as it was almost quarter end and we needed to make our numbers.'[15] This one decision will probably have cost the client over £100,000. As all these firms are each earning many hundreds of millions from consulting in the British public sector, here's a lot more money that we the taxpayers will have to find to pay our government's consulting bills.

Profit-Booster 4 – Charging and Expensing Overhead

Charging for overhead
This next practice may seem quite small, but it can be very rewarding. Normally, clients expect the consultancies' extraordinary fees to cover the costs of the management consultancies' own offices and staff. However, in one major consultancy an extra 10 per cent was automatically added to consultancy fees to cover overhead costs. So, if an ordinary consultant was being charged out at say £250,000 a year, the client would also be billed for another £25,000 to pay for administrative overhead. That's enough to pay for at least one full time administrative employee to support each consultant. Yet, according to data from the British Management Consultancies Association, there is on average one support employee for every four to five consultants.[16]

To give an example I experienced, the London office of a major consultancy had about three hundred consultants and around forty to fifty administrative support staff – secretaries, receptionists, human resources, accountants, marketing support, resource managers, trainers, information centre researchers and document production. Yet, with the 10 per cent add-on, we were charging for the equivalent of about 300 administrative staff – hence the salaries of up to 250 support staff were not being spent. That's a lot of extra profits for the consultancy directors and partners.

Expensing overhead

Even though they already charge extra for overhead, to squeeze even more money out of their ingenuous clients some consultancies have instructed office staff to keep timesheets, where they try to book as many extras as possible to projects over and above the £25,000 per year already earned by adding the extra 10 per cent to consultant fees. At one of the world's largest consultancies we were even instructed to keep logs of all telephone calls made from the office so that these could also be charged to clients. Thus clients find themselves paying for administration costs that include photocopying, faxes, stationery, secretaries' time and all sorts of other small but significant items – all making the clients poorer and the consultancy bosses just that delightful little bit richer.

In consultancy, we call this 'double dipping' – being able to charge twice for one thing. Although perhaps this is 'triple dipping' – the margins on consultant fees are already quite sufficient to cover overhead costs, then you charge an extra 10 per cent over and above consultant fees to pay for the same overhead costs and then you have the gall also to expense as much overhead as possible – all in all, a very profitable little process.

Profit-Booster 5 – Flat Rate Expenses

When a consulting project is sold, another small but not wholly insignificant money-earner is to agree with the client that expenses will be around, for example, 10 per cent of fees. So, for every £7,000 paid weekly for each consultant, the consultancy will invoice the client for another £700 in expenses. The deal is that at the end of the project there will be a reconciliation between the 10 per cent paid by the client and the actual expenses incurred. The client will be charged more if the expenses exceed the 10 per cent or reimbursed for any difference if they are less.

Now, of course, the 10 per cent (or whatever figure is chosen) is usually a huge overestimate. Most consultants do not manage to spend £700 per week on travel, accommodation, food, booze and entertainment. So this leaves the consultancy two options:

1. It can come clean at the end of the project and reimburse the client for the money invoiced, collected but not spent, having gained the interest on this money for many months in the meantime.

2. It can be slightly more imaginative. It can take a bunch of expenses from projects that have got into trouble either because their clients may be less generous with expenses or because more manweeks were used and more expenses generated than expected. It can then pass these over and shove them on to a project where the consultancy has got the client to agree a comfortable level of expenses or where the client is less than assiduous in auditing the expenses charged by the consultancy.

Thus an unsuspecting client can end up covering losses the consultancy has made on other projects for other clients.

I remember one project for a key supplier to the MoD where we had estimated 12 per cent expenses. So each month the client was paying us our full fees plus this extra 12 per cent to cover our expected level of expenses. But in spite of the team's best efforts to use as much of the client's money as possible, we were actually only running at about 7 per cent. The vice president in charge of the account informed the rest of the consultancy that he had room to soak up expenses both from other projects and from our head office, rather than paying lots of money back to the client. Although I was merely a humble consultant on another project, we had some great dinners at luxurious restaurants and some other lavish social pleasures at that client's expense.

Very occasionally, clients would audit our expenses and if they found some real horrors, we'd just say there had been an administrative error and refund the minimum necessary to keep the client happy.

Many consultancies working for the public sector take a more straightforward approach to making money on travel expenses. They agree a level of 'reasonable' travel expenses with their government clients. Each month the client pays this in addition to the consultants' fees. Then the consultancy puts huge pressure on its employees to keep their travel expenses well below the level the government department is paying, so the consultancy makes a profit on its employees' travel. I have been informed that this is the policy of a consultancy that is one of the world's largest IT systems companies and a major supplier of consultancy services to Her Majesty's government.

Profit-Booster 6 – Overcharging

This is an old favourite and one without which any list of more questionable management consultancy money-earners would be incomplete.

Most consultancies have different weekly billing rates depending on the seniority or experience of the consultant. For example, a simple consultant may cost a client a mere £5,000 or so a week, a project manager £7,000 to £10,000 and a partner or vice president £15,000 to £20,000 a week.

On the grounds that some consultants might be promoted during a project, the consultancy decides to charge out their services at one grade above their actual level for the whole period of the project. During discussions around pricing projects, I've often heard vice presidents and partners saying about an ordinary consultant, 'he/she will really be working at a senior consultant level, so we ought to charge them at senior consultant prices.' However, while they are eager to have clients pay higher fees for that consultant, they too often forget to pay the hard-working consultant at the same level. It is only well into or even at the end of the assignment that the consultant gets the promotion that the client has being paying for during the preceding six to twelve months. A slight variation on this method was described in an email I received recently: the sender claimed that while working for a British government agency 'staff were "accidentally" charged out at higher grade rates on many lines of work and staff from regional offices (where rates were about 70 per cent of London) were "seconded" to London and then charged to the client at premium rates'.

Profit-Booster 7 – Tax Avoidance

Many consultancies have a fairly creative relationship with their tax authorities. While most companies tend to make at least some effort to give the impression of being good corporate citizens, you'll often find that consultancies do not suffer from such scruples – usually so much money flows in so easily that, once they've got their hands on it, their owners become quite loath to give it away. The American giant Accenture, probably one of the largest suppliers of consultancy services to the British government, was reported to have only paid around 7 per cent of its profits in tax from 1997 to 2000 compared to an average of 36.9 per cent paid by the biggest companies in America. Moreover, despite having more than 2,500 stock-holding partners and more than 80,000 employees in 75 countries around the world, Accenture was, according to the same reporter, head-quartered in Bermuda where the gargantuan consultancy had all of three employees![17] The reporter described Bermuda as 'an offshore jurisdiction, which has been condemned by lawmakers as a place companies go to avoid paying tax'. I think one can be forgiven for suspecting that the Bermuda incorporation has more to do with tax minimization than the tiny island being a key consulting market for mighty Accenture.

An employee of a major British consultancy emailed me to allege tax avoidance in their firm, 'the firm publishes accounts but they are a joke. They utterly fail to give the true value of the tax breaks, investment income, captive insurance income, referred income from partner firms, equity shares of partners in associated companies in Jersey, Isle of Man, Switzerland, British Virgin Islands, Bahamas or Bermuda.' In fact, this practice of apparent tax avoidance by consultancies has become so widespread in the US, that Congress tried to bring in legislation preventing any consultancy involved in tax avoidance from getting government work. Accenture, for example, was reported to have been facing the loss of more than $600m of US government business if this legislation had been passed and, following a vote in Congress in 2004, almost lost a $10bn US Homeland Security project.[18]

80,000 Lambs to the Slaughter?

Perhaps consultants' huge fees and their other ways of extracting money from the taxes we pay the government would be acceptable if these consultants always delivered an appropriate level of value. Sometimes, of course, they do. But all too often consultants are inadequately qualified, their work is of questionable quality and the pressure to meet their sales and billing targets causes them to push gullible government departments into paying many millions for work that is of little value and even unnecessary. Moreover, far too often, the flow of money to consultancies is accompanied by massive job losses in the organizations that these consultancies have just 'helped' or 'modernized' – for example, if the proposals of the Gershon Review are implemented, over 80,000 public-sector employees will find that their services are no longer needed.

I've worked for a broad range of management and IT systems consultancies for almost a hundred clients across the world and we and our competitors have found many new and fashionably sophisticated ways of expressing and packaging what we do – productivity improvement, profit improvement, activity-based management, lean manufacturing, business process re-engineering, enhancing shareholder value, strategic realignment, rightsizing, benchmarking, supply chain optimization, speed to value, business transformation, overhead value improvement, value engineering, post merger integration, implementing an internal market, achieving synergies, transformational outsourcing and so on. But all too often, when management or IT systems consultants are paid to enter an organization, a significant percentage of the staff soon find that their services are surplus to requirements. This link between consultants' well-being and people losing their jobs was made clear when a senior executive of McKinsey said, during a rare television interview explaining how McKinsey worked, 'usually when a consulting firm is known to be coming into a company, let's say McKinsey, it is announced that they are coming in to do a study, there is considerable concern and alarm among the people in the company because they expect that probably one of the results will be that people will lose their jobs, because very often that is what is needed.'[19]

Since New Labour began its consulting spending spree, however, this euphemistic double-speak has risen to new heights of excellence and absurdity. At the BBC, we had Lord John Birt's 'Producer Choice' – this meant increased administration of £140m a year, budget cuts and a reduction in front-line programme-making staff. In the MoD there was 'Modernising Logistical Support' supported by McKinsey – 3,000 jobs lost and several critical repair facilities closed. In the NHS, there is 'Patient Choice' – budget cuts, ward closures and reductions in numbers of operations. There are PFI hospitals – invariably with fewer beds and therefore fewer staff than the hospitals they replace. The NHS are also giving us 'Commissioning a Patient-Led NHS'. This plan should result in 300 primary care trusts being reduced to about 100, 28 strategic health authorities coming down to 11 and around 6,000 to 9,000 jobs lost with redundancy costs of £320m – money which will have to be taken out of budgets for front-line patient care.[20] Throughout government there are 'Strategic Partnerships' – private companies taking over all kinds of services from hospital cleaning to running schools – and all with similar results: increased administration costs and drastic cuts in the numbers of front-line workers. In fact, any time the government mentions the word 'choice', this usually means fewer staff and less choice. Any time the New Labour government talks of 'partnership', this means money being siphoned off from front-line workers to pay for new managers and to give private sector companies guaranteed profits far in excess of what they could earn in normal competitive business markets. And any time the government refers to 'service', this is New Labour speak for granting a monopoly arrangement to one of its favourite consultancies inviting them to plunder the public sector at will.

Currently, consultancies are casting around for a new and socially acceptable euphemism to disguise the fact that the latest profitable trend in government business is all about consultancies making millions while people lose their jobs. The trend is 'outsourcing' and then 'offshoring' public-sector activities.

In December 2005, the Department for Work and Pensions (DWP) reportedly issued a briefing paper to senior staff. This informed them: 'In line with the continuing need for government departments to reduce costs, proposals are being made by service providers to undertake work for or on behalf of the department overseas. This could involve the transfer of part or even all of the functions of a DWP area to a centre located outside the UK. This is referred to as *offshoring*.'[21]

So far, the new names for this practice seem a little transparent – 'rightshoring' from Capgemini, 'bestshoring' from EDS and 'anyshoring' from BearingPoint.[22] Some public-sector staff have tried to oppose being offloaded to an IT company that they would never have applied to work for. In Swansea and Bradford bitter battles were fought as staff struggled to maintain their jobs. In Swansea, for example, 70 out of 135 council IT workers were being moved to a large outsourcer. Apparently showing deep concern for the careers of those involved, a council official said, 'our ICT staff will join one of the world's leading IT companies, where they will be able to develop their skills and careers.'[23] However, many outsourced staff tend to find that outsourcing happens in two stages: first you get bounced from your public-sector job to the outsourcer, then a few years later – usually when some kind of employment rights protection period has expired – you find that someone in India or another low cost economy is doing your job and you are no longer needed.

Lest anybody feel that I am being overly negative about the latest consulting service being offered to the British government, I will allow one victim to tell their story of the experience of being outsourced to a company that has a multi-billion-pound outsourcing deal with a central-government department and many more outsourcing contracts with local authorities. We'll call that company 'Massive Systems'.[24]

My recent layoff has opened my eyes to the dangers of off-shoring. With a well paying job and a degree in hand I believed it wasn't my problem. How wrong I was! In August 2004, Massive Systems announced their 'distributive delivery business model'. 'Distributive delivery' is a euphemism for off-shoring labour. Massive Systems was going to move jobs to India, Poland, Malaysia and communist China. It was my job as subject matter expert to train my replacements within six to nine months. Training was performed through a telecommunication audio/video portal to India and communist China. Each session was recorded for management and trainees. If for any reason training was deemed intentionally inaccurate, I could be terminated for 'cause' with no severance pay. Layoffs were scheduled in several waves – in October 2004, March 2005, July 2005 and October 2005. Out of 2,700 employees, 75%–85% will be terminated.

I was terminated in March 2005. On that day I was given a document to be signed within 45 days. If I signed, I would be waiving my rights to sue my former employer, Massive Systems, or their executives. Secondly, I could not defame my former employer, Massive Systems or their executives. I was also required not to mention the waiver agreement to anybody except my spouse and my lawyer. If I do not agree to the terms, I will not receive my severance. If I do agree to the terms but violate any clause within the waiver, I will be sued for the reimbursement of severance pay and associated damages.[25]

One specialist research service predicted a significant rise in outsourcing due to the government's plan to make major cost savings in public services: 'the Gershon Efficiency Review, which aims to save £21.5bn from the public sector by 2008, along with plans to cut 80,000 Civil Service jobs, will force managers to outsource more.'[26] Those departments providing the most critical public services seem to be those which will see the greatest rise in outsourcing – Education a forecast 131 per cent increase, NHS 164 per cent and Defence 282 per cent. These figures will justifiably horrify anybody who believes there is a difference between providing essential public services and just running an organization using the cheapest sources of labour in the world purely to make as much money as possible. In 2005, just one of the major suppliers of outsourcing services to the New Labour government was reported to be trying to hire 30,000 new staff in India – a useful figure for people to bear in mind when the outsourcing consultancies come calling with their offer to improve public services delivery and enhance the career prospects of those employees lucky enough to be moved from the public sector to work for the outsourcer.

So, if you are one of the 80,000, remember the consulting money machine chosen by our government does not care about the many tens of thousands of lives it affects and sometimes destroys – its only aim is to keep on making money for those in charge of the machine.

CHAPTER 6

Adding Value or Cost?

The tens of billions spent on consultants' efforts to transform public services and government departments should, if they are providing value for money, translate into improvements in public-sector productivity. Some studies do show that some public services have begun to perform more effectively following a rise in overall public-sector spending under Gordon Brown of around £50bn and an increase in staff numbers of 637,000. Others unfortunately indicate that productivity in the public sector has actually fallen. In March 2004 the Cabinet heard that, using traditional methods of calculation, productivity in the public sector had fallen by 10 per cent since 1997,[1] over which period public-sector spending on consulting had gone up sevenfold.[2] While measuring such an abstruse concept as public-sector productivity is notoriously difficult and traditional methods were known to be flawed, the apparent drop in productivity offers anything but reassurance. Following this revelation, a government review was hastily established to examine how the figures for public-sector productivity should be calculated. In 2005 with the New Labour new calculation methodology, things looked a lot rosier – NHS productivity was now estimated to have increased by over 27 per cent between 1995 and 2003, while in education productivity had supposedly gone up by 9.4 per cent over the same period.[3] But statistics produced by the Reform Group, using the old methodology, pointed towards a picture of declining productivity. According to the Reform Group data, productivity in the NHS declined by around 9.5 per cent between 1995 and 2003 and in education it fell by about 10 per cent.

However, the most easily measurable and marked effects of all the consultancy and IT systems seem to have been significant rises in the numbers of administrative and non-front-line staff. The figures are quite daunting – since 1998 the NHS numbers are up by 66.1 per cent, education up by 47.1 per cent, the police up by 33.6 per cent and the prison service up by 31.3 per cent.[4] In 2005, despite an efficiency programme to reduce administration, the government admitted that it was £200m over its administration budget and that in the previous year alone the number of administrators had not decreased but had increased by around 17,000.[5]

Perhaps the worst example of administration costs going totally out of control is in the government department that has probably received more consulting and IT systems support per employee than any other part of government – the Child Support Agency (CSA). The CSA's ten thousand or so employees have been given over £450m of management and IT systems consulting support – a quite unbelievable £45,000 per employee. Yet, in spite of all this 'help', the Agency was reportedly managing to collect £1.85 for every £1.00 spent on administration. In comparison, the Australian CSA, which probably hasn't benefited from so much management and IT systems consultancy, manages to collect about £8.50 for every £1 in administration costs.[6] So abysmal is the CSA's performance that many people were calling for the CSA to be scrapped. By the end of 2005, even the Prime Minister seemed to agree.[7] If, as is likely, the CSA is gradually shut down and its responsibilities are progressively handed over to the Inland Revenue and debt-collection agencies, this will represent a quite staggering example of bureaucratic ineptitude and a totally inexcusable waste of taxpayers' money. Naturally, at no time has there ever been any suggestion that compensation could be sought from the consultancies that have given us this utter fiasco.

With so much money being spent by New Labour on consultants, there is a need to try and pin down exactly what taxpayers are getting for all the billions that are being handed over on our behalf. There has only been limited research into success levels of pure management consulting. There has been much more analysis of the results of IT systems consulting. For both types of consulting, the figures are worrying. Indications are that around 30 per cent of management consulting is successful. For IT systems consulting, the success rate is comfortably below 20 per cent and some studies suggest that it may even be below 10 per cent in the British public sector. Given these low rates of achievement, it's worth looking at why both management and IT systems consultancy so seldom deliver the value that was originally promised.

Management Consulting

One study conducted by the Cranfield School of Management asked 640 consultants whether they thought they brought value to their clients and also asked 170 clients whether they believed they received value from their consultants.[8] There were considerable differences of view between the well-paid consultants and the clients who paid them. A healthy 71 per cent of consultants said they brought value to their clients. Unfortunately only 36 per cent of clients happened to agree.

Yet, in spite of the general dissatisfaction with consultants' work, many managers are so dependent on them that they keep on buying their services. As one of the authors of the research said, 'some consultants are so embedded in the culture of the organization that the client believes he has to go through them to get anything done.'

A situation you frequently see in the public sector is that quite senior managers appear to be in awe of consultants. They seem to have been browbeaten into believing that consultants have some special knowledge that none of the millions of public-sector workers can possibly possess. This is a line that has been continuously peddled by New Labour and their consultants as they repeatedly talk of the Civil Service's inability to deliver and of the need to instil competition and private-sector management methods in public services. This sense of inferiority being instilled in public-sector managers was described by an MP on the Public Accounts Committee: 'I have been saying for some time that the public sector has lost its self-confidence at least in relation to these kinds of projects.'[9] This allows even the most junior, inexperienced and incompetent consultants to run riot in areas like healthcare, education and defence, giving advice that everybody knows is nonsense and making changes that everybody knows will be harmful. Yet everybody keeps their heads down and nobody dares reveal that the emperor has no clothes. The author of the Cranfield Business School report described a typical situation: 'I know a chief executive who won't do anything without asking the consultant. He acts on the consultant's advice, against his own best advice in the company.' The author also noticed the same fear of criticizing the consultants: 'people don't want to speak out on this issue. There is a taboo about it.'

Some more recent, but less statistically based research by a Harvard Business School professor and world expert on the management consulting industry concluded that consultants privately admitted that about 20 per cent of their work was really excellent, about 60 per cent was tolerable but of little value and around 20 per cent was 'junk'. He believed that the focus on short-term profitability rather than on maintaining professional standards was the main reason for the low standard of much consulting work: 'in the professional services world, however, principles were sacrificed for cash. With one or two really rare exceptions, professional firms are not places that are driven by values and ideology any more. They are driven by almost a caricature of short-term financials.'[10] A popular recruitment website regularly contains emails from practising consultants concerned that they have not really been providing much value for their clients. One example read, 'sometimes I know I have helped the client or done great work, but it just doesn't seem we are worth the millions that they pay us and I've been on enough projects where it is often apparent that we are not.' Another admitted, 'at least half of all the consulting projects I have seen have been underwhelming in their impact. Consultants can do great stuff but the bulk of work we sell is nonsense that clients should be doing themselves.'[11]

Why Management Consulting Often Fails to Deliver

There are many very talented management consultants working in the British public sector who are dedicated to providing the best possible results for their clients. Yet too often they are prevented from delivering value and are even put in ethically questionable situations by the way the consultancy industry works. There are four main reasons why about 70 per cent of organizations get disappointing results from their consultants: utilization targets, 'warm body' selling, pushing products and wrong issue consulting.

Utilization targets
In many consultancies, executives' bonuses depend on their reaching certain 'utilization' targets – usually about 70 per cent. This means that 70 per cent of their consultants' time must be sold to clients. Failure to achieve the utilization target can result in a consultancy director or partner losing several hundred thousand pounds of bonus, so consultancy directors are under tremendous pressure to sell their people's time, whether clients have problems to be solved or not. Thus many consultants find their talents wasted by being put to work on projects that are just lucrative 'billing slots' sold to keep utilization levels up but with little practical value for their clients.

'Warm bodies'
Many consultancies have just a few experienced experts in each of their areas of work, while most of their employees are what we call 'warm bodies' or 'billing fodder'. The consultancy's profitability depends on being able to sell teams mostly

made up of lower-paid 'warm bodies'. This allows their more highly paid experts to work on several projects at once and sell new business at the same time. So they only have time to visit each of their projects occasionally. Of course, with proper direction from the experts, the 'warm bodies' can provide good work. Though too often the warm bodies may be of dubious quality. As a consultant at the world's largest systems consultancy wrote on meeting the latest intake of new recruits (green beans), 'The green beans have arrived and oh my god I suggest you start shorting your stock – these 2005 new hires are absolute monkeys. These new people are absolutely stupid. What the hell was HR thinking?'[12]

Government departments would get much greater value if their consulting teams were mostly made up of more experts and fewer 'green beans'. As the British government increases its spending on consultants, armies of warm bodies and green beans, most of whom have absolutely no public-sector experience and many of whom don't even have any work experience, are being foisted on government departments to tell them how they should organize and run themselves. It's tempting to conclude that this will result in fewer services being delivered at higher cost.

Pushing products
Quite a few consultancies are 'product-focused' rather than 'solution-focused'. This means that they are interested in selling you their 'product' – the services that they already know how to deliver. This focus on selling their product can prevent them actually trying to find the right solution for your particular organizational issues. Moreover, if your consultants are part of an IT systems supplier, they will probably be under huge internal pressure to sell you IT systems work even if you don't really need it. I was with a consultancy that was bought by a huge IT systems supplier which is now working on over £4bn of British government contracts. Our executives' bonus structure was changed to encourage them to sell IT systems and IT outsourcing. I remember the numerous internal arguments we had when we were pressured into convincing clients

that only by buying IT systems from us or outsourcing activities to us would they be able to improve their organizational performance, even though we knew that sticking in a new system or outsourcing would be of little use to them. We were also clearly instructed always to try and sell a client expensive new computer systems rather than help them improve what they already had in place. So good salesmanship can often lead to clients implementing organizational changes and new computer systems that give them relatively little value and are not what they ought to have bought. Clients can also end up outsourcing functions that they should have kept in-house – and once a client has outsourced something to you, you really have them by the balls. Numerous local councils have found themselves paying millions to get out of onerous IT systems and outsourcing contracts that were giving lousy service. For example, Bedfordshire County Council reportedly paid £7.7m of taxpayers' cash to prematurely break its £250m twelve-year outsourcing deal;[13] and a consortium of five councils looks like it will have to carry on paying millions to a systems supplier for a system that most of them will never implement, because after three years of largely fruitless efforts, the supplier can't get the system to work.

Wrong issue

One problem frequently facing commercial companies and government departments that buy consultancy is a lack of capability in the top management team. However, there are few management teams who will be honest enough to admit that they are not up to the job. So, when faced with difficulties, they will tend to blame other factors like their employees, their computer systems, their organization structure and so on. Clearly in such situations, if a consultancy takes millions for providing new organization structures, new IT systems or employee training without solving the weaknesses at top management level, their interventions will be of limited value. But there are few consultants who will put their revenue at risk by telling a client's top management that they need to radically change the way they manage. In fact, the

weaker the management of a department are, the easier it is
to sell them consulting and systems that they don't really
need. So most consultants will just take the money to do
what their clients think they want, in the full knowledge that
their work will be highly profitable for the consultancies but
of little real benefit for their clients.

Consulting in Action

The New Labour government's drive to modernize the public
sector by paying consultants to introduce competition and
drive down bureaucracy displays all of these pitfalls. A consultants' idea, which has not been properly evaluated, is being
forced on to organizations as diverse as health, education and
the military. Huge teams of warm bodies are being sent in to
implement the modernization agenda. Moreover, in larger
government departments there is a multitude of consultancies
all trying to sell as many consulting manweeks as possible and
all working simultaneously on different and often contradictory projects. There is little interest in actually understanding
what improvements really need to be made in the various
public services. And the consultants are only too eager to take
the money for supporting the New Labour cause without ever
questioning the value it will bring.

A good example of what can happen when management
consultants sell the idea of bringing private-sector management
practices, markets and competition into a public-sector organization was seen when Tony Blair's former unpaid strategy
adviser, Lord (John) Birt, became Director-General of the BBC
and applied there the same kind of 'modernization' that New
Labour and their consultants are expensively spreading
throughout almost all areas of the public services. Birt paid
the leading US consultancy McKinsey and other consultancies
tens of millions of pounds of the public's money to 'modernize'
the BBC by implementing a kind of internal market, in which
departments bought and sold services to each other. This
would apparently cut down waste by bringing clear-minded

commercial thinking into a supposedly bloated, bureaucratic public service organization.

As with most subsequent New Labour consultant-driven 'modernization' efforts, the work at the BBC was declared to be incredibly successful. When questioned about their use of consultants, the BBC claimed that by spending only £6m on consultants, they had achieved an impressive £255m in savings on administration. Some time later, when the truth eventually came out, it appeared that the BBC had actually been spending over £20m a year on management consultants and that their administrative costs had not decreased by £255m – they had in fact gone up by £140m. This pattern of surreptitiously giving vast sums to consultants, trying to disguise how much has been paid and attempting to paint the episode as a stunning triumph of managerial excellence is a recurring feature of most of New Labour's failed projects. Although I have already told this story in *Rip-Off!*, it is worth repeating here as it is very likely that something extremely similar is happening in most of the government departments that have been encouraged by the New Labour modernizers to open their doors to management consultants.

Two commentators have written such eloquent accounts of what appears to be a disaster for this organization and a goldmine for the executives and the consultants involved, that rather than trying to paraphrase their work, I'll let them tell this amazing story in their own words:

> Lord Birt became director-general in 1992 with a mission to reform and improve the BBC. He believed the solution was management restructuring and McKinsey were commissioned at vast expense to recommend radical change. McKinsey and Company Inc. is a secretive management consultancy with a formidable reputation . . . McKinsey takes itself terribly seriously. Priced at £500,000 a year, a McKinsey adviser is hugely self-confident, intellectually precise, elitist, puritanical and obsessed with systems and structures. Like a cult, advisers encourage an aura of mystique and exploit the fears and power-jealousy of nervous, insecure executives running huge companies and organizations.

A devoted disciple, Birt allocated McKinsey a permanent office at Broadcasting House ... A major transformation occurred in 1996 with the implementation of an 'internal market' at the BBC. A typically complex McKinsey project, it divided the corporation into dozens of new departments with extra 'business units'. Producers now had to negotiate with each unit to book a facility for a programme. This increased red tape and burdened producers. 'I've got an identity crisis,' said one at an internal conference. 'I started off as a production business unit. A couple of months ago I became a resource business unit and a couple of days ago an orchestral business unit. What does this mean?

None of the BBC's top management or staff were consulted by Birt ... about this radical new system. It was almost as if McKinsey was running the BBC. 'Birt always seemed to trust McKinsey's rather than his own management,' said John Tusa, former head of the BBC World Service. 'Perhaps it was because they were completely obedient.' Programme-makers deeply resented the McKinsey culture. They claimed that millions were wasted on 'management counselling' and 'role-playing' in business negotiations. One exercise in 'working together' involved cutting out paper frogs and pretending to sell them to each other. Such training activities soaked up £15m a year. A bizarre new language known as 'Birtspeak' was now used by BBC executives. Birt himself was likened to a McKinsey clone.

Hiring McKinsey was supposed to cut costs at the BBC, but bureaucracy and the number of administrators increased. Executives doubted they were getting value for money, but the fees paid to McKinsey were kept a closely guarded secret. Only Birt and personnel director Margaret Salmon knew the amounts as they were buried under 'operational expenditure' in the BBC budget. In 1999, chairman Sir Christopher Bland acknowledged that the BBC spent up to £22m a year of the £2.2bn budget on advisers. When asked why the BBC had not previously released the figure, he replied: 'We were probably a little coy about it.'

But all good things eventually come to an end – even for McKinsey.

The new director-general was not so shy about his view of McKinsey. He immediately axed 75% of the budget for outside consultants. 'This is public money,' said Dyke. 'The public only give it to us legitimately on the grounds that we spend as much of it as we can on services for them.'[14]

This picture of a seemingly runaway chief executive pursuing some great but inappropriate new vision with the obsequious help of his pet, well-paid consultants is reinforced by another independent outside commentator:

But it's McKinsey's work at the BBC which is now being seen as the first major crack in the armour of perhaps the most illustrious organization in consulting. The BBC's problems run deep, and to many observers the presence of McKinsey has made them deeper. The corporation has employed the Firm on a fairly regular basis ever since John Birt announced Producer Choice, his blueprint to re-engineer the BBC two years ago. . . . BBC observers are arguing that Birt has lost touch with what's really going on. Programme-makers in particular are finding the difference between what the BBC says it is doing (as recommended by McKinsey) and what is actually happening to be huge.

One example, just last year Margaret Salmon, the BBC's director of personnel, announced that the corporation had spent £6m on consultants, but went on to say brightly that this expenditure had resulted in savings of £255m, which was now going into programme-making. Programme-makers were immediately suspicious: all they knew was that their budgets were being pared considerably. Finally when the BBC announced in April that it had run out of money for new programmes and would have to freeze all commissioning, the sceptics were vindicated. The promised £255m was nowhere to be seen. It had appeared somewhere in a McKinsey report, but was a classic consultant fudge: by reclassifying the same spending under different headings, large theoretical savings could be made.

Under a photo of the happily smiling John Birt, this report went on to conclude:

> The BBC now costs more to run while employing less people than ever before. The 'savings' have turned out to be an extra staff cost of £140 million compared to four years ago.[15]

The expensive and apparent failure of Birt and McKinsey to convert the BBC to their great new management idea was so massive that it attracted extremely passionate criticism from a wide range of observers. The following very personal comments about Birt give a powerful picture of the type of senior managers and politicians who appear to become almost dependent on management consultants rather than working directly with employees and civil servants to achieve their goals: 'It is not as if Birt's failings weren't apparent . . . during his tenure as deputy director-general. Birt's shortcomings of excessive dogmatism and ponderous decision-making were clear well before his appointment. His interaction with colleagues was minimal. His presentations were laboured. His sense of humour and fun were nil. As initiative after initiative poured out from Birt and his myrmidons – from Producer Choice to Bi-Medialism in the News – the message was clear: this was top-down, imposed change, externally driven by Birt's beloved management consultants.'[16]

I suspect many people in the NHS, the MoD, the Department for Work and Pensions, the Passport Agency, the Inland Revenue, the Department for Education and Skills, and around 2,500 other government departments[17] will recognize a similarly futile scenario being played out – with our money – in their organizations.

Why IT Systems Often Go Wrong

The picture is even worse when it comes to IT systems consultancy. The largest international study of IT systems, the Standish Report, examined over 25,000 IT systems in 13,000 organizations worldwide and found that considerably fewer than 30 per cent of IT systems were successful. The definition of success used by the Standish Report was quite generous – if an IT system cost twice as much as budgeted *and* took twice as long to implement as planned, this was judged to be a success. The Report classed 73 per cent of IT systems as failures because they cost *more than twice* their original budgets *and* took *more than twice* as long to implement as originally planned.[18] Some recent research suggests the success rate of new IT systems in Britain may be much lower: 'An Oxford University/*Computer Weekly* survey of IT projects in Britain found that only 16% were considered successful.' Another survey gave even more worrying results: 'A British Computer Society study of projects judged only 3 out of 500 a success.'[19]

One of the worst results I've ever seen was when a part of the British government paid its technology consultants around £1bn for a major computer systems implementation. In addition to the £1bn cost, the organization also had to pay their systems provider about £138m a year in service costs, which moved the organization from having made a profit for the last twenty years or so into making a significant loss. The more we delved into the history of this enormous systems project, the more concerned we became about its massive costs and questionable results. I took a meeting with the programme manager to discuss the situation. Laughing, he admitted to me without any embarrassment that the whole expensive exercise had delivered 'diddly squat'.[20]

Nobody in the organization seemed overly concerned at this disaster and fortunately nobody outside, like the press, had realised the true scale of the catastrophe. When I tried to warn the organization concerned that a similar new project they were starting up with some other technology consultants showed all the signs of heading in the same direction, I was warned never to mention this again as it was none of my business. In his last book, the late Anthony Sampson described how many of the large systems suppliers seemed able to milk their British public-sector customers: 'Mandarins were easily baffled by computer companies, which bombarded Whitehall departments with high-pressure salesmanship and lobbying, and which had always had special scope for exploiting ignorant clients with their incomprehensible language and expertise.'[21]

My concerns about how some major IT systems consultancies operate are reflected in emails from consultants at one of the world's largest systems consultancies. One written in 2004, three years after the public share offering (IPO) which made millions for each of their partners, said, 'we have gone from a firm which focuses on doing the right thing to a firm which focuses on what we can legally get away with. There is no question that the IPO has destroyed our culture along with thousands of careers. Partners, on the other hand, have made out like bandits laughing all the way to the bank.' Another consultant from the same company wrote, 'I'm ashamed to say we've changed into an AFAB (Anything For A Buck) culture.'[22] Even though these emails may reflect the views of only two disgruntled employees it could make one suspicious about whether they are right.

There are many reasons why IT systems projects in particular spin so hopelessly out of control. Over-optimistic ambitions, inadequate project management, continual changes in specification and poor communication between designers and users must take some of the blame. But there have been so many total fiascos and they have occurred so consistently, that it seems there must be something fundamentally wrong with the way most systems projects are sold and run. My experiences working alongside over 40,000 IT systems consultants and assisting IT systems projects that have got into trouble have led me to believe that there are five basic and serious causes of the many public services IT systems fiascos – incompetent buyers, contract structure, supplier over-stretch, reinventing the wheel and civil servants' ignorance of the law.

Incompetent buyers
A frightening number of large organizations, particularly government departments, simply have no idea how to buy large computer systems developments nor how much they

should pay. This makes them easy prey for the large systems houses eager to sell massive programmes to their clients. I was recently with a project manager at the consultancy which allegedly had the AFAB culture. In his long career, he had only ever met one client who, he felt, had skilfully managed his IT systems suppliers. When we talked about selling to the public sector, he just laughed and talked about how easy it was to get them to buy whatever the consultancy wanted to sell. At an IT industry conference in 2005, the lead legal counsel from one of the world's top three systems suppliers talked about British government buyers of IT being 'unsophisticated', 'inconsistent' and 'inexperienced' and joked about how this allowed the consultancy to earn huge amounts of money. Unfortunately there were no members of the press around who could have done a 'Ratner' on this particular gentleman's revealing comments.

Contract structure
Too many IT systems are still developed based on what we call 'Time & Materials' contracts. On such contracts, the supplier is paid on the basis of how much time and resources they use – so the more time and resources they use, the more money they get. Thus they have no incentive to finish any systems project within a tight time-frame or with carefully controlled use of resources. If they were on contracts with a fixed price and penalties for cost and time overruns, then many more IT systems might see the light of day faster and at much lower cost than is the case now. Many other IT systems projects may appear to be based on a fixed price and fixed time-frame contract. However, when you look at the small print, you tend to find a whole series of 'get out of jail free' clauses – clauses that, at the slightest excuse, allow the system provider to claim that the client has made changes to the specification, and so the suppliers continuously increase the cost of the project and the time taken. These projects are often called 'partnerships', although they are rather unequal partnerships as in every single case the consultants get the money while the client gets the systems disaster. At a conference in 2005, a commercial

lawyer, who had served as an adviser to the Customs and Revenue and the police, described these partnering contracts as 'a licence to permit cost-plus and death by change control'. He meant that on supposedly fixed price government contracts, you could always increase the price as much as you wanted by continually claiming that you had to make changes for which the client should pay extra on a 'Time and Materials' basis.

Hence we see most systems providers making stupendous profits year after year in spite of the fact that many of their projects end up costing hundreds of millions more than initially budgeted and taking years longer than planned, if they ever work at all. And, of course, with government IT projects, every few hundred million squandered on the latest fiasco mean a few hundred million less that can be spent on providing essential services like health, policing and education.

Supplier over-stretch

New Labour are pouring so much money into new IT systems as the 'silver bullet' for reforming the way public services are delivered, that most systems consultancies are faced with a major problem – where to find competent consultants with relevant experience to staff their huge new government projects. Some consultancies are seeing their business double, triple, even quadruple every year as they get ever more public-sector work. This places a massive strain on these companies to meet the promises they have sold. In fact, the experienced consultants these companies so desperately need don't exist, so the IT systems providers are having to make do with whoever they can get. I have seen many IT systems consultancies, while doing public-sector work, start up their project with as few experienced people as possible, then when the project is running, quickly move the few experienced staff on to their next project. Naturally, the results of this are disastrous as project after project overruns on time and cost due to the lack of experience of the people left working on them. Then when public-sector clients start to raise their concerns about lack of progress, the consultancies try to buy time by muddying the waters – for example, by blaming their clients for the problems, accusing people they are working with of delays and incompetence, claiming their clients did not make their specifications clear and so on. The consultancies know that few of their public-sector clients have the knowledge or will-power to hold them to account for their failure to deliver and so usually get away with enormous time and cost overruns. In many cases, they even succeed in charging their public-sector clients extra money to fix the problems that were caused in the first place by the consultancies' blatant lack of experienced staff.

Reinventing the wheel
Although their products or services may be very different, most organizations do fundamentally similar things. They make or buy something, put it in a box and sell it; or they make or buy something, put it in a shop or website and sell it; or they transport passengers; or they handle people's money. In the case of government departments, they take some skill, knowledge or service (cancer surgery, taxation, social services), provide it to citizens and manage their own costs and budgets. So most organizations, in the private or public sectors, need similar things from their systems – acquiring products or skills, attracting customers or identifying the people they should serve, managing information about customers or citizens, cost control and billing, HR management, financial accounting and so on. For example, the £450m system for the Child Support Agency is unlikely to be hugely different from the types of systems used by debt-collection companies. Yet, as the hundreds of millions price tag, the system's failure and the ensuing administrative chaos all show, a whole new system was built rather than an existing system being adapted. Moreover, at the start of 2006, the government is even talking of handing many of the CSA's responsibilities over to private debt-collection companies that use precisely the kind of IT systems the CSA should have adapted for its use in the first place. In another case of extravagant wheel reinvention, the MoD was reported as having abandoned an IT systems development project after spending eight years and £41m to achieve nothing. The MoD then bought an adapted off-the-shelf replacement system for

just £6m.[23] Similarly, after three years of largely futile work on developing a new IT system, a local council found to its surprise that small changes to its existing system would give the results the new system had so far failed to provide.

It is simply not in the IT systems consultancies' interests to provide you with a fast, cheap adaptation of existing systems when they can earn hundreds of millions convincing you that you need your own specially designed new system.

Civil servants' ignorance of the law

A slightly depressing aspect to the whole British government IT systems debacle is that the government has not only utterly failed to manage its IT systems projects in a professional way, but has also failed to enforce its own legal rights as a paying customer of the IT systems consultants. In Britain, case law around the duties and obligations of IT systems suppliers and consultants has undergone a seismic shift over the last ten years or so. In the early 1990s, buying systems was very much a case of *caveat emptor* (buyer beware), and organizations seldom had any right of recourse against their IT suppliers, however disastrous the results of those suppliers' work. A series of over 100 legal judgements has since changed this to something that more resembles *caveat vendor* (supplier beware). The 1994 case of *Streets Heaver* v. *Stephenson Blake* (an IT consultancy) laid out the duties of anyone being paid as an 'expert' for their advice and services. This stated that an IT consultant must inform you whether your business analysis actually meets your operational requirements, whether its systems will meet your operational requirements, whether both your staff and its staff are capable of successfully completing the project and whether your original budget is sufficient to meet your objectives. While the 1995 case of *St Albans Council* v. *ICL* (now Fujitsu) established that an IT systems supplier must inform its client of exactly what its system will provide, what it will not provide and what are the 'consequential effects' of the things that the system will not provide.

Unfortunately, government departments and their expensive city lawyers do not seem to have a clue about their legal position when setting up contracts with IT systems suppliers. In an analysis of over 500 IT systems contracts, many of them entered into by government departments, one group of specialists did not find one single contract that effectively took account of the 'duty of care' and other legal obligations on IT systems suppliers. In meetings with government departments for one company I worked with, we frequently found ourselves having to explain to government lawyers the legal obligations of IT systems suppliers. Many government lawyers seem to be unaware that there have been any changes in the law in the twenty years or so since most of them left law school. Even when the lawyers are aware of the changes in the law, they have usually not understood the implications these changes have on the way that IT systems projects should be bought and managed. Moreover, when systems suppliers clearly fail to meet their legal obligations, the government virtually never seeks to enforce its legal rights. On one consultancy's website, the company claims to employ '70,000 experts'. While some people may see this as just puffery, the statement that employees are 'experts' actually has legal significance. If these 'experts' fail to deliver to their promises, having claimed they are 'experts', the consultancy can be sued for their failure.

What is worse is that the government, probably unintentionally, prevents government departments from effective buying of IT systems. The approaches to buying IT systems that the government promotes through organizations like the Office of Government Commerce (OGC) and through its official OJEU (Official Journal of the European Union) buying procedures are great for buying photocopiers, paperclips, envelopes, mineral water dispensers, desks, comfortable chairs, filing cabinets, hole-punchers, staplers, staples, rulers, pencils, biros, coffee, tea bags and all the other essential items to keep a bloated bureaucracy comfortably supplied. But they are quite unsuited to buying complex services like IT systems consulting for at least three reasons: they actually prevent the IT suppliers from understanding what is really required from the new system; they prevent public-sector buyers of IT systems from getting the benefits of their legal position; they hugely erode the legal responsibilities of systems suppliers to the public sector. Too often on public-sector projects, we find that the intelligent way of buying IT systems is contrary to government department procedures and so departments ignore our warnings and knowingly go ahead with IT contracts that are doomed to failure from the start. It will probably not be a great surprise that it is consultants who are largely responsible for designing the government's procedures for buying consulting services – a process which pretty much removes all the legal responsibilities from the consultants to deliver to their original promises.

Overall, it seems to me that many IT systems failures have more to do with the dubious ethics of the consultancies supplying the systems rather than the inherent technical difficulties in the systems' development.

The Winner Is – The British Taxpayer!

Perhaps one of the most graphic demonstrations of the enormous gap between the value that the consultants claim they bring, and the costly reality experienced by the taxpayers who witness the decimation of our public services, can be seen in the results of the 2005 Management Consultancies Association (MCA) awards. Summing up the awards, one industry journalist wrote a gushing article entitled, 'The winner is – the public sector and the British taxpayer!'[24]

Capgemini won an Outsourcing Gold Award for its work with the Inland Revenue. Capgemini was praised for creating 'a global ecosystem of technology partners as a means of facilitating greater access to innovation' and for using its 'Transformational Outsourcing service, which helps clients boost performance against key business objectives and bring their IT in closer alignment with business needs'. As it handed over more than £4bn of our money to Capgemini, the Inland Revenue seemed delighted with its new supplier: 'we need a technology partner who can help us meet our huge challenges and I'm confident we have found such a partner,' said Sir Nicholas Montagu, former chairman of the Inland Revenue.[25]

As we saw in Chapter 1, this was the same Inland Revenue that gave us the family tax credits disaster which impoverished many thousands of poorer families, led to some people losing their homes and jobs, and enabled possibly the largest benefits fraud in British history. Admittedly, Capgemini inherited most of the systems from its predecessor, the almost ubiquitous EDS, but the benefits fraud took place after Capgemini took over running the system and it seems odd that they should have the Inland Revenue's confidence and be winning awards if they were in any way associated with any part of the disaster.

Another MCA Gold Award went to the consultancy Boxwood for their work in helping the Metronet Consortium on their £17bn contract for upgrading London Underground's infrastructure. Boxwood were credited with having 'instilled a culture of improvement that is inspiring the company'. Metronet's director Andrew Cooper seemed more than satisfied with his organization's performance ('it's a standard by which others can be judged'). Yet at the same time as the MCA awards ceremony took place, official figures showed a 43 per cent increase in signal failures in the first four months of 2005 – on some lines, signal failures more than doubled. Nevertheless, Metronet was awarded £9m in performance bonuses as, in order to attract private-sector firms, the government had agreed lower performance targets for the private sector than those that had previously existed for London Underground. While tube users fumed at the continuous daily disruptions, one senior tube manager was reported as saying, 'the whole thing is a farce. Commuters have every right to be furious with the government. Millions are being paid in bonuses while at the same time we put up notices most days telling passengers there are delays or no trains at all.'[26]

A Gold Award for 'Change Management' was handed over to Capita for their work in helping the Department for Work and Pensions (DWP) replace the Minimum Income Guarantee for pensioners with a new entitlement, Pension Credit. Again, we saw an apparently extraordinary effort from Capita: 'the resulting performance improvements in pension centres included a 37% increase in deployment of effort and a 41%

increase in case-clearance capacity across the service.' Naturally, the client was delighted: 'Capita's approach has challenged our thinking and helped us make lasting improvements in our operational management capabilities.' This success was lauded in the write-up for the MCA award: 'Pension Credit was launched on schedule and without incident. The target of 2.4 million recipients was achieved on time.'

However, it appears that things were not quite as successful. For example, overpayments due to errors and fraud reached £280m in the first year. The government preferred to boast about the take-up of the credit ('lifting record numbers of pensioners out of poverty'), though the experience of DWP employees told a different story. Forced to cold-call pensioners, who were understandably reluctant to answer personal questions, the 2.4 million take-up target was, according to staff, reached by not removing dead pensioners from the records.[27] Once again, an example of New Labour successfully hitting targets as a result of its consultants might appear to owe more to creative accounting than actual achievement.

CHAPTER 7

PFI Paradise

Another Policy, Another Bonanza

No single government policy better epitomises the handover of
public services to the vested interests of the consultancy
industry than the Private Finance Initiative (PFI). First announced by Tory Chancellor Norman Lamont in his 1992
autumn statement amid the gloom of a recession and in the
shadow of the government's massive 'Black Wednesday' losses
on the currency markets, the plan was for private companies
rather than a cash-strapped public sector to pay for new
schools, hospitals and other services. The companies would
then run them for anything up to fifty years, recouping their
outlay through annual charges to the taxpayer. The clear
political advantage was that the public spending commitments
created under these agreements, unlike the government borrowing that would traditionally have been required for such
investment, would not count as public debt – more of which
the struggling Exchequer needed like a hole in the head. But the
snag with PFI is that it costs private companies much more to
borrow the money needed than it would the government,
increasing the costs that are ultimately passed on to public
services. What's more, the private companies controlling the
assets are guaranteed income for providing additional services

for decades. All told, as is now becoming painfully clear in health and other services, the expenses that taxpayers (and the children of today's taxpayers) become committed to under PFI vastly exceed the burdens imposed by traditional investment. The promise to pay these extra costs, however, magically vanishes from the government's books; a sleight of hand that would become New Labour magician Gordon Brown's favourite trick, ably helped by his glamorous assistants in the consultancy industry.

The idea of PFI was reported to have come from young Tory hopeful, David Willetts,[1] whose thoughts eventually emerged as a pamphlet for the Social Market Foundation think-tank entitled 'The Opportunities for Private Funding in the NHS'. Regrettably for the great Tory thinker, his ideas translated into little action under Lamont and his successor Kenneth Clarke, both of whom, though keen on the policy, were all too aware of the scope for the private sector's profits to drain the Treasury's coffers. Two years after Lamont's launch of PFI, in a speech to the CBI Clarke reinforced the two conditions for PFI schemes: the private sector must really take the risks involved and the taxpayer must receive value for money.[2] This was too onerous for the nervous banks and construction companies that needed to be persuaded of the prospects of making some serious money. Although a couple of billion pounds' worth of deals had been signed by 1996,[3] there wasn't sufficient interest in the scheme for it to gain any significant momentum under the Tories.

The choice facing New Labour as it took power in 1997 was relatively straightforward. The option of funding investments in schools, hospitals, roads and railways from public borrowing, at relatively cheap interest rates, had the fatal flaw that the debts would appear on the books. Incoming Chancellor Gordon Brown, anxious to convince a sceptical City of his economic credibility, was committed to keeping borrowing down, and in July 1997 published his 'golden rules': one limiting his spending to no more than his income over the economic cycle; the other restricting public-sector debt to a 'prudent proportion' of the country's gross domestic product, assessed as 40 per cent. But having inherited debt of 45 per cent[4] – with expectations but no guarantees that it would fall – he could not afford any more borrowing to fund the new government's investment plans. The answer to the dilemma was to sprinkle the magic dust of PFI on the problem.

In Opposition, New Labour had understood the limitations of PFI – shadow ministers who would go on to embrace the policy in government had roundly condemned it shortly before. As shadow Chief Secretary to the Treasury, Alistair Darling had pointed out the dangers of PFI: 'But this lack of control will become a very real problem within the next two to three years if in fact PFI takes off. Apparent savings now could be countered by the formidable commitment on revenue expenditure in years to come.'[5] Soon he was in the Treasury, however, and later funnelling huge amounts of public money into PFI as Transport Secretary. Ideological as well as economic objections also faded away. No New Labour minister would again call the initiative 'privatization by another name', as shadow Health Secretary Harriet Harman had in 1996 by declaring that 'when the private sector is designing, building, financing, operating and running the hospital, and employing the doctors and nurses, that is privatization and that is what the Conservative government are all about.'[6] The one prominent Labour Opposition front-bencher who had not spoken out against the scheme was Gordon Brown, shrewdly realizing perhaps that, despite the views of his colleagues, he would be relying more on PFI than the Tories ever did.

By the end of 2005, so central had PFI become to government policy that contracts with capital value (the cost of the facilities before interest and service charges) of nearly £50bn had been signed, committing the taxpayer to annual payments of up to £7.5bn for at least twenty years to come.[7] The costs would fall in some of the most sensitive areas, notably in the National Health Service where the extra burden would be borne by cash-strapped hospital trusts struggling to cope with reforms designed to usher in more competition. But even these PFI costs may pale next to those to come from future contracts: while the NHS was already struggling with hospital deals worth £2bn by December 2005, the government had given the go-ahead for £15bn more.[8] The Ministry of Defence similarly renewed its commitment to PFI at the end of 2005[9] and had several deals in the pipeline, the largest being the £13bn Future Strategic Air Tanker project. And the Department for Education and Skills had committed to £2bn–£3bn a year for a school rebuilding programme under PFI.[10]

Although crippling many public-sector bodies, committed irreversibly to expensive deals spanning a generation, the great PFI splurge is a dream come true for consultants, who rack up huge fees by backing all horses in the complex bidding process that precedes every deal. Consultants within the big four accountancy firms are the main beneficiaries. By 2005 PwC had been employed as consultant, either for the public or the private sector, on 174 projects with a total capital value of £31.4bn. KPMG wasn't far behind with 98 deals worth £16bn, while Deloitte had advised on 78 deals coming in at £21.3bn and Ernst & Young 128 at £11.7bn. Apart from the banks providing their own brand of advice on financing, the next most powerful firm, Grant Thornton, had advised on just £4bn worth of deals, and no others had more than £2bn to their name. Thus the near monopoly that had for years ratcheted up prices in the accountancy market was transposed directly by the dominance of the 'Big Four' firms on to the state-sponsored PFI market.[11]

While the consultants give no indication of what they earn on PFI deals, an early study showed that the first fifteen NHS trust hospital PFI deals generated fees for advisers – paid by the taxpayer – of 4 per cent of the capital value of the deals, of which over half went to financial and other consultants.[12] With almost £50bn of contracts concluded by the end of 2005, a similar rate would have generated income for advisers of £2bn, giving more than £1bn to consultants. And as all the bidders on each deal also require expert advice, the lawyers' and consultants' bonanza is likely to be four to five times what the government gives directly to consultants on the taxpayer's behalf. So estimates of around £10bn for advisers, with about £5bn for consultants (just on deals already signed), might not be too far off the mark. And as the complexity of deals increases, the costs of consultants are going up. In September 2005 the Major Contractors' Group estimated the bid costs for each bidder on a PFI hospital were coming in at around £11.5m, about 6 per cent of the value of a typical deal.[13]

Tilting the Playing Field

Sweeping into office in May 1997 on a huge majority, but with awkward twin pledges to keep borrowing down *and* increase investment, New Labour desperately needed the accounting trick of PFI. But how to deal with the hesitation of the companies on which pulling off this sleight of hand would depend? Even if many had been won over to New Labour, they remained sceptical of a party that only two years earlier had been promising re-nationalization of certain industries. And, the strict conditions that the Tory Chancellor Clarke had attached to PFI, that risk must be transferred to the private sector and deals must provide value for money, stood in the way of the investment programme Blair and Brown were desperate to unleash. So how could companies that were already wary of PFI under the Tories be persuaded to sign contracts for anything up to fifty years with such a government? The solution was to put the new Paymaster General, millionaire and seasoned businessman Geoffrey Robinson, in charge of reinvigorating the programme.

Such was the urgency of the task that Robinson announced a review of PFI just six days after the election victory, beaten only in the Chancellor's list of priorities by independence for the Bank of England. His review team didn't hang about either and six weeks later had produced the blueprint for a renewed push for PFI. Following the review, the Tories' worthy but politically limited private finance panel, stuffed with bankers and builders, was immediately replaced by what was to become a preferred type of New Labour quango: a taskforce. The Treasury PFI Taskforce, to give it its full name, ensured that every angle was covered. It brought together policy and projects specialists, including lawyers, bankers, consultants from PriceWaterhouse, Coopers and Lybrand and Nicholls Associates, and industry specialists. Launching the taskforce, Robinson's enthusiasm for PFI seemed to be clear: 'Today is an important step forward in harnessing private-sector finance and expertise to fulfil the government's determination to deliver high quality value for money projects in the public sector. I am pleased to see such a range of talent and experience coming forward to contribute to achieving the immense benefits to be gained from good PFI and Public–Private Partnerships.'[14]

The Chief Executive summed up the approach of his taskforce: 'This is a really strong team of young Turks; they have the qualifications, the experience in PFI deals and, above all, the feel for what the private sector wants from the PFI to be a really effective bridge between the public and private sectors.'[15] In short, it would make sure that PFI offered the private sector just what it wanted if it was going to play the game.

The taskforce set about issuing a series of 'technical notes' designed to ease the tortuous PFI process and make it more attractive to the market. For example, no limits were placed on the profits to be made by the private sector if the expensive financing they had built into contracts suddenly became cheaper. Future PFI liabilities were to be discounted by 6 per cent, significantly greater than the cost of money to the government and current or expected levels of inflation. But perhaps more importantly, the taskforce proposed that fewer risks needed to be taken by the private sector, with the public sector retaining more. Fifteen different types of risk were identified. Each time one of these was taken on by a PFI contractor, a complex formula was applied to increase the (theoretical) cost of the public-sector alternative – allowing PFI operators to charge more while simultaneously improving the chance of the deal appearing value for money and thereby getting the go-ahead. Another accounting trick allowed spurious adjustments to be made to the way in which value for money of a PFI proposal against the conventional government-funded alternative was calculated, including factoring in an ever-flexible 'optimism bias' assumed for public schemes.[16]

The PFI deal, under this taskforce of bankers and consultants, soon got a whole lot better for the industry, and private-sector scepticism quickly turned to salivation as the financiers, builders and consultants eyed the returns on offer from PFI, which in some cases give margins of over 50 per cent. To oil the wheels of the PFI programme, the wise counsel of PFI consultants was warmly welcomed under Treasury Taskforce guidance entitled 'How to appoint and manage advisers to PFI projects', which urged the use of success fees (payable when the deal is signed off) and instructed public-sector bodies: 'Don't underestimate the complexity and difficulties of a PFI negotiation and make sure the key individual advisers are present at all important meetings.'[17]

There was little evidence to substantiate government claims of more efficient procurement under PFI and the official fiddle factors these claims spawned. Perhaps the most often quoted by ministers, and put into Treasury guidance in 2003, was that, 'Previous research has shown that 70 per cent of non-PFI projects were delivered late and 73 per cent ran over budget.' These numbers, repeated authoritatively in Parliament to demonstrate how the old inefficient methods of procurement were being swept away, emerged from a 1999 study from the Agile Construction initiative, funded by one of the main PFI players at the time, Balfour Beatty. The data used weren't included in the report which, in any event, was intended not to estimate procurement methods but to develop methods of measuring them.

But whatever the truth about procurement under traditional funding methods, PFI was not about to herald a bright new efficient dawn. With all the dubious adjustments in the calculation methodology tilting procurement decisions in favour of private finance, and various other sweeteners such as VAT breaks and 'PFI credits' from central government on offer, the competition between the methods was not so much on a level playing field as on the side of a mountain.

The Unacceptable Face of Capitalism

PFI certainly started to deliver in New Labour's first years – for the consultants and the burgeoning private finance industry, if not the public relying on it for services. Hospitals across the country, from Durham to Dartford, Calderdale to Cumbria, proved to be goldmines for the consortia behind them, all encouraged and advised by a growing band of consultants who had also seen the rich pickings on offer. By the end of 1998, contracts for eight major new hospitals had been signed, with capital value around £726m, where none had been achieved under the Tories.[18]

All naturally required the services of consultants to advise public-sector staff unfamiliar with the arcane world of the Private Finance Initiative and its complex tendering and contract negotiation processes, not to mention the financing of deals that would last decades. Technical, financial and legal consultants were needed by both the private-sector bidders and the public bodies, generating an unprecedented feeding frenzy which was stimulated by their clients' confusion over PFI. Crucially, the consultants who had developed the methods through which the value for money of proposed deals would be assessed, and had then helped to enshrine them in official Treasury Taskforce guidance, became the key advisers to the public bodies as they crunched the numbers. Unsurprisingly, time and again PFI emerged as the preferred method for building and running major public infrastructure.

PFI quickly proved to be another source of potential conflicts of interests for the Big Four. In scores of cases a firm acting for the public body commissioning the PFI deal also counted at least one of the bidders, often the successful one, among its valued clients for auditing and consultancy services. The accountants also happily continued their lucrative sideline in performing local authority and health trust audits on behalf of the Audit Commission while advising authorities on taking up the PFI deals that would form a crucial part of their affairs to be reviewed in later years.[19]

Despite official insistence that PFI schemes would only go

ahead if they gave value for money, the early projects proved to provide anything but. The leading academic in the field, Professor Allyson Pollock at University College London's School of Public Policy, showed that costs of PFI projects escalated dramatically from the first stage 'outline business case' to the final figure. At the Norfolk and Norwich Hospital, the capital cost went up from £90m at 'outline business case' to £200m, at Swindon from £45m to £148m,[20] while the annual expenses placed on their trusts for the use of premises went up by at least 12 per cent in every case,[21] an additional burden that was soon to lead to deficits and the scaling back of clinical work. The boast often made of PFI, that extra financing costs would be offset by the benefits of private-sector efficiency, was exposed as the myth that sceptics had long believed it to be.

Within a couple of years the full extent of the Treasury's generosity in setting the rules of the PFI game became apparent. While many doctors, nurses and school teachers could already feel the pinch, when the PFI companies started to cash in some of their chips it became clear to many outside the public sector where the extra costs were going. Leading the way was a consortium of Tarmac and Group 4, which in 1999 re-financed its borrowings to take advantage of the markets' growing faith in PFI and corresponding willingness to lend more cheaply, realizing a £10.7m gain on top of the £17.5m they were expected to earn anyway.[22] In 2003 the companies behind two of the early hospital PFI schemes – the very first one at Dartford and Gravesham, another at the Norfolk and Norwich Hospital – re-financed their contracts, crystallizing the benefits of the lucrative deals in the form of £33m and £115m windfalls respectively, with the returns to investors soaring to 56 and 60 per cent. In each case only around a third was handed to the NHS because Treasury guidelines at the time, effectively drawn up by the industry for the industry, demanded not a penny back for the taxpayer. The trusts, furthermore, could only take their shares as reductions in their enormous obligations over future years. When the Public Accounts Committee came to look at the Norfolk re-financing, chairman Edward Leigh resorted to Ted Heath's description of

1970s tycoon Tiny Rowland in describing the outcome as 'the unacceptable face of capitalism'.[23] It was quite acceptable for the consultants, however, as every significant change in the contract or the financing demanded their involvement. At Dartford and Gravesham, for example, Ernst & Young had stepped in to advise the hospital trust while PwC were helping the PFI companies.[24]

Beyond details of isolated cases, only in 2004 did clear evidence emerge of the margins generated across a range of contracts for the PFI companies. The Association of Chartered Certified Accountants showed that between 2000 and 2002 shareholders in the early PFI hospital schemes were making returns of over 100 per cent, while similar excess emerged in the other major area of PFI spending in the 1990s, roads. The report highlighted huge differences in costs of funding, the private companies' borrowing at around 10 per cent rather than the 4.5 per cent cost of government debt at the time, for which they were compensated by receiving payments based on inflated estimates of risks carried by the private sector.[25]

How had such returns, and corresponding expense for the taxpayer, been generated when the extra costs that soon emerged should have been foreseeable, preventing the waste in the first place? The answer is the fiddle factors available to the architects of the deal, egged on by their consultants, and the absence of any meaningful checks on their work. In 2002 a paper from the *British Medical Journal* showed how the 'public-sector comparator' (PSC) was always significantly cheaper than the PFI proposal, until various risk and optimism bias adjustments were made, following which – hey presto! – the PFI scheme invariably appeared to be marginally better value for money, often by just a few pounds. This benefited all parties: hospital trusts and other public bodies knew, in the words of Health Secretary Alan Milburn, 'it's PFI or bust.'[26] So if they didn't play along, they would not get their new building; while the contractors and their advisers guaranteed themselves a much healthier stream of income than they had ever achieved under boringly traditional public procurement methods. As the assistant head of the NAO put it some time later, 'if the answer comes out wrong you don't get your project. So the answer doesn't come out wrong very often.'[27]

Never more clearly was this unholy convergence of interests illustrated than at the West Middlesex hospital where consultants to the health trust, KPMG, found that the PSC was slightly cheaper than PFI. This result was overturned when the advisers 'encouraged the trust to revisit these figures' through a series of 'risk workshops'.[28] An extra £12.5m-worth of risks was duly found to add to the PSC, happily taking it above the estimated cost of the PFI contract.[29] And it wasn't long before the costs hit home: in 2002 the hospital had to close a ward to accommodate the mushrooming deficit to which the PFI deal had contributed.[30]

Never Mind the Quality

So much for the alleged cost-efficiency of the Private Finance Initiative, but what about the quality of the infrastructure built under it? Here too it wasn't long before patients, doctors and nurses began to smell a rat (and worse). The first fourteen PFI hospitals saw 30 per cent bed reductions, while numerous other defects began to emerge. An 'independent' report on the first completed PFI hospital, the Cumberland Royal Infirmary in Carlisle, detailed failure to adjust to a hospital that had been built with fewer beds on the strength of dealing with patients more quickly[31] (and of course more cheaply for the PFI company managing the hospital). The BBC reported that: 'The hospital has been plagued by reports of blocked sewerage pipes which spewed out waste into sinks, flooding in the maternity unit, overheating in the atrium and of a patient injured after falling in the hospital's revolving door. Many patients have complained about the atrium – a centrepiece of the hospital. On one occasion, temperatures reached 110 degrees Fahrenheit in the hospital. And in May, there was a power failure, during which nurses had to manually ventilate some patients. There were also basic design faults, such as disabled services being placed at the back of the hospital away from the car park. A new one has been built, but the door to the unit is not suitable for disabled people to use.'[32]

Other hospital deals demonstrated how the necessity of using the Private Finance Initiative trumped the needs of the communities they were supposed to serve. Existing functional hospitals that could have been renovated were ditched in favour of new buildings that were more amenable to the requirements of lucrative PFI deals: a large capital outlay and something big to rent back to the public body for a juicy annual fee. Thus the new hospitals in Norwich, Edinburgh and Swindon were out of town and considerably less convenient for patients – all because the wishes of the PFI companies, despite often fierce local opposition, had prevailed. In Swindon, what started out as a £45m refurbishment of the St Margaret Hospital in the town centre turned into a £96m new hospital on a greenfield site convenient for the M4 but not for anyone having to make their own way there without a car.

By far the greatest opposition to the upheaval imposed on an unwilling community came in Kidderminster, where a valued hospital was to be downgraded as part of plans for a £87m PFI infirmary in Worcester, achieving the remarkable feat of drastically reducing acute admissions (and beds) while increasing the catchment population. By June 2000 activists had taken control of Wyre Forest council, covering Kidderminster, in the form of a new political party called Health Concern. Greater triumph for the group was to follow when, in May 2001, Health Concern's chairman, Richard Taylor, stood as an independent candidate at the 2001 general election and was elected with a 17,000 majority on a platform of opposition to the closure of Kidderminster hospital.[33] Joy was short-lived, however, as the power of PFI overcame democratically expressed rejection of the deal when the enlarged Royal Worcester Infirmary opened in 2002. Three years later, the trust was struggling with a growing deficit, while Taylor reported the ludicrous position the PFI contract had imposed on the cash-strapped hospital: 'about 10% of the £20 million that the acute trust in my area has to save is accounted for by the surcharge negotiated into the PFI contract for a bed occupancy above

90%. With less beds, this occupancy is inevitably and predictably often exceeded.'[34] Perhaps the NHS managers negotiating the contract didn't understand the implications of what they were signing up to, but one would be curious to see what advice they got from their expert advisers. The consultants behind the deal were the country's largest PFI consultants, PwC.

Although the National Health Service had been the main target of New Labour's early PFI assault, it wasn't the only one. Other services might not have had the same place in the public's affections but that didn't mean they weren't ripe for the PFI treatment. Along with hospitals, roads and IT, schools and prisons were also demanding more investment and provided fertile ground for PFI. Pupils soon paid the price as a series of uninspiring and often dysfunctional buildings was erected to fit the PFI formula, as developed by the experts and consultants swarming round the project. This led to an Audit Commission review in 2002, which concluded that the sample of twenty-five schools were 'statistically speaking, significantly worse'. In return, there was no evidence that PFI was proving any cheaper or quicker.[35]

When it came to prisons, there may have been less sympathy, but the situation was equally serious. While schools had teachers whose services couldn't be outsourced under PFI and hospitals had doctors and nurses in similar positions, prisons could be privatized wholesale with private finance. The PFI company could provide all the services, including employing the guards. This allowed some money to be saved, leading to a relatively positive National Audit Office report on the first seven PFI prisons in 2002, even though the young offenders institution at Ashfield, run under a PFI deal by Premier Prisons, had been branded the 'worst' prison in the country by the chief inspector of prisons.[36] But it emerged that the savings came from cutting staff wages, with private guards earning 30 per cent less than publicly employed ones, leading to lapses in professionalism and a staff turnover of 25 per cent, going up to 40 per cent for the worst prisons such as Ashfield.[37] Several investigations showed how poorer standards fed greater abuse in privately run prisons and detention centres. But the social and ultimately financial costs would never feature in any PFI calculation.

The Consultants Fight Back

With New Labour's first term drawing to a close, and with PFI widely rumbled as an expensive way to make sub-standard investment, the government found itself facing increasingly hostile questioning on the policy just as it hoped to take the initiative to another level. Thankfully some helpful consultants were on hand to provide the answers that would be parroted at critics for years to come and clear the way for a second term New Labour PFI splurge.

Once again the loyal Arthur Andersen came to the government's aid when in January 2000 the Treasury commissioned a report from the firm. Andersens concluded that PFI projects were 17 per cent cheaper than conventionally procured ones, allegedly through taking risks away from the public sector.[38] This was music to the government's ears: not only did it give a simple statistic that could be used to beat back any opposition to PFI, it also endorsed the official rationale for the scheme – risk transfer – in the first place. The study was, however, deeply flawed. In the 29 projects considered by Andersens, most of the reported savings came from just three schemes, while all had been selected by civil servants, who weren't independent of PFI; the extra financing costs assumed for PFI were drastically less than independent experts showed to be the case in practice.[39] The Andersen findings were even shamelessly exported to developing economies as various government ministers used them on trips to South Africa and Turkey to promote British PFI companies. Loyal New Labour politicians regaled audiences with selective tales of allegedly successful PFI deals, using Andersen's unreliable estimates of cost savings – regardless of the consequences of privatizing infrastructure in countries where people could even less afford to pay the price than taxpayers in Britain could.[40]

No sooner had the Andersen report been comprehensively rubbished and discredited, than the largest PFI consultant, PwC, stepped in to offer support. 'Public Private Partnerships: A Clearer View' proved to be no more than a series of testimonials from a selection of public-sector managers, who had committed large amounts of public money to the initiative and weren't about to admit their own misjudgements, and from a few people in the private sector responsible for delivering services under PFI and likewise firmly on the gravy train.[41] Yet minister after minister used the consultants' 'studies', which were in fact little more than PFI puff pieces, to support the scheme while ignoring the more numerous and more rigorous critiques produced by academics such as Allyson Pollock at University College London and Jean Shaoul at Manchester University, that exposed the delays, costs and defects in projects. The Prime Minister himself relied on the PwC report. Responding to Scottish Nationalist MP Annabelle Ewing when she questioned the disgraced Andersen's report's credibility, he simply referred 'the hon. lady to the PricewaterhouseCoopers report on the PFI, which found that it was excellent value for money'.[42]

Despite the manifold weaknesses of PFI – the expense, the inflexibility, the social and environmental costs – the country's main public spending watchdog, the National Audit Office (NAO), has never asked the obvious question: is it worth it? Several individual cases have been looked at, and the NAO has even identified glaring examples of outrageous cost overruns. But the focus has always been on identifying lessons for future PFIs with no challenge to the policy itself, and whether it should simply be ripped up. General enquiries have been nearer to opinion surveys than hard analysis and have invariably given proponents of PFI, especially government ministers, something to cling on to in support of the scheme.

As PFI became entrenched the NAO appeared to move closer to the consultants and the industry. It appointed a 'head of PFI development' who produced upbeat reports with titles such as *Managing the partnership to secure a successful partnership in PFI projects*, while the watchdog's senior staff became a feature on the PFI conference circuit alongside industry representatives. In the summer of 2004, for example, the NAO entitled its own conference *The new agenda: how PFI/PPP is adapting to deliver future success*. The chairman of the NAO and his head of PFI development were joined on the platform by representatives of Partnerships UK, consultants PwC and KPMG and other PFI beneficiaries.

The Treasury did, however, at least appear to take a hard look at PFI in 2003 when even the government started to recognize some limitations. While the Treasury's 2003 paper 'Meeting the Investment Challenge' put certain constraints on the policy, such as ruling it out for very small schemes, it was accompanied by the entrenchment of distorted methods for calculating value for money that effectively guaranteed PFI would have to be chosen for major deals. Such methods were said to be endorsed by three reports: two from the NAO showing vastly better construction performance under PFI, both of which were simply yet more surveys of project managers responsible for PFI deals; one from another PFI consultancy that had advised on PFI deals with capital value of £1.3bn by July 2005. The latter report's 'optimism bias' adjustments of up to 28 per cent for standard buildings in favour of PFI were shown to be based on inappropriate samples and comparisons of cost overruns from completely different stages in the procurement process.

A further highly technical but equally powerful adjustment, which could favour the PFI route by over 20 per cent, was built into the process on the advice of consultants at KPMG. The theory was that because they took on more risks than conventional suppliers, PFI companies would make more profits and thus pay more tax, a windfall for the Exchequer that ought to be set against the cost of a PFI deal when comparing it with the public-sector alternative. But the calculations ignored such vital issues as PFI companies' abilities to avoid tax, the way they were funded and all sorts of tax allowances that the experts at KPMG should have known about (and which was presumably why the Treasury commissioned the firm).

Bad for Your Health

With accountancy, tax and procurement rules all heavily slanted in favour of PFI, some of the most ambitious and grandiose projects began to emerge. The value of individual hospital projects soared from the £100m mark to several hundreds of millions, with deals of over half a billion pounds given the go-ahead in Manchester, Birmingham, Leicester and London – home to the largest ever in the form of the £1.1bn St Bartholomew's and London Hospital contract. At the end of 2005 Department of Health statistics showed that commitments for future hospitals under the Private Finance Initiative dwarfed what had been invested in those already up and running. PFI hospitals with a capital value of £2.1bn were already open while approval had been given for a further £15bn worth (of which £2.8bn had been irreversibly signed off).[43] The commitments to expenditure on lease and service payments for up to thirty years under these contracts would be many times that amount, while on what evidence is available of their fees, the advisers and consultants would be in line for further pay days worth at least half a billion pounds from the health service alone. (Just to illustrate the bias towards PFI in hospital construction, hospital deals agreed under conventional procurement methods since May 1997 total just £500m, less than 3 per cent of the total approved so far under New Labour.)[44]

It slowly became clear, however, that the large, inflexible PFI deals the government had been suckered into didn't work in the reformed health service of Labour's third term. Hospitals would compete for the 'business' of treating patients and be paid largely according to how successful they were in attracting the sick, while their expenditure on huge PFI deals was fixed for a generation regardless of how much use they had for the facilities. Towards the end of 2005 increasing numbers of trusts lumbered with multi-million-pound annual PFI commitments were running up unsustainable deficits. Managers of the Queen Elizabeth Hospital in Greenwich warned that the predicted £20m deficit for 2005/6 could climb to £100m if its PFI burdens (which had immediately increased its costs of using its premises by almost 300 per cent)[45] weren't restructured.[46] At the same time the regulator of one of the government's flagship foundation hospital trusts blamed a £17m loss at University College Hospital in the first six months of the year partly on 'higher-than-anticipated facilities management costs' under its PFI deal[47] (its premises costs had similarly ballooned under PFI). The consultants who had advised these hospitals on their crippling PFI contracts – and who, in line with Treasury Taskforce guidance, had presumably been rewarded with 'success fees' – were KPMG and PwC respectively. In an ironic twist (but one that was naturally very lucrative for the consultants) KPMG was called in by University College London Hospitals (UCLH) to look at the mess its PwC-assisted PFI deal had contributed to, while PwC was grappling as auditor with the KPMG-assisted mess at the Queen Elizabeth. The words of economic commentator John Plender about investment bankers could equally apply to PFI consultants: 'they take fees for putting Humpty on the wall, fees for pushing him off, and fees for putting him back together again.'[48]

The demands of patient choice, 'payment by results' and enormous outgoings to the PFI companies have been widely recognized as irreconcilable. The NHS Confederation reported in November 2005 on the expense and inflexibility of PFI: 'the big bang solutions don't work very well. It's bad enough trying to predict what the price of fuel will be in 30 years let alone what healthcare will look like,' it explained.[49] There were signs that the government was getting the message too. In June an indiscreet head of capacity at the Department of Health had admitted, 'I've seen some awfully grand PFI schemes that are starting to give us a real problem in our capacity mapping'.[50] By the end of 2005 the number of deals signed off was five, against plans for the year of ten, while rumours circulated that the private finance unit of the Department of Health had stopped approving schemes for final sign-off.[51] It seemed the government had belatedly realized that PFI didn't work for hospitals. By then, however, hospitals were already reducing numbers of operations and closing wards to cope with deficits and ruinous, decades-long PFI commitments.

The only question that remains is whether the £12bn worth of deals approved but not signed off will go through, or whether New Labour will be forced into one of the biggest public policy climb-downs in history. In January 2006, the Department of Health denied there was a moratorium on new PFI hospitals, but admitted a 'reappraisal' was being carried out.[52] The planned £1.1bn St Bartholomew's PFI hospital, promised for five years, has been placed under review because it appears unaffordable, as have a £761m scheme in Leicester, a similarly huge hospital in Birmingham and projects in Hillingdon and Plymouth. Health Minister Patricia Hewitt insisted there was no suspension of the PFI programme and that she was merely ensuring the taxpayer got value for money. It's a shame New Labour didn't think of that when they gave the go-ahead for the billions of pounds' worth of public expenditure under PFI in the first place. Instead the crucial financial questions were left to the consultants advising the NHS trusts, who were never likely to suggest putting the brakes on the PFI gravy train.

Whose Interests?

The limitations of PFI have already been repeatedly exposed. Even the Department of Health seems to be getting the message that the expense and inflexibility of PFI doesn't fit a changing and financially stretched NHS. But other departments, ably advised and sometimes with their PFI units run by consultants, persist with the policy and have tens of billions of pounds already committed to schemes.

By September 2005 a total of 725 PFI projects had been signed, with hundreds more in the pipeline. The signed deals alone had a combined capital value of £46bn.[53] But even these colossal figures mask the future commitments imposed on taxpayers under PFI, as payments for interest and services provided under the agreements, often involving the privatization of key functions such as hospital cleaning, multiply the total future outgoings just on deals already concluded by the end of 2005 to over £140bn at today's prices.[54] As the programme looks set to expand yet further, government departments report over £9bn worth of deals (which might be expected to add up to £50bn more in total expenditure) likely to move to completion by March 2007.[55]

After the health service, the most prolific PFI spenders are local authorities, who have seized on PFI's ability to help them get round borrowing constraints to provide everything from housing to street lighting, libraries and, most enthusiastically of all, schools. Under the direction of the Department for Education and Skills, by 2004 local authorities were signed up to 121 schools PFI projects with capital value of £2.9bn. The effect was not only to burden local council taxpayers but also to throw the building of new schools into chaos and leave thousands of schoolchildren waiting for classrooms. Many of the 121 contracts were not for single schools but for groups that proved more cost-effective for the PFI companies and consultants – regardless of whether the deals suited the local communities. At the end of 2005 the experience of schools in Exeter was all too familiar. Of the town's five schools lumped together in one deal, three failed to open in time, with children in at least one school forced to wait a year for decent facilities.[56] Yet despite repeated setbacks and several indications that the construction industry has neither the capacity nor the ability to deliver the government's PFI demands, the government persists with the policy. Already the plans to re-build or refurbish all secondary schools – as part of the £2bn–£3bn Building Schools for the Future programme, mainly under PFI – are behind schedule, with no deals signed in the first year when £2.2bn should have been.

The single biggest Whitehall investor in PFI, boasting the largest contracts, is the Ministry of Defence (MoD), which has 52 signed schemes worth £4.25bn on its books. In the pipeline are deals that, in terms of payments, will dwarf those already signed up. The Defence Training Review deal pencilled in for the combined Armed Forces is estimated to be worth £19bn, while the Future Strategic Air Tanker PFI (providing planes to refuel fighter jets in-air) is expected to generate £13bn for the PFI companies.

Such faith in PFI might suggest that earlier defence schemes had been successful, but that's not even the view of the MoD's own ministers. In 2004, defence procurement minister Lord Bach launched a review of PFI, following routinely critical National Audit Office reports on large-scale procurement, by admitting: 'we accept that not all our privately financed projects have run smoothly. There is considerable scope for improvement in the process.' The review was left to Nick Prior, the head of the department's PFI unit, previously a consultant with the MoD's main PFI adviser PwC, who seemed to un-ashamedly contradict his (by now former) minister and the findings of every NAO report by concluding: 'it is clear that the discipline and rigour that private finance brings to public-sector procurement plays a critical role in the delivery of these large and complex projects on time, to budget and to speci-fication.'[57] Once again a consultant, this time within govern-ment, came to the rescue of the discredited Private Finance Initiative to ensure it maintains its hold on public investment.

Yet with Gordon Brown's self-imposed golden rule, to limit government debt to 40 per cent of gross domestic product, hanging precariously in the balance, the accounting sleight of hand offered by PFI is more appealing than ever to a Chan-cellor conscious of his economic legacy. But to flatter his figures future generations of taxpayers will be saddled with huge debts by the PFI programme. Today, we see hospital after hospital reducing medical services to pay off their PFI charges. If the schools PFI programme comes anywhere near the level planned by New Labour, parents should probably start saving up now to buy books, computers and other supplies for schools, as we increasingly find education budgets are being given to PFI suppliers rather than being spent on children's educational needs. And if the MoD are allowed their planned PFI spending spree, one shudders to think of all the essential military equipment that will not be bought for our servicemen and women, because defence budgets are being diverted to provide profits and often 'super-profits' for the PFI companies and their consultants.

Ten years after he introduced PFI, Norman Lamont surveyed the monster he had created and declared, 'It was never intended to be a way of simply finding alternative finance, and I think it is dangerous because the reality is that private finance is more expensive.'[58] From the other end of the political spectrum Roy Hattersley summed up how the policy had turned so grotesque under New Labour and its consultants: 'Stephen Byers told a Labour conference that the government would not allow vested interests to stand in the way of PFI. Does he not realise that vested interests invented it?'[59]

CHAPTER 8

Revolving Doors

Blair gives the first push

The influence of business on public policy-making is as old as government itself, with ruling parties of all colours susceptible in varying degrees to the blandishments of commercial interests, but it is under New Labour that the process has been most explicitly and actively encouraged. In the first of many addresses to the Confederation of British Industry, in November 1997 a newly elected Tony Blair left nobody in any doubt over his intentions as he proclaimed his 'great commitment and enthusiasm, right across government, for forging links with the business community'.[1]

Even as Blair spoke, just six months into his first term, these links were being forged through taskforces led and staffed by businessmen (and some women) looking at welfare, regulation and the Private Finance Initiative, among other topics. As the new government settled in, the number of people moving into its various departments on secondments and short term contracts multiplied, while Whitehall's top jobs – permanent secretary positions – were opened up to private-sector applicants (with Civil Service pay scales expanded sufficiently to meet their demands). From day one the Prime Minister spoke of 'modernizing government' and, as a crucial part of that, importing more commercial expertise.

From the start, consultants took advantage of the new openings to further their careers, largely as secondees in departments such as Trade and Industry and the Treasury, advising on issues ranging from tax to procurement, all of which were of immense interest to their employers. The big government spending departments proved equally welcoming hosts: the Ministry of Defence, for example, took secondees from firms earning tens of millions on contracts they were handing out. By 2001 it had received such help from employees of Price Waterhouse (as it then was), PA Consulting and Ernst & Young.[2] A year later the then Lib Dem trade spokesman Vincent Cable pointed out that 300 people had been seconded from industry into the Civil Service under New Labour, scores of whom came from the consultancy firms. 'Some of this is good and useful . . . but there's [sic] some blatant and worrying conflicts of interests,' explained Cable (who, as a former chief economist at Shell, was not naturally averse to business input to government), before accusing the government of creating 'crony capitalism'.[3] Three years on, by mid-2005, the secondment of consultants into government had only accelerated. In the two departments that were most open about numbers, the Treasury and the Department of Trade and Industry, there were twenty-seven employees of consultancy firms working on issues ranging from tax policy to the Private Finance Initiative to managing government investments.[4] It wasn't all one way traffic either, although it took the consultants slightly longer to return the hospitality. In April 2001, for example, a senior civil servant from the Ministry of Defence left for two years at the IT company EDS,[5] forging the kind of relationship between the government and a large IT consultancy that cannot have harmed the firm's chances as it went on to bid for, and win, a £4bn contract in 2005.

Favoured consultants were particularly welcomed as advisers on improving government performance. When the Chancellor announced a Public Services Productivity Panel in 1998 to 'bring in outside experts, senior business people and public-sector managers to advise the Government on ways of improving the productivity and efficiency of government departments and public-sector bodies', two of the five members were partners in prominent consultancies KPMG and PA Consulting. Not to be left out, places on the panel were soon to be found for partners from McKinsey and PwC as well as the recently retired 'global managing partner' of Andersen Consulting, the firm that not long before had failed spectacularly on the government's national insurance records system.[6] Panel member Dame Sheila Masters of KPMG was asked to review NHS estates, IT and personnel management, John Dowdy of McKinsey examined defence logistics, and Claire Spottiswoode of PA Consulting looked at police efficiency. Over the following years, although the individuals would not have been responsible for the choice of supplier, all their firms went on to win lucrative contracts in these crucial policy areas.

All change please

The courtship between consultants and government in Labour's first term blossomed into marriage, whether for love or money, upon the party's re-election in May 2001 on a promise of transforming public services. Unshackled from the self-imposed spending restrictions of its first term and with the country's infrastructure crying out for investment, the government adopted 'delivery' as its watchword for domestic policy. The Civil Service, in the words of the Labour manifesto, 'needs to reform to make it more effective and entrepreneurial'. 'What counts is what works,' parroted Tony Blair and his loyal ministers. And who better to get things working than the 'can-do' consultants rather than the unreconstructed pen-pushers of the Civil Service?

Central to the delivery agenda were changes at the heart of government that saw the creation of a nerve centre within the Cabinet Office, containing a strategy unit, delivery unit and e-government unit, the latter charged with harnessing the potential of information technology to the government's public service ambitions. All were soon to become dominated by consultants. In the strategy unit alongside 'blue-skies thinker' Lord Birt – who as noted earlier combined the role with a position as adviser to McKinsey for nearly four years – was an 'independent adviser' from McKinsey, Nick Lovegrove, and one of the firm's old boys, Adair Turner. In the delivery unit the crucial position of health adviser went to a former IBM and PwC consultant, Adrian Masters, while at the closely linked No. 10 Policy Unit the Prime Minister's adviser on transport, Matthew Elson, was recruited from McKinsey.

By 2004 the e-government unit was run by Ian Watmore, the former UK managing partner of Accenture. When the civil servant in charge of the delivery unit, Sir Michael Barber, moved out to become a consultant with McKinsey, Watmore – whose CV could also boast the presidency of the Management Consultancies Association – was eased into his position. By this time yet another McKinsey consultant, David Bennett (who was reported to have sold the idea of a massive IT initiative for the health service, which became the *National Programme for IT*, to the Prime Minister)[7] had been recruited to run the Downing Street policy unit, reportedly on Lord Birt's advice.[8] By the end of 2005 both the Prime Minister's policy and delivery teams, from which emanated most of the government's domestic programme, were being run by consultants.

Away from the centre, the government departments responsible for implementing the strategies and policies coming from Downing Street were themselves increasingly turning to consultants to meet their 'delivery' obligations, as Table 1 shows (see pages 164–8). Reliance on the over-priced Private Finance Initiative for nearly all large-scale public investment accounted for much of the demand, as did the burgeoning IT programmes across the public sector. Senior – sometimes the most senior – investment roles in health, education and defence were handed to consultants during New Labour's second term, effectively ensuring that the kind of measured analysis of proposals that civil servants would traditionally attempt would be abandoned in the consultancy-led dash to spend cash. The 'scars on my back' that the Prime Minister complained about when discussing public service reform told of frustration with the instinctive scepticism of the Civil Service. By contrast no countervailing criticisms were made of the consultants whose enthusiasm to get things done, so admired by Blair, was always financed with other people's money. It therefore came as no surprise when, in May 2005, control of the National Health Service's *Connecting for Health* project was given to a consultant from Deloitte, Richard Granger.

Faster and faster

Blair spelled out the rationale for his Civil Service reforms in a speech in 2004 to mark the 150th anniversary of the report commissioned by prime minister William Gladstone from Stafford Northcote and Charles Trevelyan, which laid the foundations for the modern Civil Service – professional and selected on merit rather than patronage. 'The principal challenge is to shift focus from policy advice to delivery. Delivery means outcomes. It means project management,' announced the Prime Minister.[9] And that meant bringing in the consultants, an unsurprising conclusion from a Civil Service Reform Board within the Prime Minister's strategy unit which counted Lord Birt as one of its central figures.

Conversely, the rapidly intertwining interests of Whitehall and consultants meant that the inside knowledge and networks of a well-connected former mandarin or government minister would adorn any consultancy firm. The numbers of politicians and civil servants moving to 'the other side' soon mushroomed. For younger officials the promise of multiplying their Civil Service salaries on the back of the consultants' exorbitant fees proved highly attractive. For those at the end of careers in the higher reaches of the public sector, an advisory role with a major firm would nicely supplement their pension or form part of a 'portfolio' of interests commensurate with their lofty status. By 2004 such grandees were to be found gracing the advisory boards of most of the major consultancy firms. In early 2006 even the most senior of all recent retirees, former Cabinet Secretary and head of the Civil Service Lord (Andrew) Turnbull, who had done so much to push the Prime Minister's reforms, became a senior adviser to American management consultancy Booz Allen Hamilton.

At the end of 2005 all indications were that the revolving door between consultancy firms and Whitehall would spin yet more quickly. Indeed this was clear government policy: even the cursory, largely cosmetic, limits placed on ministers and top civil servants taking up private-sector posts in order to avoid conflicts of interest were set to be dispensed with. Tony Blair had appointed a former Department for Transport Permanent Secretary (who himself had gone on to chair a rail and bus company) to review the operation of the Advisory Committee on Business Appointments, which polices the moves of senior public figures into business, with a view to easing already lax restrictions.

Britain's most senior civil servant, Turnbull's replacement as Cabinet Secretary Sir Gus O'Donnell, presented the benign face of the interchange between public and private sector, by explaining, 'We need to . . . bring in talent from elsewhere to get the best blend of experience working in other parts of society so that they [civil servants] can develop wider perspectives.'[10] But the part of society that shares his enthusiasm most is the consultancy industry, and it comes with its own, usually financially motivated, 'perspectives'.

Power to the (Consulting) People

Towards the end of New Labour's second term the influx of management consultancy talent was most keenly felt at the very heart of government. As the Prime Minister asserted his control on policy and the 'delivery' agenda through the placement of consultants to the highest positions, their former employers became an essential part of the policy-making and implementation apparatus. Where once the firms had won government contracts with a convincing sales pitch, their involvement at the centre of any significant structural or policy reform was now taken as read. No major change in the machinery of government or of public services was undertaken without resorting to a consultancy firm. Organizing public services became less an important role of a democratic government and more a function to be bought in from those considered the specialists. And whereas civil servants may traditionally have been expected to question the need for the consultants' services before spending taxpayers' money on them, with consultants themselves directing matters from Whitehall, the advisers' entrée was guaranteed.

A spate of contracts for New Labour's new favourite, McKinsey, in 2005, illustrated the consultants' omnipresence. As the Inland Revenue and Customs and Excise prepared to merge following recommendations from the then Treasury Permanent Secretary Gus O'Donnell, in January 2005 the firm was brought in to develop and implement the new organizational model (which is now an incomprehensible but thoroughly McKinseyian jumble of customer units, corporate functions, operations and product/process groups). Soon after, as the National Health Service sought to become a 'patient-led NHS', McKinsey was brought in to help with 'creating a commissioning market', while most of the other 'workstreams' in the process had been assigned to consultants from PwC, PA Consulting and Flute Consulting.[11] By the end of the year the organization of the Cabinet Office itself appeared to be at the mercy of the consultants as McKinsey were employed to create 'a more strategic human resource function for the civil service and to help assess the strategic capabilities required in the Cabinet Office more generally'.[12]

Away with Victorian Values

The essential flaw in the practice of repeatedly awarding lucrative consultancy contracts stems from the process of decision-making at the centres of government departments, where the consultants' methods – the imposition of radical change based on idealistic and often simplistic models – perfectly match the priorities of a government keen to take credit for major change but much less interested in the problematic practicalities. Thus the tendency for departments increasingly staffed by consultants to turn to consultants whenever confronted with re-organizing public services or implementing challenging policies, while sidelining the sceptics, accelerates the demise of considered and democratic reform.

Some, meanwhile, have voiced concerns over just how the government hands out the top positions. Reacting to the government's rejection of his proposals for independent panels to have the final say on senior appointments, the chairman of the Committee on Standards in Public Life, Sir Alistair Graham, pointed out that it 'will not help public concerns about mistrust and cronyism to go away'.[13]

Sir Alistair's words, whether intentionally or not, echoed those of Gladstone's reformers, Northcote and Trevelyan, 150 years earlier when they described the Civil Service they were asked to review: 'numerous instances might be given in which personal or political considerations have led to the appointment of men of very slender ability, and perhaps of questionable character, to situations of considerable emolument, over the heads of public servants of long standing and undoubted merit.' Gladstone duly implemented their recommendations for a professional Civil Service recruited strictly on merit and 'possessing sufficient independence, character, ability and experience to be able to advise, assist and, to some extent, influence, those who are from time to time set over them'.

One hundred years later, with the Northcote–Trevelyan reforms having stood the test of time remarkably well, the then Cabinet Secretary gave the definitive view of a senior civil servant's job: 'It is the duty of a civil servant to give his Minister the fullest benefit of the storehouse of departmental experience; and to let the waves of the practical philosophy wash against ideas put forward by his Ministerial master.'

Under New Labour today, however, the patronage eschewed by Northcote and Trevelyan has returned as 'the waves of the practical philosophy' that civil servants could be relied on to supply to ministers prove far too awkward for politicians who don't want to hear about the limitations of their initiatives. Consultants can quite easily be brought in to give a demanding government whatever it wants without making any waves, while they have no 'storehouse of departmental experience' that might point to difficulties ahead. In the rush to 'deliver', critical scrutiny is most readily dispensed with, and there is no more effective way of doing that than placing favoured consultants in charge of spending the money.

As the consultants thus take control of large swathes of public spending – from health to social security to defence budgets – they assume the authority to channel billions into the coffers of their erstwhile employers (whose ranks they are more likely than not to re-join later in their careers in order to resume life on salaries in the high six figures). Consultants who temporarily became civil servants holding the public purse strings nonetheless remain consultants and are unlikely to question the value of employing or retaining consultants. Former Whitehall officials simultaneously enrich themselves and lend respectability to the revolving door by moving in the opposite direction, while the senior colleagues they leave behind, who are responsible for employing and monitoring consultants, increasingly have one eye on the opportunities a grateful consultancy industry may offer them at some point in the future. It's a far cry from the ideals of Northcote and Trevelyan. And the winners every time are the consultants and those who jump on their bandwagon.

Below are some of the senior people who have moved from consultancy firms to government, and in the opposite direction, since May 1997. The armies of lawyers and bankers who have moved into public-sector positions in the last nine years are not mentioned, nor are the multitudinous more junior appointments and transfers.

The Ins and Outs of Government

Table 1

Consultants turned public servants	Consultancy position	Public-sector appointment
Richard Abadie	Partner, PwC	Head of PFI policy, HM Treasury
Lynton Barker	Managing partner, PwC (UK), later president of Management Consultancies Association	Public Services Productivity Panel
Lord Steve Bassam	Consultant, KPMG	Government minister in the Lords
David Bennett	Partner, McKinsey	Head of Downing Street policy unit
Lord (John) Birt (see also Table 2)	McKinsey adviser	Prime Minister's 'blue-skies thinker'
Keith Burgess	Retired global managing partner, business services, Andersen Consulting	Public Services Productivity Panel
Liam Byrne	Consultant, Andersen Consulting	Labour MP, junior Health Minister
Natalie Ceeney	Consultant, McKinsey	Chief executive, National Archives
Paul Corrigan (see also Table 2)	Independent consultant managing public service change programmes	Special adviser to Health Secretary (architect of foundation hospitals and independent treatment centres)
Stephen Dance	Director, property consultancy firm DTZ	Director Partnerships UK (though 51% owned by the private sector, 'PUK' has a 'public-sector mission')

Consultants turned public servants	Consultancy position	Public-sector appointment
Dr Penelope Dash	McKinsey consultant, formerly consultant with Boston Consulting	Director, Monitor (independent regulator for NHS foundation trusts)
John Dowdy	Director, McKinsey	Public Services Productivity Panel, examining defence logistics
Matthew Elson (see also Table 2)	Consultant, McKinsey	Transport adviser, Prime Minister's policy unit
David Goldstone	Consultant, Price Waterhouse	Member, Treasury Taskforce, later finance director of PUK and acting chief executive Partnerships for Schools (responsible for school PFI programme)
Richard Granger	Partner, Deloitte	Head of NHS National Programme for IT
Patricia Hewitt	Director of research, Andersen Consulting	Ministerial posts including Trade Secretary and Health Secretary
Paul Jones	Director, systems integration, Atos Origin	Chief technology officer, NHS *Connecting for Health*
Simon Leary (see also Table 2)	Consultant, PwC	Head of Dept of Health's strategy unit
Nick Lovegrove	Director, McKinsey	Strategy adviser to Prime Minister
Adrian Masters	Consultant with IBM and Price Waterhouse	Director of health team in Prime Minister's delivery unit, then head of strategy at Monitor

Consultants turned public servants	Consultancy position	Public-sector appointment
Sheila Masters	Partner, KPMG	Public Services Productivity Panel, examining performance, estates and IT development in NHS
David Newkirk	Former partner, Booz Allen Hamilton	Member, DTI energy group board
Nick Prior	Director, project finance, PwC	Head of PFI unit, Ministry of Defence
Ben Prynn	Consultant, Price Waterhouse	Member, Treasury PFI Taskforce
Rosemary Radcliffe	Head of economics, Coopers & Lybrand	DTI Competitiveness Taskforce
Dr Martin Read	Chief executive, Logica CMG	Member, DTI strategy board
Lord (Colin) Sharman	Chairman, KPMG International	Government-appointed author of 'Holding to Account' report on public-sector accountability
Claire Spottiswoode	Associate partner, PA Consulting	Public Services Productivity Panel, examining police force efficiency
Dr Timothy Stone	Chairman, KPMG PFI advisory services (in charge of KPMG PFI consulting)	Member, Dept of Health Commercial Directorate advisory panel Member, DfES advisory panel on Building Schools for the Future (school PFI programme) Member, Sustainable Procurement Taskforce Adviser to MoD on £13bn Future Strategic Tanker Aircraft PFI deal. Adviser to MoD
Tony Whitehead	Consultant, Coopers & Lybrand	Member, Treasury PFI Taskforce

Consultants turned public servants	Consultancy position	Public-sector appointment
Ian Watmore	Chief executive, Accenture	Head of e-government then head of Prime Minister's delivery unit
Alan Woods	Chief executive, Siemens plc	Led government review of EU procurement

And going the other way, from government to consultancy:

Table 2

Public servants turned consultants	Public-sector position	Consultancy role
Lewis Atter	Head of transport team, HM Treasury	Director, corporate finance KPMG
Sir Michael Barber	Head of Prime Minister's delivery unit	Expert principal, McKinsey
Lord (Joel) Barnett	Labour peer	Chairman Atos Origin (UK)
Stuart Bell MP	Church Commissioner representing government	Consultant to Ernst & Young
Lord (John) Birt (see also Table 1)	Prime minister's 'blue-skies thinker'	Adviser to Capgemini
David Blunkett	Education secretary, Home Secretary, Work and Pensions Minister	Consultant with Indepen business consultancy
Paul Corrigan (see also Table 1)	Special adviser to Health Secretary (architect of foundation hospitals and independent treatment centres)	Independent consultant (until recall to No. 10 in late 2005 to deal with health reforms)
Matthew Elson (see also Table 1)	Transport adviser, Prime Minister's policy unit	Transport bid director and board member, Atkins Management Consultants

Public servants turned consultants	Public-sector position	Consultancy role
Lord (Geoffrey) Filkin	Home Office, Education and Constitutional Affairs Minister	Adviser to Capgemini's government and public-sector practice, Director Accord plc (includes Accord Consulting)
Baroness (Margaret) Jay	Health Minister	Senior political adviser to Currie and Brown, construction consultants active in PFI
Lady (Barbara Thomas) Judge	Chairman, UK Atomic Energy Authority, member of DTI strategy and Dept for Constitutional Affairs boards	Director, PA Consulting
Simon Leary (see also Table 1)	Head of Dept of Health's strategy unit	Consultant, PwC
Sir Nicholas Montagu	Civil servant at Department of Transport responsible for rail privatization, chairman of Inland Revenue	Member, advisory board PwC
Chris Riley	Director, analysis and strategy, Dept for Transport	Consultant, Oxera Consulting
Sir Steve Robson	Managing director finance and industry directorate, Treasury	Adviser, KPMG
Derek Scott	Prime Minister's economic adviser	Chief economist, KPMG
Jonathan Spencer	Director General, Dept for Constitutional Affairs	Consultant, Capgemini
Lord (Andrew) Turnbull	Cabinet Secretary and head of Civil Service	Senior Adviser, Booz Allen Hamilton Director, Frontier Economics (economic and regulatory consultancy)
Eithne Wallis	Director General, National Probation Service	Senior partner, Fujitsu Services

CHAPTER 9

We've Seen it all Before

We are now almost ready to look at the biggest civil consulting project that has ever been attempted anywhere in the world – the massive National Health Service *Connecting for Health* programme. But before we tackle this monster in the next chapter, it is worth looking at a small selection of typical New Labour government IT systems-led consultancy efforts. By conducting post-mortems on just three of the many disasters that have occurred, we can identify the kinds of things you should absolutely never do when running a large IT systems consulting programme. This might give a useful (and possibly slightly entertaining) context against which we can examine what the potentates at *Connecting for Health* are up to as they spend liberal amounts of our money for our benefit.

Doing Justice an Injustice

The first project I've chosen is the development of the Libra system for the magistrates' courts, but there are many others that would have revealed a similar picture. Libra is a relatively small affair – budgeted at £146m and now projected to exceed £400m, though at the time of writing almost nothing is yet working. Although I talk of doing a 'post-mortem', actually the project is not dead. It has been in the intensive care ward for the last seven years and is still looking pretty blue in the face. But with the right treatment – another few years in intensive care and lots more of our money – it will unfortunately probably survive, although in a considerably misshapen form.

Of course, it's easy to have 20/20 vision with hindsight and smugly criticize people for their actions when the awful consequences eventually become clear. But I believe that on this project, as with almost all government consulting and systems projects, the warning lights were flashing so brightly and the sirens were howling so loudly at every single step, that the government department responsible had ample opportunity to change course. Unfortunately for us, the taxpayers, all these opportunities were wilfully squandered. In fact, in common with most other similar projects, it seems that on Libra the more the disaster warnings sounded, the more those responsible pulled the wagons together, blocked their ears and eyes and, in a state of total denial, pressed on, hurling huge amounts of our cash into a bottomless pit. The problem was that once millions, tens of millions, even hundreds of millions had been spent, there would be too much loss of face for the bureaucrats to pause and reflect whether maybe they had got things a little wrong. I believe we are seeing exactly the same behaviour on the massively more expensive NHS *Connecting for Health* programme.

A Rocky Start

Britain has 42 local Magistrates' Courts Committees. These are independent bodies, answerable to the Lord Chancellor for their performance and responsible for the effective administration of the country's some 380 magistrates' courts. These courts handle around 95 per cent of criminal cases prosecuted. The Lord Chancellor's Department (later called the Department for Constitutional Affairs) had been trying to get a common IT system into the courts since the late 1980s. In 1992, the first attempt to get national case-working software, to replace the many incompatible systems in use, failed and the

Lord Chancellor's Department took legal action against the supplier Price Waterhouse. The case was settled in 1995 when PricewaterhouseCoopers agreed to pay the Department £1.3m. The next effort was in 1993 when the Department started an in-house project using Admiral and the FI Group. This also failed and cost the Department £6.8m.

Seemingly undeterred, the Department launched the Libra project and started looking for potential suppliers. By 1998, only two suppliers had shown interest in the contract – EDS and ICL (later Fujitsu). In May 1998, EDS withdrew and ICL was told that it had been named as the 'preferred bidder'. Initially, ICL, had submitted a price of £146m, but in October this went up by £38m to £184m.

At the same time, ICL was having major problems with another government IT systems project for the Benefits Payment Card. ICL had been unable to meet its promises on this project and had proposed to the government that for the project to continue ICL would either have to similarly raise its prices by 30 per cent or extend the contract for five years. In May 1999, the Benefits Card project was cancelled, with the government writing off about £700m of our money as the parties agreed not to sue each other. Before signing the Libra contract, the Lord Chancellor's Department had had the opportunity to examine the contract for the Benefits Card so they could learn from the mistakes made on the previous project and even reconsider ICL's suitability as a supplier. However, there were no other suppliers interested in producing Libra, so in December 1998 the Department had signed a deal with ICL for a ten-and-a-half-year contract for £184m.

Several warning signs were already clear. Firstly, if you had so conspicuously failed in your first two attempts to get a system going, you might think about changing your people and the way you approached things, in order to make a success of the third try. Not so the Lord Chancellor's Department. Secondly, if you want to put an extension on your house, when you invite a few builders round to look at your plans and all but one shake their heads and say, 'sorry mate, I wouldn't touch that with a barge-pole,' you might be tempted to review your plans to find out what you were doing wrong that so scared all but one of your potential suppliers. Not so the Lord Chancellor's Department. And, thirdly, if the only builder who is prepared to work with you is doing a major job on the house next door, and one night that house unexpectedly collapses into a pile of dust and rubble, you might think of questioning the professional expertise of the builder involved. Not so the Lord Chancellor's Department. As the Public Accounts Committee (PAC) later commented in what must have been the understatement of the year, 'the possibility that the problems with the Benefits Payment Card project might have reflected on ICL's technical competence to deliver the Libra project was not adequately investigated.'[1]

In a review of an NHS project some years earlier, when several bidders similarly withdrew from the race for the contract, the PAC felt that the sight of IT consultants rapidly running away from a government department's brilliant new scheme should have acted as a signal to the department involved that something was amiss. On this previous case, the PAC were surprised that, 'the fact that two major suppliers did not believe it was feasible did not act as a warning.'[2] However, ignoring common sense and lessons painfully learnt by at least one other government department, the Lord Chancellor's Department and their suppliers ICL decided to use our money to boldly (and lucratively, for the consultants) go where others feared to tread.

The Road to Ruin

Things started to go pear-shaped pretty much from the start. ICL got into difficulties when they found out that they had not properly examined the MASS software they had been intending to use and so had to start writing new software. In October 1999, ICL asked to renegotiate the deal as it was forecasting a loss of £39m. The Department agreed and in May 2000 signed a revised contract giving ICL longer to develop the system with a new higher price of £319m – a 73 per cent price hike.

In spring 2001 ICL informed the Department that it was having financial difficulties with the new £319m contract. The company now claimed it would make a £200m loss on the deal in spite of the recent huge price increase. ICL threatened that it would walk away unless the Department agreed to cover this projected multi-million pound loss. Negotiations dragged on for about a year until in July 2002 the Department signed a new contract with ICL. Now, for a price of £232m, ICL would just provide the infra-structure for the project and only for eight-and-a-half-years. The Department would have to find someone else to provide the software and yet another supplier to do the implementation. In January 2003 the Department signed a separate contract with STL to provide the core software application to support court work (case management, accounting and administration). In the same year the Department signed a contract with Accenture to roll out STL's software into magistrates' courts. Meanwhile, staff numbers on the project team were increased from around 30 to nearer 100, resulting in even greater costs.

In June 2004, the director of the Libra project wrote to Justices' chief executives, who run the administration of the courts, reassuring them that all was well ('the overall project remains very much on track'). But by the autumn of 2004 strange and unpleasant noises were coming from inside the project team. A letter from the Department to Justices' chief executives now said that the system was 'not fit for purpose' due to software bugs and to the fact that, even though its running speed had been increased tenfold, it was still running too slowly. Nevertheless, the project director seemed full of optimism when describing the situation to the outside world: 'Our planning is second to none. We are on top of what we are doing. We can handle the way things are progressing.'

He also added, 'Rest assured that the project continues to be managed for success.'[3] Current estimates are that the system will eventually be implemented more than a year late in early 2006 at a cost of well over £400m – a substantial increase on the original 1998 ICL bid of £146m. One is therefore led to assume that a £250m overrun is what the Department de-scribes as 'success'.

The Worst We Have Ever Seen

The Libra project attracted the attention of the National Audit Office and the Public Accounts Committee (PAC). The PAC concluded that, 'This is one of the worst PFI deals that we have seen.' They had a fairly wide range of criticisms of the Department and its ill-fated project. Some of these were what most normal people would call 'no-brainers'. But an ordinary taxpayer's no-brainer may be a devastatingly brilliant revelation to a naïve civil servant buying an IT system from infinitely more wily systems consultants. For example, the PAC pointed out that it was difficult to 'maintain competitive tension' when there was only one bidder in the race to obtain the contract. The PAC felt that having only one bidder did not put the Lord Chancellor's Department in a particularly strong negotiating position and should have alerted the Department that something might possibly be wrong in the way they were approaching the project: 'A single bid for a major complex project is seldom likely to achieve value for money. That only one bid was received should have alerted the Department to the fact that its project may not have been sufficiently well designed to attract competition.'

But some of the other PAC criticisms were more useful. One concerned the way the Department dealt with the whole issue of ensuring that the implementation of a new IT system was somehow linked to improving the way the future system users worked in order to get some operational and financial benefits from the hundreds of millions the system would cost. As the Department did not have direct authority over the system users, the independent Magistrates' Courts Committees, it felt it did not have the power to get them to change and standardize the way they worked. So instead of first developing a commonly agreed and more effective way of working with the Courts Committees and then designing an IT system to support it, the Department decided not to talk to the people who would use the system and went off and started building a new IT system that did not reflect how the future users either worked now or would work in the future. The PAC wrote, 'The

Department recognized that the design of a best business process model should normally come before seeking an IT solution. The Department chose to develop IT first because it did not have the authority to impose such a model on the independent Magistrates' Courts·Committees. But the lack of a coherent model allowing IT solutions to be integrated with business processes increased the risk of project failure.'

Presumably, the Department hoped that once the system was installed, some mysterious and magical process would take place whereby all the users were suddenly transformed into happy, efficient, contented employees all working in exactly the same way and all grateful to the Department for providing such a wondrous system to make their working lives more productive and more fulfilling. Scratch the surface of *Connecting for Health* and you will find a similar logic underpinning the monster that is being created for the lucky employees in the NHS.

Another recommendation highlighted the problems government departments have had managing large IT systems projects and suggested that such projects should be split up into smaller, more manageable pieces: 'The success or failure of an IT implementation often depends on its scale and complexity. We have recommended that departments should carefully consider whether projects are too large and ambitious to be undertaken in one go. Departments should think carefully about breaking up big IT projects into manageable pieces that can be delivered incrementally.'

Compared to *Connecting for Health*, Libra was only a £146m (becoming a £400m+) minnow – the NHS project is more than a hundred times as large. For the sake of our health service, one hopes that the powers that be on *Connecting for Health* have learnt some of the lessons of Libra.

Passport to Confusion

In July 1996, the Passport Agency decided to introduce the digital passport to increase security and to replace their existing-ing computer system to improve efficiency. Under pressure from the Home Office to 'involve the private sector in running their non-core business', in the summer of 1997 the Agency signed a deal with Siemens Business Services to supply the new computer system, and with Security Printing and Systems Ltd to produce the new passports. Unfortunately, the contracts with these two new suppliers were so badly structured that when things went wrong, the Passport Agency was left bearing around 80 per cent of the cost. But when things went well and passport applications were a million a year higher than Agency forecasts, the suppliers took all the benefits.

By the summer of 1998, factory testing of the new system revealed major problems. In particular, it was found that it was taking system users much longer to produce a passport with the new system than with the old one. However, as system development was already delayed, the Agency decided to cut down the time for testing in order to launch the system on the original planned date.

In October 1998, the system went live at the Agency's largest office, Liverpool. The results of launching an imperfectly designed and largely untested system were predictable – production of passports at Liverpool went down from the previous level of 30,000 a week to around 8,000 a week. Nevertheless the Agency decided to press ahead with implementation and on 16 November the new system went live at the Agency's other large office, Newport. By late 1998, the Agency had lost the production of about 400,000 passports and they decided to halt the roll-out of the system to their smaller offices. To try and deal with a backlog that eventually reached close to 565,000 applications, the Agency had to recruit and train 300 extra staff. Meanwhile, three and a half million calls to the Agency went unanswered. However, the Agency waited three months before informing the Home Office that there was a problem. Naturally, as soon as news of the delays became public, people wanting to travel sensibly submitted their applications earlier than they might normally have done, and this created an increase in applications and thus further problems for the Agency already struggling to cope with the backlog due to the introduction of the new system. The Agency had to pay £12.6m in overtime and new staff costs because of the problems. Moreover, due to the Agency's new system, the costs of production rose by £2 per passport. The failure of the Agency to successfully implement the new system did not lead to any disciplinary action against or job losses for the civil servants responsible. As the PAC reported: 'We asked the Home Office and the Agency whether anyone at a senior level had lost their job because of the Agency's problems. The Home Office had considered the position of the Agency's Chief Executive, but he retired as planned on 2 September, and no one else within the Agency lost their job as a result of this crisis.'

Once again, we can see some familiar lessons: ensure the contract does not give the taxpayer all the costs and the suppliers all the benefits; design a system that makes the users' job easier, rather than more difficult; test the system properly before implementation; choose a small controlled environment for the first implementation; have proper contingency planning in case there are problems with the implementation. As with all such reports, the PAC concluded that there were important lessons to be learnt: 'We believe this case offers salutary lessons for all organizations providing services direct to the public.'[4]

Criminal Records Bureau (CRB)

The CRB system is interesting because the project was run by the Passport Agency, who should have learnt the lessons from their recent experience. Yet one member of the PAC felt that once again the civil servants and their consultants had repeated the errors of the past. The MP noted that, 'Appendix 2 is a comparison of the Passport Agency Report and the Criminal Records Bureau Report and it makes quite interesting reading.' He then continued by saying, 'as you go through it looks pretty similar.' The new Chief Executive of the Passport Agency naturally denied any similarity between the two projects and claimed that he had learnt the lessons of the previous disaster, but had unfortunately fallen into new traps with the

CRB project: 'I came to this as the incoming Chief Executive coming in after the crisis. We discussed it and your Committee produced a set of lessons. This analysis was produced by the National Audit Office to see whether we had taken them on board. The conclusion I have drawn from this is that each situation is different and whereas we did avoid falling into the traps which the Passport Agency had fallen into in 1999, there were other traps instead.'

However, reviewing what happened on the CRB, it is not obvious that mistakes made on the two projects are so different. The CRB was initiated in 1999 to improve protection of children and vulnerable adults by widening access to criminal records so employers and voluntary organizations could make better informed recruitment decisions. It went live in March 2002, seven months later than planned, and the computer system encountered serious problems straight away. Backlogs in processing applications soon built up, peaking at nearly 300,000 by October 2002. When the system was finally working, those involved claimed another great success. But they failed to mention a few not unimportant details. For example, the service they were providing was but a pale shadow of what had originally been planned. Some key parts such as Basic Disclosure, the Identity Verification Process and checks for those looking after the elderly were quietly dropped from their range of services. In addition, success was 'achieved' by changing their targets – target times for Standard Disclosures were increased from one week to two and for Enhanced Disclosures from three weeks to four. In fact, so worthless was the service now being offered at twice the original budget that a member of the PAC reviewing the project pointed out a criminal would have to be pretty stupid to be caught out by the CRB: 'The only people who might be prevented from employment after what is going to be £400 million-worth of taxpayers' money would be people who are incompetent at filling out the form or people who were so dozey [*sic*] that they do not realize what they are telling you.'[5]

At the start of 2006, so hopeless was the service offered by the CRB that a scandal broke in the Department for Education and Skills over the number of identified sex offenders (possibly more than 150) that were allowed to work as teachers – they should have been identified and prevented from this by the CRB.

There seem to be five key mistakes made on the CRB project which are quite similar to those made on Passports and Libra. One striking similarity to Libra was in the PAC's use of superlatives to describe the performance of the civil servants responsible. While Libra was 'the worst they had ever seen', the CRB was 'one of the most incompetently let contracts this Committee has seen'.

Worked on assumptions and didn't talk to customers
Although the CRB did have some high level contact with the heads of the organizations that would use their services, they did not talk to the actual users till just before the new system went live. This was a bit unfortunate as the civil servants assumed around 80–85 per cent of customers would use the phone and the rest would contact them over the Internet. When they eventually did conduct customer research, it was discovered that most of their customers would contact them in writing – a channel they had not even intended to offer. This led to a panicked change in their whole set-up in order to offer a paper channel, a drastic reduction in the service to be offered and a price increase of some £200m. This echoes the Passport Agency's working to an assumed volume of four million passports a year, even though there was clear proof that actual demand would be nearer five million and the government was introducing a new children's passport which would increase volumes even more.

Didn't listen to suppliers
The CRB asked suppliers to provide a system where virtually all contacts from the users would come in by phone and not in writing. Two of the three companies bidding believed the assumptions to be wrong and put in bids based on at least one half of user contacts being paper-based. Dismissing the two bids which did not fit their assumptions, the Passport

Agency bureaucrats chose the supplier who agreed with them, just as in the case of Libra. In their arrogant belief that only they were intelligent enough to diagnose the service they should offer, they did not think to reconsider their assumptions in the light of the concerns of two out of three bidders.

Didn't manage suppliers effectively
Once the project was well under way, it was discovered that the initial assumptions were wrong and that the service would have to be completely redesigned. At this point, the civil servants did not think of going back to the other two bidders to see if they could offer a solution. They just kept with their original suppliers, Capita, and, as with ICL on Libra, saw the price double. Moreover, the CRB were paying their suppliers a fixed price per application, as with passports. So when volumes on paper applications were higher than expected, the supplier got increased revenue, while the Agency got no benefits from economies of scale.

Didn't improve the processes
Although the project had to completely change direction following the discovery that most users would choose a paper channel, it was not thought necessary to re-engineer the business processes till just before the system went live – predictably, chaos ensued. As with both Libra and passports, there was no attempt to use the introduction of a new system as a basis for improving current work processes. (In fact, with passports, this led to passports taking longer to produce with the new system than before.)

Didn't do a pilot
Although a pilot had been planned, this idea was abandoned because the project was running late. When a pilot was eventually done, it was too late to make any changes and the system went live long before it could handle the volumes of work that it should have been able to support. In the same way, delays on systems development meant no proper testing was done with either Libra or passport (and the passport system

was implemented in the largest office without any pilot being conducted first).

Never Listen, Never Learn?

In 1999–2000, before New Labour's programme to modernize the delivery of public services really got going, the PAC reviewed twenty-five government IT projects to try and understand if there were any common lessons to be learnt from the long series of failures. The twenty-five chosen included some real corkers – an MoD project abandoned after £41m had been spent over eight years, one for the NHS binned after blowing £32m and another after wasting £43m, £190m a year lost when a Benefits Agency system hit the dust and £48m that went up in smoke when the Department for Education actually succeeded in getting a system going but unfortunately with no measurable results. An ordinary taxpayer might be tempted to think that it would be obvious if a system was going to work or not after just a few million pounds had been wasted. Unfortunately for us, it's only after many tens of millions have disappeared that civil servants and their hungry IT consultants see the paucity of their achievements.

The conclusions reached by the PAC, though not terribly profound, at least set some basic ground rules that have since been expertly ignored by all those who should have shown some interest. The PAC found a number of lessons that should have been learnt from the consistent run of disasters. These included such warnings as:

- No project should be started unless there is a clear business case. Projects should not be launched to meet vague, vacuous political point-scoring
- Involve influential users closely in the design and implementation
- It is critical to ensure contracts with suppliers are professionally drawn up and that competitive pressure is maintained to prevent overcharging and profiteering

- Split larger projects into manageable pieces and try to avoid a 'big bang' implementation approach
- Always pilot and test new systems before implementing them
- Avoid monolithic multi-year systems developments as rapid changes in technology will probably make most systems obsolete soon after (and often before) they are implemented
- Take care in managing consultants, avoid giving them too much control and don't pay consultants twice – once to make a botch of things and then again to sort out the mess they have made
- All failures should be reviewed and the lessons learnt should be acted on in planning future IT systems

It might be instructive to bear these in mind as a simple checklist as we move on to look at the largest project of them all, the project that could make or break our health service – *Connecting for Health*.

CHAPTER 10

Welcome to *Connecting for Health*

We've seen some impressively big projects, each costing many hundreds of millions of pounds, each wasting hundreds of millions more and most failing to deliver anything like the levels of service that were originally promised. But nothing can compare with the NHS IT systems programme that has been going on since October 2002. Previously called the *National Programme for Information Technology* (NPfIT) this has been renamed *Connecting for Health* (CfH).

A successful CfH would have an immensely beneficial effect on healthcare in Britain. It would provide comprehensive, up-to-date and immediately accessible medical information on all patients, thus dramatically improving doctors' ability to diagnose and treat them. It would contribute to drastically reducing the annual 980,000 'patient safety incidents' and 2,000 deaths from medical and prescription errors. It would free up time for clinicians to spend looking after patients instead of looking for medical records. It would greatly reduce bean counting, administration and paperwork by hundreds of millions of pounds per year, which could then be channelled into patient care. And it would automatically provide a wealth of healthcare information to target and measure the progress of performance improvement initiatives and to assist future healthcare planning. Conversely, in terms of cost, scope, potential for wasting money and potential for having a catastrophic effect on the NHS, which is probably our most critical public service, CfH far surpasses any previous New Labour scheme for modernizing the delivery of public services. It is almost a hundred times larger than most other New Labour projects. So if it goes wrong, with the all too depressingly familiar sight of budgets and timescales spiralling hopelessly out of control, our government will have caused the largest haemorrhage of taxpayers' money from essential front-line services into the pockets of management and IT systems consultants in British history.

Connecting for Health: a Brief Guide

Between 1998 and 2002, a series of studies and reports identified the need for the NHS to drastically improve its use of IT systems. Perhaps the most significant was the April 2002 Wanless Report. It compared the inadequate use of IT in the NHS with the 'improvements in performance and efficiencies gained from new technology seen in other spheres of industry and in other health services'. It recommended 'an increase in IT investment; stringent centrally managed standards for data and IT; and better management of IT implementation in the NHS, including a national programme'. This led to a document called *Delivering the NHS Plan* which 'developed a vision of a service designed around the patient offering more choice of where and when to access treatment'. In June 2002 *Delivering 21st Century IT Support for the NHS – a National Strategic Programme* set out 'the first steps including the creation of a Ministerial Taskforce and recruitment of a director general for the National Programme for IT'. In October 2002 the *National Programme for Information Technology* (NPfIT) was formally established with (ex-Deloitte consultant) Richard Granger's appointment as the director-general of NHS IT. Its task was 'to procure, develop and implement modern, integrated IT infrastructure and systems for all NHS organizations in England by 2010'. In June 2004 another document, *The NHS Improvement Plan: Putting*

People at the Heart of Public Services, detailed 'the priorities for the NHS, including the purpose of NPfIT'. A month later the NHS Information Authority was merged into the NPfIT creating one body for managing IT within the NHS. In April 2005 CfH was established.

In addition to supporting existing NHS IT systems, CfH has six main 'products' that it plans to deliver. These are:

- NHS Care Records Service (CRS) – building a central database with electronic patient records. This will lead to one unified electronic medical record for each patient to replace today's inefficient mix of paper and electronic records often duplicating each other and often held in different places.
- *Choose and Book* (C&B) – an electronic booking system allowing GPs to offer each patient they refer to a hospital a choice of four to five hospitals and enabling them to make the booking immediately on-line. This is intended to replace the current process where patients often get a limited or no choice of hospital, where appointments are made by phone or letter and where the patient seldom gets much choice of a date and time that suits them.
- Electronic Transmission of Prescriptions (ETP) – allows prescriptions to be sent electronically from the prescriber to the dispenser and then to the Prescription Pricing Authority. This will reduce the reliance on paperwork for the over 325 million prescriptions issued each year.
- New National Network (N3) – this will provide IT infrastructure, network services and broadband connectivity to support the systems being implemented as part of CfH.
- Picture Archiving and Communications Systems (PACS) – this system will allow the replacement of film-based radiographic images by electronic images. Digital images will then become part of each patient's electronic medical record and there will no longer be any need to print on film and to file and distribute images manually.
- General Medical Services Contract, Quality and Outcomes Framework (QOF) – a data collection and management system allowing payment of GPs, analysis of information,

targeting of improvement initiatives and measurement of hospital and GP performance.

What Will it Cost Us?

When looking at where the money for CfH will come from, for the sake of simplicity CfH can be divided into two main parts – the smaller of these by far is what the government pays from central funds in order to build up the basic infrastructure and systems. The larger part is what health authorities will have to provide to get the new systems up and working in their areas. The money from health authorities is money that is being taken from their local budgets, thus leaving less for patient care.

The government has already awarded around £6.5bn of contracts to a very small, select group of about seven consultancies – many of whom have placed their people in influential positions within government or have been generous contributors to the New Labour cause. This £6.5bn is often quoted in the press as being a lot of money to spend on IT systems. However, it is fairly modest compared to the other associated costs of the programme. So far, we only have a number of estimates for the total cost – the government has never categorically stated precisely how much we will pay for the whole adventure. Most estimates suggest that individual health authorities will have to pay between four and five times the cost of the basic £6.5bn infrastructure – so around another £25bn to £30bn of money that could be used for front-line patient care – to upgrade and adapt their systems for CfH to function.[1] Management consultants are expecting about £10bn to come their way for 'change management projects to ensure the successful implementation of NPfIT'.[2] In addition, in 2003 the head of the NHS predicted huge training costs: 'there are recent articles indicating that other healthcare systems are investing six times the amount in training that they are in the IT systems themselves, and it will have to be in that sort of order if you take the true costs into account.'[3] By the beginning of 2006, the figure of £50bn was being mentioned as the likely total cost of the programme.[4]

The total annual budget of the NHS is around £70bn. So whatever the final cost of CfH, it means that over the next few years a huge amount of money is being taken out of, and will continue to be taken out of, patient care to fund the CfH programme. Assuming about one million employees in the NHS will be affected in some way by the programme, CfH is going to cost over £35,000 per employee – that is really quite a lot of money for management and IT systems consultancy. In fact, with CfH we are seeing consultancy support per health service employee that is almost on the scale of the £45,000 per employee paid to consultants during the catastrophic Child Support Agency programme.

This is already causing some concern and even turmoil at a local level, as health workers see their hard-pressed budgets being diverted from valuable hospital medical consultants to expensive but probably less essential IT systems consultants.[5] In October 2005, I had a meeting with the IT director of a regional health authority. He was at his wits' end. He had IT systems consultants from the huge multi-national consultancy that had the CfH contract for his area crawling all over his department telling him what he had to do to prepare for CfH and continuously coming to him with demands for money to 'upgrade' or change his systems and data to make them 'compatible' with CfH standards. He was not allowed to see the contracts CfH had agreed with the systems consultants as these were apparently 'commercially confidential'. So he could not find out whether the consultants' requests for cash were justified or not. Additionally, he could not find out whether their hourly rates were appropriate, though he personally felt they were exorbitant and much higher than those of the local companies he would normally use. Yet under pressure from the CfH organization, he had to go to his chief executive and get the funds transferred from front-line patient care to pay the IT consultants whenever the consultants asked for more money.

As many hospitals faced funding problems in late 2005, the

Health Secretary resisted demands to bail out NHS hospitals that were heavily in the red and avert a winter crisis. As one newspaper reported, 'dismissing calls for more money, she said, "No – there is more money going into the NHS than ever before." ' She went on to point out that if hospitals were in financial difficulties, it was probably because they were wasting taxpayers' money: 'I don't know whether Marx ever said waste is theft from the working class, but he should have done, because it is. We have asked them to pay higher national insurance contributions. We have got to give them maximum value for money.'[6] The Health Secretary clearly had no time for poor and wasteful management of public-sector money when she also said, 'I want to make it clear that inefficiency and poor financial management are not acceptable.'[7] Although there was no money available to help hospitals avoid closing wards and reducing patient care, the Department of Health did at the same time manage to find almost £100m to offer as financial incentives to various medical professionals who could show that they were using some of CfH's new IT systems, so that the government could claim that CfH was the stunning success it most clearly was not. In the same month, the Health Secretary also blamed doctors, rather than her own department, for a shortage of flu jabs to protect those who were most at risk.[8] So there seems to be an emerging pattern of government claiming that we are truly fortunate to have such a wondrously effective department as the Department of Health while asserting that all problems in the health service are due to wasteful hospitals and incompetent doctors. Such political posturing can ring a little hollow to the people on the ground who are experiencing cost-cutting, recruitment freezes, reductions in numbers of beds and corresponding reductions in numbers of operations.

Progress So Far

How is CfH progressing? Actually, it is difficult to say. Firstly, because although CfH issues an impressively shiny Business

Plan full of such high-sounding fashionable management gob-
bledegook as its 'mission, values and strategy', the document
contains many more photos of happy healthcare workers than
figures explaining how much money is being or will be spent.
Moreover, although the Business Plan details all the remarkable achievements of CfH, nowhere does it compare these
achievements with an original schedule. So we cannot see if
they are on target, behind or ahead. Not only is the Business
Plan less than informative, but it is also almost impossible to
get any information from the CfH organization about what is
happening. A cult of secrecy seems to have descended over the
project. This got so extreme that journalists from one of
Britain's leading computer publications, which had been critical of the way CfH was being run, were allegedly banned
from attending a CfH press conference.[9] Requests for information on whether the project is going off schedule are met
with a stony silence or patronizing denials. Answers to parliamentary questions are also either singularly unenlightening or
else consist of reams of figures detailing CfH's many achievements – reminiscent of Soviet newsreels claiming over-performance against the five-year grain production plan, while most
people are going hungry. The suspicions that something truly
horrible is happening behind the CfH iron curtain is not helped
by the fact that the publication date of the NAO report on the
project keeps getting put back. One journalist voiced their
doubts about the length of time it was taking to produce the
NAO report when they wrote, 'it is not unknown for government departments to deliberately spin this process out to delay
what they perceive to be potentially embarrassing reports.'[10]

Most failed IT systems projects (and remember that a study
of over 13,500 organizations showed that this is around 73
per cent of all IT projects) go through four well-known and
exasperatingly predictable phases. First there is a huge **ambi-
tion** to 'revolutionize' and 'transform' the working practices
of the lucky future system users. CfH certainly gave us that:
'We will deliver a twenty-first century health service through
efficient use of information technology.' Then there comes
pride as the leaders of the great venture mistakenly equate the

sight of huge numbers of consultants, being paid huge amounts of money, with making real progress towards delivering a system that meets users' needs. Again, CfH has demonstrated this: 'The National Programme for IT has a strong record of achievement. For example, since our inception two years ago, we have mobilized a skilled workforce capable of meeting the challenge.' By this time tens of millions have usually been spent. Now the project can go two possible ways. Very occasionally, it delivers working prototypes and systems that match the original promises, in which case the worthies in charge are usually only too happy to continually advertise their tremendous achievements to anyone with the time and energy to listen. Alternatively, and much more frequently, endless problems start to surface: it is discovered that the business processes being computerized have not been fully understood; that the complexity of the system has been drastically underestimated; that the hardware is found to be inadequate; that response times are ludicrously slow; that the initial budgets look like pocket money compared to the fortunes that are now being poured into the consultancies' bank accounts. And those responsible eventually come to the horrible realization that, 'Oh, shit! We got it wrong. It's not going to work!' But by this time so much money has gone up in smoke and so many reputations are on the line, that there can be no turning back. The project is in a hole and in their desperation to try and sort out the mess, everybody just keeps on digging faster rather than pausing to check whether they are actually digging the right kind of hole in the right place. Meanwhile, the tens of millions turn into hundreds of millions as the consultants, who had previously apparently agreed a reasonably fixed price for the work, now start billing the client, in this case the government, by maintaining that every bug and inadequacy they fix is new work for which they need to charge extra. Anxious to avoid a bust-up with their suppliers which would leave them both high and dry and looking particularly inept, the civil servants are trapped and have to keep on handing over millions of our money in the hope that something can be salvaged from the wreckage so that their careers can be protected. This is when the third phase – **secrecy** – kicks in. Given the iron curtain that seems to have been erected around CfH to prevent anything but the official line leaking out, it's hardly difficult to guess that inside the monolith all is not light and joy and popping champagne corks.

Close to delivery, things generally change yet again for most of these kinds of projects, and *Connecting for Health* doesn't seem to be any different. By the end of 2005, one piece of the system should have been close to delivery – the *Choose and Book* system for GPs to make hospital appointments for their patients. Planned to cost £65m, this first system has now cost over £200m. In 2004, it managed to make 63 hospital appointments compared to a planned 205,000. In 2005, despite the fact that the Department of Health pulled £95m from front-line care to give to any doctors who used *Choose and Book*, only about 0.7 per cent of hospital appointments were made using the system and in most cases created extra paperwork that had not been required before. Of course, CfH denied that there were problems with the system, denied *Choose and Book* was over budget and claimed it was always intended to cost £200m. (It is odd that when the press first reported that *Choose and Book* would only cost £65m, the CfH press office didn't correct this apparent 'inaccuracy'.) In the light of the Health Secretary's comments about hospitals being in the red due to their own waste and mismanagement, it is interesting to note that the total budget deficit for NHS hospitals in the 2004/5 financial year was around £140m. Coincidentally, this almost exactly matches the current £140m overspend on *Choose and Book*. Though, of course, as we know from CfH, this £140m was not overspend at all, it was always in the budget. This reminds one of the congenitally incompetent MoD bosses claiming that their £6bn overspend was not 'overspend' either, it was just a £6bn 'level of disappointment'. Let us hope that we do not get similarly huge, or even larger 'levels of disappointment' at CfH.

This brings us to the fourth phase of failing or failed IT systems projects – **blame**. This is when the original budget has been overspent by millions, tens of millions, hundreds of millions or even, as will be the case with CfH, billions. Years after the planned date, either nothing is yet installed or else some sort of system may be working, but it does incomparably less than was originally promised, is tortuously difficult to use and is probably costing more per transaction than the previous, largely manual way of doing things. At this point, those responsible for the system's implementation blame those who work with it for continually changing their requirements and for not using it properly. Although by November 2005 CfH was far from completion, a rather unsightly public spat had already broken out between the director of the programme and the head of the NHS. Richard Granger reportedly wrote to a senior civil servant at the Department of Health claiming 'Choose and Book's IT build contract is now in grave danger of derailing (not just destabilizing) a £6.2bn programme. Unfortunately, your consistently late requests will not enable us to rescue the missed opportunities and targets.'[11] So that's the predictable bit about changing user requirements being responsible for the cost increases and delays. Additionally, in an interview with a computing magazine, the director of CfH said, 'Low usage is not something I can do anything about.'[12] And there we have the equally predictable criticism of users for not using the marvellous new system that has been developed especially for them.

When a complex public-sector project goes well, those involved are usually seen enthusiastically clapping each other on the back and smiling delightedly for the cameras as they contemplate their forthcoming knighthoods and lucrative positions as highly paid, top level advisers and directors – they are not usually knifing each other in the back by sending accusatory emails in an apparent attempt to shift responsibility for an impending disaster. This altercation could be seen as yet another sign that CfH is decidedly moving into the 'Oh, shit! It's not going to work!' period and is casting around for somewhere convenient to hang the blame, while everyone inside the project struggles to fix the unfixable before the outside world spots the meltdown. Of course, when talking to the press, CfH claim that all is well in the best of all possible worlds. But given the careful control on information from the project, one could suspect that there is an ever widening chasm between what is said by CfH spokespeople in public and what they really believe.

Learning from Past Mistakes?

The NHS and IT systems have not, in the past, been the happiest of bedfellows. There have been two major NHS IT strategies in recent memory. In 1992, the NHS developed a strategy to 'ensure that information and information technology are managed as the significant resources they are and that they are managed for the benefit of individual patient care as for the population as a whole'.[13] Despite its lofty intentions, it seems that the 1992 NHS IT plan turned out to be something of a damp squib when words had to be turned into actions. The PAC noted that: 'Design and implementation of the 1992 NHS IT Strategy demonstrated many of the key failings we have seen on public-sector IT projects generally. In particular: the absence of an overall business case; errors in business cases that were produced for individual programmes; failure to identify interdependencies between programmes leading to a lack of cohesion; and failure to set budgets for the full costs involved. The NHS executive decided not to set specific, measurable, achievable, relevant and time-related objectives for the six main projects and programmes. Neither did they consider how the projects related to one another.'

As part of the ill-fated 1992 plan, a project to standardize IT systems in the Wessex Regional Health Authority was abandoned after about £43m had been spent. A flurry of civil lawsuits and allegations of criminal fraud ensued. The NHS then waited four years before reviewing what had gone wrong, slightly limiting its ability to learn from the unfortunate experience. In 1990 following a severe attack of NIHS (see Chapter 1), the NHS decided that the US clinical coding standards were not suitable for Britain. It then went on to waste about £32m trying to develop its own new electronic language for health. By 1998, the NHS had given up and just adopted the US clinical coding standards after all. And at least £10m was lost when the West Midlands Regional Health Authority supplies division junked their plan to set up an electronic trading system because 'proper market research was not carried out, suppliers were not consulted, estimates of supplier take-up were significantly overstated, potential customers were not consulted and the royalty projections were unrealistic'.[14]

In 1998, the NHS launched a package of new and existing IT projects and service aspirations called *Information for Health – An Information Strategy for the Modern NHS 1998–2005*. Reviewing the 1998 Strategy, the PAC felt that the NHS had learnt something from previous mistakes, but expressed its concern that, 'again the NHS chose consciously not to make the objectives specific or fully measurable, leading to a failure to clearly link targets to objectives. There is no full business case for the strategy.' It was also felt that the 1998 Strategy 'risked a similar lack of cohesion' to the 1992 plan.

Is CfH definitely and expensively heading for the same fate as virtually all other New Labour projects? Or could it still turn out to be a shining example of best practice showing that our Civil Service have, as they repeatedly claim, learnt from past mistakes?

One thing the government seems to have found out from their impressively long list of IT screw-ups is that civil servants are not capable of running major projects. So, in hiring Richard Granger for CfH, the government seems to have made the effort to find someone from the private sector who already had a track record of successfully delivering large, complex projects. As Sir John Pattison, then head of the NHS, said to a House of Lords select committee: 'What we have done is to secure for ourselves Richard Granger, who is Director-General of NHS IT. He comes from the private sector. He has experience of putting in large computer systems. We can look at the experiences of the Passport Office as one experience; we can look at the experience of what Richard Granger installed for congestion charging in London as another experience; and say that we may well have somebody who is capable of delivering on time and on price something that works.'

Sir John Pattison, who would have retired well before the results of CfH were apparent, for better or for worse, then went on to explain that the new Director-General had been drafted in due to a lack of capability in project management in the public sector: 'However, if I may just make a personal comment, I cannot exaggerate the value of Richard Granger to this programme, and the likelihood of its success. These are skills and experience which we simply do not, or have not had up till now in the Department of Health and the NHS. We are good, and we have introduced somewhere in the NHS everything that we want to install, but we have never done it on a scale that is implied as necessary and correct in order to support the National Health Service. So he is bringing in people who we would not automatically have brought in and did not know about, and I think that is increasing the likelihood of success of this enormous project.'

The other major change that shows CfH have learnt something from previous projects can be seen in the way they have structured their contracts with suppliers. For almost the first time on a government project, CfH have imposed major cost penalties on suppliers if they miss critical project dates. Moreover, they are also applying them. BT were reported to have paid £4.5m in penalties in 2004 and to be facing further fines in 2005. BT denied that the £4.5m had been a fine and insisted it had just been an 'adjustment of payments'.[15] The Director-General of CfH, however, seemed fairly unambiguous in his views of BT's performance. He accused them of having made 'a very shaky start' to the contract and of being 'behind the original contracted schedule'. Moreover, he said, 'their project management wasn't good enough, the people they had on the job weren't good enough and they still have some distance to go there.'[16] Nevertheless, whether the £4.5m was a fine for late delivery or 'adjustments of payments', in theory this new tougher stance should push IT systems suppliers to perform better than they have done on previous programmes.

However, this approach has been derided within the IT

industry. At a conference in November 2005, the chief legal counsel of one of the world's top three systems consulting companies explained that the problems on government projects stemmed from the limited management capabilities of the civil servants running the projects and so would not be solved by the imposition of fines: 'The changes in the style of the process were typified by the NHS NPfIT Programme procurement in 2003. This can be summarized as the "big stick" rather than the partnership approach to procurement. At a recent meeting of industry trade body Intellect's healthcare group, Richard Granger, Director-General of the £6bn NHS NPfIT told his audience that he wants to "hold suppliers feet to the fire so that the smell of burning flesh is overpowering". Suppliers have expressed concern to the OGC that the Government is increasingly relying on punitive contracts and the inevitable fines (which have already begun at NPfIT), rather than developing its own programme management capacity and becoming the "intelligent customer".'[17]

Of course, given the typical business practices used by the larger consultancies, one should take such protestations of innocence with a not inconsiderable pinch of salt. Too often, civil servants' inexperience and incompetence have suited the consultancies as they have enabled consultancies to double, triple and even quadruple their prices once they got their public-sector contracts signed. Some consultancies even boast that the way they make money from public-sector contracts is to submit a low bid, in the full knowledge that the government contract will be so full of holes that it offers the consultancy a captive client and an almost unlimited licence to raise prices once the project has begun. However, there is probably also some justification for the IT company's chief legal counsel at the conference going on to accuse the government side of, among other things, 'lack of clear senior management and ministerial ownership and leadership, lack of skills and proven approach to project management and risk management, lack of understanding of and contact with the systems supply industry at senior levels, too little attention to breaking development and implementation into manageable steps, inade-

quate resources and skills to deliver'. Failings from the government side that, as we have seen, seem to be a recurring feature
of large public-sector consultancy programmes.

Sadly, as I review and also discuss with experts and insiders
how CfH have designed and set up their programme, it seems
that, apart from these two areas, they are taking exactly the
same approach as previous catastrophic projects and so wilfully repeating the mistakes of the past. It is said that one sign
of madness is to carry on doing the same thing and to expect a
different result. Unfortunately for us taxpayers and for our
health service, CfH seem determined to follow in the ill-fated
footsteps of their unfortunate predecessors, while somehow
expecting the results to be quite different.

CHAPTER 11

Heading for Meltdown?

With most government IT systems, there is an inherent tension between what is good for the politicians who eagerly launch the projects, the civil servants who end up running them, the management and IT consultants who earn a more than comfortable living from them and what is best for the people who will use and be affected by the systems being developed. The politicians want bold, headline-grabbing policy initiatives – Patient Choice, Targeting, Strategic Service Delivery Partnerships, Agenda for Change, Patients' Charter and so on. They are not interested in the practical difficulties of implementation – that a 'Strategic Service Delivery Partnership' can actually mean creating a local monopoly that drains hundreds millions from NHS front-line services and makes the so-called 'partners' obscenely rich. They don't want to hear that 'Patient Choice' is meaningless as most people will just go or can only go to their local hospital. They haven't got time to concern themselves with the fact that almost every new hospital built under a PFI or PPP scheme has fewer beds and fewer services than its NHS predecessor, thus giving patients less rather than more choice. Civil servants involved in these large programmes have repeatedly been shown to be out of their depth and are mostly interested in their own longer-term career interests rather than value for money for the taxpayer. After all, governments come and go and policies change with the inevitability of the seasons, so few civil servants are going to put their heads above the parapet and say a particular policy dreamed up by cabinet ministers and their self-interested consultants is absurd or impractical. They ideally want to hand the whole problem to a large systems supplier on the principle that the larger the supplier they choose, the less likely they personally will be blamed for making a wrong decision – what we used to call the 'nobody ever got fired for buying IBM' principle. As for the large systems houses, they want big projects with fast start-ups. They want millions spent quickly. But all the systems users and NHS patients want is radical improvements in the quality of care – whether there are IT systems involved or not is, for them, immaterial. So, in running a programme like *Connecting for Health*, the people responsible have a fairly complex task of finding the right balance between the usually conflicting interests of the various parties involved.

Against the background of CfH's aims, and what has been seen to go right and wrong on other government IT projects and on other NHS projects, I propose to examine in some detail how the overall CfH programme and each of its six products are being designed and implemented. My aims are to see how well CfH management have balanced the interests of the main stakeholders and to assess the likelihood of success or otherwise of this critical programme that is going to consume over £30bn of our money and have a major impact on the quality and quantity of healthcare that we all receive in the future. First we'll look at the seven main concerns I have with the whole way the overall CfH is being managed and then we'll examine each of the six main products in the programme to evaluate their robustness.

Judging by past reactions to other critics, I have no doubt that my analysis will be ridiculed by New Labour's spin-doctors and the powers that be in CfH as being inaccurate and misdirected and that I will be held up for being mad, evil or stupid – or, most probably, all three. But then this is exactly the same kind of response that has met critics of all New Labour public service modernization disasters so far. For example, the

Home Secretary has recently accused critics of New Labour's Identity Cards of being 'simply mad' and of talking 'total nonsense'.[1] While John Prescott's Office of the Deputy Prime Minister claimed that a report critical of one of his policies (developed after spending £168m on consultants) was 'utter nonsense' and that the writers of the report were 'only interested in ill-informed scaremongering, not the facts'.[2] When the government and its agents use language like that against those who dare to disagree with them, you can be pretty sure you are on the right track. It is to be hoped, but not expected, that the government, its spin-doctors and the grandees at CfH could rise above their normal vilification of critics and provide more constructive responses to the concerns raised here.

Given the difficulty of getting accurate information from CfH, I have had to base my analysis on the limited information that is available in the public domain and on what I have been able to obtain from insiders within the NHS. Some of the leaks may be factually correct and some may be creative interpretations of reality put out by people interested in having their version of events accepted as fact. I have done my best to distinguish fact from fiction and to have my assessment thoroughly checked by reliable people with comprehensive knowledge of what is really happening on CfH. But a few inaccurate assertions may still have slipped through and I apologize for this.

The Overall Programme

Concern 1: Anyone for a Game of Monopoly?

In deciding how to design and implement new IT systems throughout the NHS in England (Scotland and Wales have so far been spared the joys of this great undertaking), CfH made the sensible decision that they should not be dependent on any one single supplier for such a massive programme. So they split the country up into five regions, called 'clusters', and asked the main IT providers to bid to become Local Service Providers (LSPs) for these clusters. Most of the leading IT firms did not have expertise in all the different areas that would be covered by the new IT systems. These areas would include systems for GPs' practices, pathology, radiology, patient record-keeping, appointment booking, electronic prescriptions, accounting and so on. So to produce credible and competitive bids, several of the big companies allied themselves with smaller niche suppliers who already had the specialist knowledge and systems the major players lacked.

CfH apparently felt that having a multiplicity of suppliers in one cluster went against their stated aim of a single suite of common IT systems for the whole NHS. The mantra at the time was that CfH needed 'industry strength vendors' and not a bunch of smaller suppliers, so-called 'cottage industry' companies. So CfH instructed the bidders to adjust their bids to exclude the smaller suppliers. This was done and the five clusters were allocated to the fortunate few massive companies – two went to Accenture and one each to BT, Fujitsu (formerly ICL) and CSC.

However, this was, I believe, a fatal mistake. It was equivalent to splitting the country into five regions and then saying to Tesco that they could have exclusive rights to run supermarkets and supply food in two regions and that Sainsbury's, Asda and Waitrose could each have one region exclusively. Why does it cost more to get standing room on a dirty overcrowded train from London to Leeds or Manchester than it does to get a seat on a flight to Barcelona or Rome for the weekend? Obviously, because certain train companies have monopolies on the specific lines, while there is competition on the flight routes to Barcelona and Rome. What CfH did was to create regional monopolies that could do what they liked and charge what they liked in their regions.

As the LSPs' contracts with CfH are apparently still 'commercially confidential' years after they have been awarded, it is difficult to get data on the costly effects of creating these monopolies, and we cannot find out what they are charging for the different services they are offering. One consequence of handing whole regions of the country over to the LSPs has been that GPs and hospitals were strongly encouraged by the LSPs to abandon systems that worked and replace them with the systems that the cluster monopoly supplier wished them to run. The Director-General of CfH once said that the programme would make use of previous work: 'this isn't about sweeping the board clean and bringing in ruthlessly standardized solutions that may provide less functionality than existing solutions. This is about making best use of the existing asset base and having a coherent integration and upgrade programme.'[3] However, people inside the NHS claim there is pressure to change systems unnecessarily: 'many practices are under pressure from Primary Care Trusts to move to LSP-provided systems.'[4] As all health systems will be hosted by the LSPs rather than in GP surgeries or in hospitals, this gives the LSPs huge power to dictate policy in their region – they decide what systems they will and will not allow. This push to standardize has allegedly caused a large amount of unnecessary system replacement for which health authorities have had to find the money. Another result seems to be a substantial increase in prices that health authorities have to pay for IT services. For example some figures suggest that while the previous providers of practice management systems for GPs would charge £2,500 to migrate a surgery's data from an old system to a new system, one of the monopoly companies was charging £5,000 and taking twice as long as the previous competitive suppliers.[5] In 2000 the Public Accounts Committee (PAC) had already warned government department buyers of IT systems to have 'adequate protection of possible abuse by the supplier of the advantageous position they are in' and advised departments to ensure 'value for money' through 'competitive pressure'.[6] In granting regional monopolies to the LSPs, the PAC's warnings seem to have gone unheeded by the worthies at CfH.

Following the decision to grant these huge regional monopolies, there was a flood of complaints from GPs who were satisfied with their existing systems. In March 2005, pressure from the users of some of the most popular systems caused CfH to backtrack and allow some smaller supplies of compatible systems back into the market. However, the power of the

holders of the regional franchises is so great that that it has
been difficult for the smaller specialized companies to prosper.
So, in spite of this policy reversal, the market is still dominated
by the four firms with the five regional monopolies.

Concern 2: Uniformity not Interoperability

One of the main justifications for the CfH programme was that
in the past the NHS had developed a whole plethora of
different systems which could not communicate and that there
was no central mechanism for ensuring successful systems
work was used across the organization. As the CfH business
plan helpfully explains: 'Historically, the NHS has not always
used or developed IT as a strategic asset in delivering or
managing healthcare. While there were good, usually local,
IT initiatives sponsored by enthusiastic visionaries, these were
generally outweighed by an overall lack of investment given to
IT at all levels. Good experiences were not captured from their
local beginnings to NHS-wide applications. This failure to
capitalize on opportunities could not be allowed to continue.'[7]

This is certainly true. But it is also a generalization that
displays a fundamental misunderstanding of the real situation.
To see what was actually happening in NHS IT systems before
CfH, you have to look at primary care (GPs) and secondary
care (hospitals) separately. In hospitals, it was absolutely true
that in some places there was a woeful lack of IT and in others
a multitude of locally developed incompatible systems that
probably caused more problems than they solved. Moreover,
there was little learning and sharing of experience among
hospitals. All this led to much NHS secondary care IT being
a lost opportunity. However, in primary care, the situation was
quite different.

In primary care, the NHS Executive introduced a process
called 'Requirements for Accreditation' (RFA) in April 1993.
This was to ensure General Medical Practice computer systems
provided an agreed core functionality and conformed to national standards. National (though limited) interoperability
standards were also implemented. After 2001, the RFA process

was due to be replaced with NAPPS (a new and improved RFA). With the latter stalling indefinitely, a number of health-care IT systems suppliers got together in 2002 and created the rather inelegantly named Healthcare Interoperability Forum (HCIF). These companies agreed common standards for data and other system aspects that meant the many different systems from different suppliers were compatible. So a market was created with multiple competing suppliers, but with compa-tible products. This led to rapid innovation, new product development and low prices.

Unfortunately, HCIF was killed off by CfH, as CfH seems to have decided to cure the whole of the NHS for a disease – lack of interoperability – that was actually in the process of being cured by the existing systems suppliers at no cost to the NHS. Moreover, CfH have come up with the wrong cure for the NHS secondary care's past failure to implement accreditation and interoperability standards. What CfH should have done was to impose interoperability standards throughout the UK in both primary and secondary healthcare and to allow a com-petitive market to continue in both areas of healthcare, en-couraging the participation of any supplier who worked to the agreed standards. What CfH did instead was to obliterate competition by decreeing that the LSPs were the single supplier per cluster and that only a very limited number of systems would be permitted. By destroying the competitive market when it created the lucrative regional monopolies, CfH have helped the big suppliers by exterminating competition and the benefits of competition. The result will be much higher prices for health authorities, less product innovation and a collapse in service levels. For example, one of the competitive suppliers quoted a time of six weeks to make some system upgrades. The quote from the region's monopoly supplier for the same piece of work was over a year.

Concern 3: Failure to Understand – Improve – Automate

Before the days of these massive New Labour system devel-opments, we used to have a simple acronym: UIA – Understand, Improve, Automate. The intention behind UIA was that if you wanted to implement an IT system, you first had to understand precisely how the future users worked today – what we called the 'As-Is'. You then should improve current work processes – to create the 'To-Be'. Finally you should design your system to support the future improved way of working. All very simple really. And in report after report, the PAC have stressed the need to improve administrative process before trying to automate them.

Looking at CfH, some of the systems that are being developed are in principle very worthy, but in an ideal world you would understand and improve the way health workers operated now before launching into a massive systems development. If so little attention is being paid to improving how the health service works now and should work in the future, we risk having the world's flashiest and most expensive IT systems without having made any significant improvements in the delivery of healthcare. This danger was clearly articulated at a House of Lords hearing which featured individuals with the wonderfully Dickensian names Dr Catchpole and Mr Spittle. As Mr Spittle said, 'there is a grave danger of going down the route of purely automating what we are doing. We have to determine the desired state.'[8] But causing change is difficult, it is messy and it takes time, so the politicians, civil servants and consultants usually take the easy route – spend the money now, build the systems and then see what happens. This appears to be what is happening at CfH.

Concern 4: 'Big Bang' Development

To simplify enormously, one could say there are two main ways of developing new IT systems – 'big bang' and 'iterative prototyping'. With big bang, you may do a small pilot just to iron out the bugs, then put in massive resources (often hundreds of consultants), build the system and roll it out to the users. Big bang satisfies the politicians' need to show things are happening, it reassures the civil servants that the whole thing will be delivered ready for them to press the button and off it will go and it provides admirably large levels of billing for the consultants right from the start of the project. Remember that in 2000, after reviewing twenty-five government IT projects, the Public Accounts Committee recommended that, 'an incremental, as opposed to a "big bang" approach to IT projects should be adopted, with regular milestones, each delivering an auditable business benefit.' In an organization like the NHS, big bang can be disastrous for the users and for patients. Big bang tends to be inflexible as regards the needs of doctors and patients. The system is designed and built using hundreds of consultants and at massive expense. If anything has been misunderstood during the design (as always happens) or if circumstances change during the build phase (as always happens), big bang systems developments are usually unable to adapt and so tend to bulldoze their way forward ignoring those bits of reality that do not fit their preconceptions. When hundreds of millions are being spent on a huge complex programme, there is little opportunity to adapt to particular changing needs. Juggernauts do not move like gazelles.

With iterative prototyping, on the other hand, you start small with a basic system – ideally based on an already working system – in a couple of test locations. You involve users and gradually build on more functionality. You go through a whole series of iterations – involving the users and adding even more functionality – until you have a system that meets user needs. Then you scale it up and roll it out. With iterative prototyping you can involve users, continuously adapt the system and make friends. But iterative prototyping can look messy to the politicians and civil servants because you don't appear to have as much central control as you do with big bang. Moreover, the really big consultancies try to avoid iterative prototyping as it starts small and so doesn't provide huge fees up front.

One of the great unsung advantages of iterative prototyping is that it is impossible to spend many tens of millions before you find out if the system is going to work or will have to be radically adjusted in order for it to work: the main problems are usually discovered after just hundreds of thousands have been spent. With big bang, as scores of previous government efforts have shown, it is usually not till tens or even hundreds of millions of our money have gone up in smoke that the problems are discovered.

CfH seems to be developing most of its systems centrally and then dropping them on to the future users in a classic 'big bang' implementation. We are already paying the price for this error.

Concern 5: Building the Church for Easter Sunday

A classic mistake made by politically driven IT systems developments is to set an impressive-sounding target that looks good in the newspapers but actually has limited relevance to real-life needs. For example, with the new CfH system, the government proudly boasts that if you live in Birmingham and fall ill while on holiday in Carlisle or Portsmouth, doctors there will be able to immediately access your electronic medical records thus ensuring you get the appropriate care. Now, most people living in Birmingham will never visit either Carlisle or Portsmouth and the few that do will probably not fall ill when they are there. In fact most people fall ill close to their homes and will be treated in their local hospitals. So while the idea of any health worker anywhere in England being able to access your medical records sounds absolutely splendid on daytime television, it may not be necessary and the costs may be out of all proportion to the benefits. What the government is doing is what we consultants used to call 'building the church for Easter Sunday' – building an IT system that is so massive that it can cope with every possible eventuality. For us this was mouth-wateringly profitable, yet usually quite unnecessary. In real life, the 80/20 rule (more often it is the 90/10 rule) generally applies – at least 80 per cent of cases can be dealt with by probably less than 20 per cent of the IT system's capabilities. So conversely, 80 per cent or more of a system's costs will be linked to probably fewer than 20 per cent of the cases handled. Often it is much cheaper and much simpler to provide a manual or small customized solution for the 10 to 20 per cent of exceptional cases that cannot be processed by a basic IT system, rather than vastly increasing cost and complexity to cope with every possible eventuality. Politicians love building the church for Easter Sunday because it shows they have thought of everything. IT consultants love over-dimensioned projects because they allow them to build much larger and more expensive systems. Unfortunately for us the taxpayers, building the church for Easter Sunday, rather than for an average congregation, hugely and unnecessarily increases the costs of the project and the risks of failure.

Concern 6: Not Involving the Clinicians

One of the other recommendations made by the PAC in 2000 was that influential users should be fully involved in the system's development and implementation. The PAC found just one successful project in the NHS, at Greenwich Health Authority. The PAC commented, 'The NHS executive told the committee that a key factor had been the involvement of a senior clinician as project director.' The PAC went on to say that they felt that 'the commitment of clinicians is crucial to the success of such projects' and that they 'agreed with the NHS Executive's view that all users need to be involved in the development of these systems'. Of the five-person CfH Board of Management in the 2005/6 Business Plan, the director of the programme is from consulting, another member comes from the management side of a health authority and the three others are from government departments already infamous for their extraordinarily incompetent handling of previous major IT systems projects. They are all 'managers' and/or bureaucrats. There is not one clinician. It seems that the NHS Executive has unfortunately just forgotten what it claimed to the PAC that it had learnt only a few years before.

Concern 7: The Great Reinvention

But perhaps the greatest concern of all is one that I mentioned at the start of the book – we may be going though a tortuously difficult and mind-bogglingly costly reinvention of something that by and large already existed. Not being a confidant of those who have given us CfH, it is difficult to know whether what was originally intended resembles in any way what is now being so expensively delivered. But there are tantalizing hints that the whole project started off as a minor operation and has turned into an attempt to build a kind of Frankenstein, likely to fall over with an almighty crash as soon as it tries to walk.

Looking back over the available information, it seems that the genesis of CfH was a report from McKinsey which saw the whole enterprise as being based on 'the purchase of off-the-shelf software' that should only have cost around £2bn to be implemented across the whole NHS.[9] If this is the case, then CfH originally began life as a sensible and low cost attempt to use and adapt existing technology which already worked – absolute best practice for IT systems development. Following this proposal, various worthies linked to CfH apparently went on a series of junkets around the world to see the required systems working in other countries' health services – primarily in the US. Then something appears to have gone wrong. Probably the usual process occurred – a severe attack of NIHS, the same condition that has affected so many other New Labour projects. I expect that, lacking the expertise to buy IT systems effectively, the civil servants preferred to hand the whole project over to the few favoured enormous IT systems companies. These companies, sensing an opportunity to earn almost unlimited amounts of money, convinced the civil servants that all the systems needed to be built from scratch to suit the NHS's particular needs. Everybody conveniently forgot that they had so recently seen systems that worked in other countries. They also conveniently forgot the previous NHS Chief Executive's claim, which I quoted in the first chapter, that all the required systems were already functioning somewhere in the NHS. And so the construction of the mighty and mightily expensive Frankenstein began. This has happened many times before and it will happen again – the hubris of politicians, the ineptitude of civil servants and the greed of consultants can only lead to one outcome and that outcome is going to be agonizingly disastrous for our health service.

Meanwhile, the Health Secretary, a previous employee of one of the massive companies bringing us this costly catastrophe announced, 'waste and inefficiency in the NHS is intolerable. A penny wasted is a penny stolen from a patient.'[10] One would assume therefore that she would agree that £10bn to £20bn wasted on unnecessarily building new IT systems is also £10bn to £20bn stolen from patients – maybe she will act to stop this massive 'theft'.

The Six Products

Care Records Service (CRS): Thick or Thin Spines?

Before the CfH programme, there were two great weaknesses with the way patient records were handled in the NHS – many were paper-based and at any one time around 15 per cent would be missing. Also, as some were paper-based and others were on incompatible IT systems, different departments would be creating records for the same patient. Clearly, this was administratively inefficient and, more importantly, meant that it was difficult for any medic to quickly obtain the full records on a patient, therefore impeding effective diagnosis and preventing patients getting the right level of care. Moreover, with this almost prehistoric method of record-keeping, there was a constant risk of vital information like allergies not being contained in all versions of a patient's documentation. So implementing a system of Electronic Patient Records (EPRs) with all data being held electronically should be a huge step forward. The CfH Business Plan lays out the benefits of EPRs: 'Clinicians will benefit from being able to access patient information wherever it is needed. It is estimated that around 80% of decisions for diagnosis or treatment are based on information, for example medical history. This means better access to a patient's records will improve diagnosis. With less time chasing records and test results, clinicians will also have more time to concentrate on providing quality care for patients.'

The intention is that all EPRs will be held on a national, centrally managed database called 'The Spine'. As the CfH

Business Plan explains: 'The Spine is the name given to the national database of key information about patients' health and care. It will form the core of the NHS CRS. It will also support other key programmes of the National Programme for IT, such as Choose and Book and Electronic Transmission of Prescriptions.'

The big question about the Spine is whether it should be 'thick' or 'thin'. A thick spine means that all information about a patient will be located on one central database so that anybody in the country with authorized access to the system could view your complete medical records. A thin spine would mean that your medical records would be held on a local database. If you were to fall ill away from your home area, a thin spine would just have an electronic card that identified you, that might hold essential information like allergies and that would direct any authorized queries automatically to the local database, which would hold your full medical records.

In a perfect world, all information on IT systems is always accurate, all IT systems connections are always up and running, response times are always rapid and all helpdesks answer the phone and respond immediately to problems. In this kind of world, having a thick spine could make sense. But anyone who has had dealings with banks, insurance companies, the Inland Revenue and other institutions holding huge numbers of records, might be aware that the world is far from perfect, that information is often far from being current, that systems are frequently either down or responding so slowly that they are all but useless. Moreover, if it is the case that more than 80 per cent of people will fall ill and be treated near where they live, there is really no need for their information to be held on a massive central database. In fact, by holding all information centrally you would be hugely increasing the number of electronic messages passing through the system and thus hugely increasing the size, cost and vulnerability of the necessary supporting telephone networks.

The one fundamental lesson we should all have learnt from the development of the Internet is that using web connectivity to link smaller local databases is cheaper, more flexible, more effective and more robust than trying to build gargantuan central information depositories. The failure of one part of a distributed network will not affect other parts. Moreover, it is easy and cheap to upgrade small portions without having to make changes to the whole structure. But with one monolithic system, one crash will often crash the whole system and to make upgrades or changes you must apply these to the whole edifice. Huge monolithic systems suit politicians who want control, civil servants who want simple answers and consultants who want money, but in a web-enabled Internet age, they are the wrong way to develop new systems. Google – probably the best-known and most effective information retrieval system in the world – is not based on a huge computer with all the world's knowledge stuffed on it. It is just a website with some very smart programmes for accessing information from millions of distributed databases. Yet the worthies at CfH apparently know better than the founders of Google and so have decided to build a thick spine and one computer system containing most of the NHS's information. This is inevitably more complex, riskier and hugely more expensive than a thin spine linking local databases. It is my contention that CfH have made an enormously expensive mistake.

Just in case anybody thinks this assessment is over-pessimistic, on Thursday, 22 December 2005, four days after some 'upgrading' during the previous weekend to put on 'additional functionality', the system was 'unavailable'. The CfH website informed users: 'Over the last weekend the Spine services were upgraded with additional functionality and a number of infrastructure changes were introduced. Unfortunately this has caused service levels for the Spine to be diminished and users are likely to experience some intermittent interruptions.'

However, CfH staff were apparently working hard to solve the problems: 'Resolution activities have progressed and throughout Wednesday night corrective actions were implemented on the Spine to improve service levels. Planning and resolution activities continue to address the remaining issues. NHS CfH and BT are continuing to work closely to bring service back to normal levels.'

These system problems also meant the *Choose and Book* (C&B) wasn't working either and in the case of C&B users were informed that 'the disruption may continue for the next few days.'[11]

Helpfully, users were informed that if they had any questions, they could email (not call) the helpdesk. There was no indication of how quickly the helpdesk would reply – if ever.

It was not until 12 January 2006, 25 days after the upgrade, that the problems were resolved. CfH did sort of apologize for the problems by blaming its suppliers, perhaps forgetting that CfH management are paid to ensure that their suppliers deliver what they promise: 'It is regrettable that our suppliers were unable to maintain full availability without interruption during the integration of the multiple systems that took place following the upgrade. It is also regrettable that the solutions do not yet appear to meet the exacting standards we require to support continuous working 24 hours a day seven days a week.'[12]

No doubt there are many more similar upgrades to come over the next few years and no doubt most will result in similar system instability. Moreover, no doubt the CfH grandees will blame their suppliers for all the problems.

Yet, if the system crashes now when it is carrying an absolute minimum of traffic, it is quite frightening to imagine what will happen when it is trying to support sixty million detailed patient health records, perhaps more than fifty million digital images, three hundred and fifty million prescriptions, nine million hospital bookings and detailed financial and management information for all Britain's hospitals and GP surgeries. A likely future scenario is all hospitals in the country having to suspend operations several times a year as the system crashes and they are unable to access patient records and digital X-rays. Meanwhile, the helpdesk will continue to refuse to take any calls as it feels that responding to emails, perhaps weeks after they are received, is a quite sufficient level of service. Had CfH chosen a thin, rather than a thick, spine these problems wouldn't happen.

Choose and Book (C&B): You'll Be Lucky

The C&B system is interesting as it probably displays some of the worst features of New Labour's IT-supported 'modernization' programme.

Firstly, C&B is driven by the headline-grabbing ideas of 'patient choice' and a 'patient-focused NHS' – GPs should give every patient referred to hospital a choice of four to five hospitals before making a booking for an appointment. On the surface, this sounds frightfully appealing and worthwhile. It shows New Labour is truly committed to revolutionizing healthcare for our benefit. But how necessary is C&B and will the costs far outweigh any benefits? Every year there will about 23.3 million incidents of people attending a hospital in Britain. Of these, 13.9 million are Accident and Emergency (A&E) admissions and 9.4 million are referrals from GPs. One could safely assume that the 13.9 million A&E cases are just happy to get to hospital, any hospital, and get treated before their pain gets worse or before they die. So they would have little use for any form of C&B. Of the 9.4 million GP referrals, probably about 20 per cent live in areas where there is only one major hospital. As one doctor wrote, if he were to offer four choices to his patients, some would have to travel over 200 miles to reach some of the hospitals offered. So that gives about another 1.9 million referrals which don't need to be able to choose a hospital before booking. Then there are maybe another 20 per cent who, because of where they live, only have a realistic choice of two hospitals. The head of the NHS had previously explained to the PAC that if the NHS was only to offer patients the choice of two hospitals, there would be no need for an IT system to support this: 'you would not need it if it was offering perhaps a choice of one or two hospitals.'[13] There are therefore another 1.9 million patients who have no need for an IT system for choosing and booking.

So, from the overall 23.3 million possible beneficiaries of an electronic C&B system, we're now down to about 5.64 million who could be interested in such a system. People who are sick would generally not want to travel a hundred, fifty, even thirty miles to a hospital if there was one closer to their home. Moreover, many of the people who go to hospital may be elderly. Here again we have a group who would generally prefer treatment as near to their homes and friends as possible. So we probably aren't far off the mark if we guess that a third of the remaining 5.64 million cases will choose their local hospital. Then add another third who will not have spent time studying the government's hospital performance league tables and so will see no reason to select an inconveniently situated hospital in preference to their local one. That leaves 1.86 million who may well want to 'choose and book', especially if they see that waiting times are shorter at a hospital some distance away than they are at their local one. Though of these, probably at least a third will still choose their local hospital even after reviewing the different choices available. That leaves us with perhaps just 1.2 million patients, out of a possible 23.3 million, who will consciously choose a hospital other than their local one and so would find C&B useful. Of course, the authorities claim that C&B will be the most popular act since the Beatles. On a test project run in London, around 70 per cent of patients opted to accept a choice other than their local hospital. However, the target group selected for the test were people who had already been waiting six months or more for a hospital appointment – if you were in pain or needed an operation and had been waiting six months for an appointment then were asked if you would prefer to go somewhere further from your home and be seen more quickly, I suspect you would also choose the faster alternative. In fact it is rather amazing that the rate of take-up was not 100 per cent.

C&B looks like costing about £200m to develop, £122m per year to run and maybe another £100m at least to make existing systems compatible. So for the first ten years of its contracted operation, C&B will cost us close to £1.5bn to make, I guess, at most 12 million appointments – a cost of over £125 per appointment. It probably would have been cheaper to just pick up the phone.

Actually the situation is worse than this. Assuming that the NHS really meets its target of running C&B for £122m a year, you can do a quick, back-of-a-fag-packet calculation: there are about 10,000 GP surgeries in England and the annual cost of C&B will thus be £12,200 per surgery. So, if we scrapped C&B right now, we could employ a junior clerical assistant at every single GP surgery for say £10,000 per year (thus providing much needed employment opportunities for school-leavers) and still have £22m left over each year to put back into front-line patient care. As is so often the case with the New Labour 'modernization' of public services, headline-hungry politicians, inept bureaucrats and voracious consultants have managed to give us a poorly working IT system that actually costs more than it would cost to do everything by hand – an extraordinarily inept result in a world where computers have such potential to automate and reduce the costs of repetitive activities.

But perhaps the real issue is this: at a time when the NHS is making drastic cuts to numbers of beds, staff and operations due to budget deficits, is spending around £1.5bn on C&B really a sensible priority? Or should C&B just be junked as soon as possible and the £1.5bn put back into paying for doctors and nurses?

Then there are the unforeseen consequences of C&B. For example, if you live near a popular hospital, you will probably find that all available appointment times are taken by people from outside the area. So, although you live near a good hospital, you will actually have to travel far from your home to a less popular hospital to get an appointment with an acceptable waiting time. Not much choosing and booking for you. Moreover, if you are elderly and on a limited pension or do not have a car, who is going to pay for your travel? Who is going to pay for your friends to travel to visit you? And are you going to want to travel when there is an adequate hospital near you? In addition, most reports say that C&B will only allow patients to book appointments up to twelve or thirteen weeks ahead. So, if a waiting list for a certain medical condition is over thirteen weeks at your local hospital, the system won't even allow you to make a booking at all. You will be forced to go elsewhere.

Additionally, a choose and book system can only work if there is available capacity in most of our hospitals. If you want to fly from London to Australia just before Christmas, you theoretically have a choice of airlines – BA, Qantas, Singapore Airlines and so on. But there is one problem – it's the holiday season and they are all sold out. So a theoretical choice of lots of airlines actually becomes no choice. In fact, if you are really intent on going, it's either spend thousands on first or business class or go via some circuitous route on a cheap airline. One will wreck your finances and the other will wreck your nerves. It is the same with choosing a hospital to treat you – if there is no room in the hospital, then you have no choice. In Germany, they have 920 hospital beds per 100,000 of the population, in France it is 834 and in Britain it is a less than impressive 413. Bed occupancy rates in Britain are among the highest in Europe at around 85 per cent. Waiting times in Britain are among the highest in Europe. Britain's hospitals are full. If you are ill, you are probably going to whichever hospital has room to take you and you will not, as the government imagines, spend your time delightedly skimming through glossy hospital brochures as you might with travel brochures when planning your dream holiday. Or else, if you can afford it, you will go private. C&B can only work in a well-funded health system with spare capacity – that is not the NHS under New Labour. C&B makes politicians look great on breakfast TV, but for most people, it will be an expensive mirage.

By the end of 2005, the C&B system was about a year behind schedule. Yet the government had set targets for how many people should be using C&B to make hospital appointments. What I understand is happening is that, rather than delay the imposition of targets till the IT system is ready, the NHS is having to set up a largely manual operation to enable GPs to offer the functions of C&B for an intervening period until the system is ready, so that GPs can reach the government's choose and book targets and the government can claim another 'success'. There is currently no information about how many millions this interim measure will cost.

As to why the system is delayed, that seems less clear. The

unsubstantiated information that I have been given suggests that the company producing C&B, Atos Origin, designed a system without properly understanding how GPs make appointments. In particular, I have been told, they failed to take account of the fact that appointments could not be made directly because all hospitals operate a triage system to prioritize the most urgent cases. So choosing and booking could not be done in the same way that you book an airline ticket – pilots are generally not allowed to decide who they want on their plane. My informant alleged that when this mistake was realized, major and expensive changes had to be made to the original design, hence some of the delays. This version of events is partially supported by one specialist medical publication that referred to C&B as 'an integrated airline-style online booking service'.[14] I have also been told that because of this misunderstanding, even when C&B is fully operational, there will still be a considerable amount of manual processing necessary. The chairman of the British Medical Association was reported as criticizing New Labour's Patient's Choice initiative and as 'dubbing Choose and Book a "fiasco" that takes no account of how GPs and hospitals work'.[15]

More evidence suggesting that the system's designers failed to understand the process they were meant to be automating comes from the first users: some surgeries found that every time they made a booking, data on their patients' records were being unexpectedly overwritten each time they received an electronic referral from the NHS spine. Hospitals were then having to manually re-enter deleted patient details. The highly respected Addenbrooke's Hospital also seemed to be struggling with the system: 'Addenbrooke's, one of the leading teaching trusts in the country, has been an enthusiastic early adopter of Choose and Book with the system now live in 39 specialities. But because of the problems with local data being automatically replaced with data from the spine, the trust now relies on paper as never before.'[16]

The satirical magazine *Private Eye* commented on C&B's apparent problems: 'Another outfit doing well out of the NHS's towering IT ambitions is Atos Origin, the company behind the

'Choose and Book' fiasco for GPs that cost £140m more than it should have done and is getting a fraction of the use intended for it. 'Choose and Book' was one of the early projects in the IT programme now run by the trendily named "Connecting for Health" NHS agency run by former Deloitte man Richard Granger. He has just appointed a new chief technology officer, Paul Jones, who joins straight from . . . Atos Origin.'[17]

One interesting aspect of C&B is that although CfH openly admit that the system is around a year late, there have been no reports of financially punitive measures against the suppliers, Atos Origin. So while poor old BT's feet are being 'held to the fire' for late delivery on their part of CfH and they have suffered a £4.5m fine or 'adjustment to payments', why does Atos Origin seem to be getting off scot free?

Electronic Transmission of Prescriptions (ETP)

With ETP, CfH seems to be on much safer ground. After all, 325 million prescriptions for over 650 million prescribed items is just the kind of process that IT systems were designed for. Massive numbers of repetitive actions are where IT systems really come into their own in reducing paperwork and the likelihood of human errors. This is truly IT system nirvana. The opportunities for making the prescription process faster and more accurate while cutting costs are immense. If ETP works, it will provide huge benefits in reducing prescribing errors, slashing paperwork, minimizing administration and improving accounting and control. ETP has apparently been successfully piloted, is now being fully tested and will be rolled out across the country when the system is found to be robust.

So all is well. Possibly. However, the unsubstantiated rumours I am hearing from within CfH paint a slightly different picture. Firstly, it appears that ETP systems already function successfully in other countries. So it should not have been too onerous or costly to have adapted one of these for the NHS. Moreover, I have been told that prior to CfH a fully working pilot version of ETP had been built in Britain. However, as this was from a small cottage industry supplier, it was scrapped and one of the big industry strength vendors was paid to reinvent what had already existed both in other countries and in the UK. Unfortunately, this new version had problems with developing what is called the 'electronic signature' – basically the PIN identification process to only allow authorized users to write prescriptions. Moreover, by the end of 2005 very few pharmacies were connected to the system. So in the first version of ETP that will be rolled out, GPs will automatically send the prescriptions through to the Spine, but the Spine will not communicate these back to the pharmacists. So patients will still have to take their paper prescriptions to pharmacies as they have done for at least the last hundred years. It is hoped that by the time the second version of ETP is implemented, the digital signature problem will be solved and more pharmacies will be connected to the network. Then we will see the undoubted potential benefits of this system. (Though it will probably have cost many times more than it should have if an existing, already functioning system had been adapted rather than a new one built.)

At the end of 2005, it was reported that the Department of Health were exploiting the obvious usefulness of the ETP system to try and force GPs to take the largely useless and unnecessary C&B system. An NHS insider wrote, 'while ETP was generally welcomed by GPs, many have proved less keen on Choose and Book. To drive wider adoption the Department of Health has come up with the ruse of sugaring the Choose and Book pill. In order to get the software for ETP, practices will have to order an integrated Choose and Book upgrade, which will then come with the electronic prescribing software bundled in.'[18] Such desperate coercive measures suggest that CfH is drowning in its own arrogance and incompetence. Incidentally, this practice of forcing systems users to take unwanted software by bundling it with wanted applications has been found by the courts to be anti-competitive and illegal. But when the New Labour government is frantically attempting to prove that its modernization of public services is a stunning success, it seems that any tactic is worth trying.

New National Network (N3)

There are high ambitions for N3. It will 'link all NHS organizations in England enabling reliable and secure exchange of
data', it will 'satisfy the current and future requirements of the
NHS', it will be a 'complete and seamless network' and it will
also save the NHS 'an estimated £900m over seven years,
relative to previous NHSnet contracts'. Anyone who has ever
worked with large IT systems will have often heard the
promises of being 'seamless', 'satisfying future needs', making
huge 'savings' and providing 'reliable secure exchange of data'.
Just the use of these words should probably set the alarm bells
ringing. However, until we see this beast in action, it's difficult
to say whether it will live up to the hyperbole. Too often, in the
public sector, the hardware and communications are config-
ured for the original versions of the systems they are intended
to support. But in development, those systems become more
complex, more data must be stored than forecast, there are
more security routines necessary and the volumes of information to be communicated have expanded exponentially. So
when the final working versions of the systems are rolled out, it
is found to everybody's surprise that the hardware and communications networks are under-dimensioned. This usually
leads to system response times that are prehistorically slow
and frequent network crashes as the whole caboodle becomes
overloaded. This normally means party time at the network
suppliers as only a healthy injection of extra cash and a
panicked rush to buy more boxes and wires can then solve
this new 'unexpected' yet predictable problem. Yet the devel-
opers should have identified the problem long before it happened. Will N3 suffer the same fate? Only time will tell, but the
current problems with the network do not bode well for the
future.

However, the main issue with N3 really concerns whether
there should be a thick or thin spine for the electronic patient
records. If the decision to go for a thick spine is taken, then a
monstrous N3 network is necessary. If, as I believe, CfH
should have chosen a thin spine and used more distributed

databases with web connections, then we may be buying a jumbo jet when we only really needed a two-seater turbo prop. Jumbo jets are much more fun to buy, especially when someone else is paying, but they do tend to be more expensive than two-seaters and when they crash they make an awfully costly mess.

Picture Archiving and Communication Systems (PACS)

Like electronic patient records and electronic prescriptions, PACS should be a major advance – moving away from unwieldy film-based processes to a modern digitally enabled way of working. Like ETP, this is using IT systems for what they are good at – the storing, transmission and retrieval of massive quantities of data. When it works, it should bring huge benefits – improved image quality, no time wasted looking for lost images, 24/7 availability and a massive reduction in administration. The only concerns with PACS are the same as for EPRs – should the electronic pictures be held as part of a patient medical record on just one central database, the thick spine, or should they be held as part of the EPRs more locally on distributed databases? If the spine is always functioning with rapid response times, accurate data and no access problems, the thick spine might work. But if there are constant network problems, data is less than current, there are interminable difficulties with access and helpdesks never bother to respond because they are overwhelmed with calls, then hospitals will find they are having to make local back-up copies of all their patients' medical records and hundreds of millions will be clawed out of front-line patient care just to give clinicians access to the data that the thick spine predictably fails to provide. I believe that the distributed database option for PACS would have been the correct decision.

Quality and Outcomes Framework (QOF)

Here we are once again on computer cloud nine. Crunching numbers, running accounting systems and producing masses of data are what computers are best at. When the QOF is up and running, we should see a reduction in NHS administration costs of hundreds of millions of pounds a year that can be put back into front-line patient care; at the same time, a plethora of new and valuable information will become available. Managing the NHS will never have been easier than it will be after QOF is alive and kicking. However, past experiences could lead one to suspect that, rather than reducing administration and management, QOF will be used to justify administration costs rising even further as NHS managers get a new toy to play with and a new excuse to set up even more unnecessary administrative departments.

Summary: the New Millennium Dome

Unfortunately, CfH is an ungainly mixture of potentially useful new services and empty political gestures. EPRs, ETP and QOF are major advances in how the NHS functions today and should result in greatly improved clinical care coupled with a radical reduction in administration costs. However, C&B is more or less just poorly thought-through political hot air that is proving to be an expensive distraction from the worthy parts of CfH. As a GP, one of the target group for the new C&B system, wrote: 'In any case, I am sceptical that the system will ever work properly. After years of upheaval in the NHS, we don't need more clever initiatives thought out by think-tanks insulated from the day-to-day trials and tribulations of using the NHS. We need to get the basics right.'[19]

With 'patient choice' being provided by C&B, New Labour and its consultants have largely misdiagnosed the problems facing the NHS and so come up with a headline-grabbing, admirably expensive but erroneous solution. But despite all the evidence of the worthlessness of C&B, the government will not backtrack as this would mean admitting a mistake and losing face. So C&B will be implemented and will result in over £1.5bn being taken from patient care to pay for a piece of political grandstanding dreamt up by New Labour and its consultants, all of whom, of course, have private medical insurance and so probably hardly even know what the initials 'NHS' stand for.

As for the parts of CfH that have real value, the decision to impose central control through using a thick spine rather than using distributed databases is, in my view, a costly mistake we will all come to regret. Just one of many indications that we are building an over-complex monster can be seen in the fact that just one small upgrade required three million manhours of work – and there are many more upgrades to come.[20] Eventually, exploding costs, endless network problems, lack of data ownership, inadequate data accuracy, slow response times, access problems and helpdesk failures will cause clinicians and health workers to lose confidence in the system and probably lead to unofficial local copies of medical information being clandestinely set up as a fall-back, thus largely negating the supposed benefits of the original thick spine decision. Towards the end of 2005, on C&B, for example, following the 'upgrade' of their systems to accept C&B referrals, we were already seeing hospitals having to make overnight back-ups of their own data to use as their reference to re-enter data after the C&B system deleted and altered key information on their patient records. While the CfH *nomenklatura* proudly display figures proving increasing take-up of their systems, on the ground we will increasingly see people introducing cumbersome, expensive, time-consuming manual and IT systems work-arounds as they try to cope with the unforeseen side-effects of appallingly bad, centrally designed CfH systems.

But perhaps the worst aspect of CfH may not be in the way the various systems, some useful, some a waste of time, are being developed. It may not even be in the massively costly reinvention of a square wheel – although the costs of this reinvention will cripple patient services for many years. The really dangerous side to CfH for patient care in the NHS is the insidious, government-sponsored creation of four IT systems monopoly suppliers and the obliteration of competition. There is already evidence that this is leading to profiteering on a massive scale as health authorities are forced to divert cash to pay for possibly inappropriate system replacements at IT systems consultant charge-out rates that are more than adequately profitable. This practice is likely to get much worse as the four companies involved realize that there are no limits on their predatory behaviour. The PAC has warned us on countless occasions about the dangers of becoming captive customers to monopolistic suppliers. It is sad that these warnings are repeatedly ignored.

By the end of 2005, the NHS was facing a deficit of £630m, three-quarters of hospitals were in the red, three-quarters of NHS trusts were denying patients recommended medical treatments as they tried to cut costs, many trusts were cutting services, beds were being reduced, over 20 per cent of trusts were making redundancies and many more were not filling vacant positions. As many as 1,700 of 2,200 university graduates in physiotherapy were unable to get jobs despite the NHS having paid £25,000 for each graduate's three year course. ('It's a crazy situation when you think that the health services have already paid £30m to £40m to see these people through university and can't now afford to employ them,' the chair of the Chartered Society of Physiotherapists said.[21]) Around 2,000 newly qualified doctors were unable to get jobs as there were insufficient hospital places for them to complete their training.[22] Yet over £200m had been squandered on a largely worthless C&B system, billions more were being thrown at IT suppliers to provide a hugely expensive, illogical and over-dimensioned IT infrastructure and many millions more were being siphoned off by the four LSP monopolies.

Eventually, we will get systems that more or less work and most will be useful. But the costs and disruption will be massively in excess of what they should have been. New Labour are in the process of building a multi-billion pound electronic Millennium Dome for the NHS at the expense of the health service's employees and patients. This will waste at least £15bn and probably nearer £25bn that could have been spent on front-line services and this will have a disastrous effect on the availability and quality of medical care in this country for many years to come.

CHAPTER 12

The Unholy Trinity

New Labour took office promising a fresh start for Britain. With the apparently 'honest bloke' Blair leading the country, the supposedly prudent Gordon Brown at the Treasury and a new generation of MPs, we seemed to have a winning team in place. Add to that fresh new ideas about the importance of public services and a strong flow of tax revenue from an improving economy and you had all the elements of a bright new dawn for the country. And yet it has all gone horribly wrong. Instead of improving public services as part of an enlightened social democratic vision, New Labour have allowed them to be desecrated by profit-seeking private-sector companies to an extent that even the most rabid Tory free-marketeers would not have imagined possible. As we shall see, even America, the hotbed of capitalism, has not permitted the plundering of public services that we are experiencing in Britain. And what has happened so far is small beer in comparison to what is to come.

This disaster is not the result of some kind of conspiracy. The driving force for the modernization of public services was probably a genuine desire by New Labour to make an historic change for the better. And yet as our taxes rise and our public services are depleted, New Labour have managed to produce the exact opposite of what they intended. Behind closed doors, New Labour politicians are probably as uncomprehending and disappointed at what has happened as anyone else. But so much money has now been wasted and so many reputations are on the line, that there can be no turning back. In fact there cannot even be a pause for reflection. So New Labour have apparently decided to brave it out by squandering billions more in an ultimately futile attempt to justify a programme that has been hijacked by New Labour's consulting 'friends' and is already thoroughly discredited in the eyes of everyone except its proponents and those who are growing rich from its continuation.

There seem to be three main companies of actors in the farce or tragedy that is being played out in the British public sector – the politicians, the civil servants and the consultants. Before moving on to proposing how we can salvage something from the wreckage of New Labour's failures, I would like to review the role of each of these in the unfolding drama.

The Politicians

Swimming lessons from the Great White
When they came to power in 1997, New Labour were rightly suspicious of the naturally conservative inclinations of the Civil Service. Under Wilson and Callaghan, Labour governments had met constant resistance from civil servants to their reforming efforts. But in replacing civil servants by consultants in the making and implementing of policy, New Labour have failed to understand that they were merely exchanging one set of vested interests for another. While civil servants may well have been a force for excessive inertia, the cash-hungry consultancies' need for money has been a powerful force for excessive, unnecessary and expensive change and for the development of ludicrously over-dimensioned and extraordinarily badly planned IT systems.

For many years, it has been fashionable and to a certain extent justifiable to laugh at the inertia of the Sir Humphreys in the senior ranks of the Civil Service. But at least their inertia provided some sort of control on government policy and meant that most policy had to go through a fairly rigorous examination before it moved from idea to implementation. By removing civil servants from the policy-making process and replacing them with self-serving consultants, New Labour not only took away some checks and balances, but also put policy-making into the hands of companies whose only agenda was to sell whatever services they could for as much as they could get. The consultancies encouraged New Labour to implement massive change, because that is what makes money for consultancies. Consultants do not make money if clients decide things are pretty much OK as they are.

Perhaps the fatal mistake that New Labour made when talking to consultants was to assume they were talking to experts in finance, organizational effectiveness, IT systems, performance management, internal markets and so on. They were not talking to experts, they were talking to people with warm bodies to sell. Consultants are not professionals like doctors. They are not people with an interest in proffering impartial advice based on years of study and work experience. They are not trying to make you healthy. They are salespeople with sales targets to meet and bonuses to be earned. They are trying to make themselves rich. When you meet with consultants, of course they will try to give you valuable advice, but they will always give that advice within the context of convincing you to buy something from them. When I sold consultancy, in any month I could be in Britain acting as an expert in IT systems implementation, in Norway as an expert in oil-rig construction, in France as an expert in theme-park management and then back to Britain as an expert in hospital management. I never lied to my clients, but the advice that my colleagues and I gave was always and only a means to obtaining large consulting and IT systems projects so that we could meet our sales targets and earn promotions and bonuses. When talking to a House of Lords committee about the modernization of the NHS, the head of the NHS stressed that they had used outside experts to advise them: 'the current programme to develop IT in the NHS stems from a seminar in Number 10 in February 2002, at which two of the major suppliers had representatives present to give us technical advice and specialist advice.'[1] Yet asking a consultant if you should change your organization structure or put in a new computer system is like asking a hungry Great White shark whether the water is warm and you should go in for a swim. Yes, the Great White will be an expert on water temperature having spent all its life in water, just as consultants are experts in their trade. However, the Great White's motives in encouraging you to take the plunge will revolve more around it obtaining its next dinner and less around it providing you with a great swimming experience. It may come as a surprise to the great and noble minds who assembled at No.10 in February 2002, but while the politicians and civil servants may have thought they were getting impartial 'technical and specialist advice', the consultants present would have been primarily focused on lining up their next meal – and, for the consultants, the bigger the meal the better.

Headlines not policies – from the Islington set
As the New Labour project progressed and as hundreds of millions disappeared into the consultancies' pockets, the government found that it was much harder than it imagined to actually get the results that all the management consultancy and huge new IT systems should have delivered. Much of the management consultancy turned out to be worthless and ended up, as it had at the BBC, in reduced services being delivered with hugely increased administration costs. Most of the IT systems were badly designed and poorly implemented, and those which were not scrapped after hundreds of millions had been wasted ended up increasing the costs of government departments while seldom improving service levels. That left New Labour in a quandary. They could either eat humble pie by admitting that all was not well and rethinking their plans, or they could try and spin their way out of the mess. Under pressure due to lack of progress and incapable of losing face, New Labour started manipulating the numbers to produce supposed 'good news' as it found that creating the impression of progress in the delivery of public services was easier, faster

and more enticing than the much more difficult and longer process of making real changes. It also fiercely stonewalled any questions about how much money was going to consultants by claiming either that this was 'commercially confidential' or that it would cost too much to collect the figures. Once New Labour and their consultants started blatantly lying and falsifying figures to prove that their failing policies were actually working, there was really no turning back. The more that was spent, the larger the lies became. However, as the millions wasted became hundreds of millions and the hundreds of millions became billions, still with paltry results, lies were no longer enough to put a favourable gloss on the unfolding catastrophe. More drastic measures were required. So we started seeing cases like that of the NHS – at the same time as the Health Secretary refused to provide additional funds to help hospitals with deficits from having to cut staff, close wards and treat fewer patients, the Department of Health found £95m to pay cash bonuses to any primary care trust that would use, or even just say it was using, the largely worthless new *Choose and Book* system.

Much has already been written about New Labour's use of spin to portray its version of a situation as reality, whatever the real facts. The importance of this preference for superficial image over meaningful action is that probably more than at any other time in British history, we have a government that does not seem to understand or want to understand the difference between a headline and a policy. 'Patient Choice' is a good example of the destructive effect of running a country by newspaper headlines rather than considered policies. First we had the catchy headline dreamt up by New Labour and its consultants. Like so many New Labour initiatives, 'Patient Choice' sounded a reasonable proposition to those who lived in million-pound houses in Islington, had friends with villas in Chiantishire and, with their private health insurance, assumed that ordinary people chose and booked beds in hospitals on the basis of the Michelin guide to the quality of catering provided by the hospital restaurant. Once the catchy headline had appeared in the press, the bandwagon started rolling. No

meaningful analysis was done. If it had been, those responsible
would have found to their discomfort that all the British public
wanted were clean hospitals, shorter waiting lists and the drugs
they needed to save their lives. Being able to choose a hospital
that was miles away from their homes never figured on most
people's list of priorities for the NHS. So first we had the
headline, then someone with no practical experience of real life
in the NHS had to explain what it meant. Soon it became a
huge multi-million pound computer system project and, after
£200m has been spent, all we have is confusion and disruption
as civil servants and their consultants try to achieve something
that sounded great in the media but was never wanted or
necessary in the first place. It has also been a massive distraction from the real job of getting more essential IT systems up
and running in the NHS.

A similar misunderstanding of the realities of life by the
Islington set seems to have been one of the causes of the Inland
Revenue's tax credits disaster. The logic behind tax credits is
based on how rich people pay their taxes – if they earn less than
expected in a year and so pay too much tax, they get a rebate; if
they earn more than expected and so have paid too little, then
they get a tax demand for more. But there is one small crucial
difference between the rich and the poor people at whom tax
credits were targeted. Rich people have spare money, poor
people don't. So if the Inland Revenue gave a tax credit of a few
hundred or even a thousand pounds to a family on the bread-
line, this family would not put it into a high interest savings
account, as rich people might. The family would probably
spend the money on trying to survive. So when, at the end of
the year, the Inland Revenue hit a poor family with a tax
demand, either because the Revenue had got its sums wrong or
because that family had managed to earn a few pounds more
during the year than had been expected based on their previous
year's income, most of the people concerned simply didn't have
the cash to pay the tax demand. Many were forced to take
extreme measures to meet the Revenue's demands for payment. Had the idea been properly thought through rather than
being hastily launched as a wonderful New Labour initiative

with a big advertising campaign, the obvious illogicality of the whole process might have been spotted.

Civil Servants – Taking Candy from a Baby

Heavily influenced by its consultants, the government decreed that the way forward for the 'modernization' of public services was through following a free market dogma of introducing 'competition' and through what were called 'the benefits of technology' – implementing massive IT systems. New Labour made it clear that the only way to cut bureaucracy and become 'customer-focused' was to learn the skills that private-sector managers supposedly had. A partner from Ernst & Young summed up the new philosophy: 'the public sector must have access to the skills needed to perform successfully in this more competitive regime: skills more commonly found in the private sector than in public service.'[2] Moreover, New Labour made it clear that it would not accept dissent from the 'vested interests' within the Civil Service, the NHS, schools, the police, fire services and so on. Under pressure to fall into line and quite out of their depth with the massive scale of the changes being proposed, civil servants made easy targets for the consultants.

There are many different ways of buying consulting and IT systems. Expert buyers would carefully assess different suppliers, would structure exactly what they need and might tend to use specialists who had already shown capability in relevant areas. Above all, they would have the confidence to take responsibility for the deal and the outcomes. An inexperienced buyer, on the other hand, might try to pass over the whole project to just one big supplier in the hope of getting a 'turnkey' solution – all the buyer needs to do is turn the key and the system would deliver the results. Experienced buyers create and benefit from competition, innovation and lower prices; inexperienced buyers reduce competition by handing the keys of the castle over to just a few big operators. Reduced competition means less innovation and higher prices.

Almost invariably, civil servants took the inexperienced

buyer approach. They did not understand the law around buying consultancy services, they did not know how to structure contracts, they did not have the capability to seek out smaller specialist suppliers with already functioning solutions and they did not know how to manage large projects. In an effort to avoid all responsibility, they tended to hand over their major projects to just a few massive suppliers and they became captive customers subject to ever rising prices from the day they signed the contract with their consultants. Around 85 per cent of all IT work for the Department for Work and Pensions goes to just one supplier, EDS. So badly managed was the procurement of work from this supplier that a spending review found that £900m of taxpayers' money could be saved just by 'realigning' the contract with EDS.[3] Overall, just eleven large IT systems companies receive more than 80 per cent of all government systems work. And on the biggest project of them all, *Connecting for Health*, the programme board have knowingly created just four monopoly IT systems suppliers each with their own reserved area of the country – one supplier even has two areas. So systems are reinvented from scratch, while specialist healthcare IT systems providers with already proven products are barred from selling to the NHS and told that, if they want to stay in business, they should sell their products abroad. The government has repeatedly claimed that it is trying to push more work to medium-sized companies. In fact, they have done the opposite – the way civil servants have bought consulting services has provided a truly incredible financial bonanza for just a few massive companies at the expense of smaller providers and of the taxpayer. We don't have competition – we have just a few robber barons sharing the spoils among them and not even allowing the scraps to be distributed among the others. Had civil servants been capable buyers, most of the work they bought could probably have been obtained for well under half the price actually paid and many more of the systems would have worked. The systems would have been based on adapting existing working technology from specialist suppliers, rather than on paying a small number of generalists with massive armies of code-monkeys to try lucratively, incompetently and unsuccessfully to rebuild what already existed.

Consultants – the Perfect Predator

The Rise of the predator

From the 1960s till around 2000, management and IT systems consultancy experienced extraordinary growth year after year. In some years growth rates were as high as 30 per cent. Perhaps the most lucrative period in consulting was the 1990s. In addition to all the normal stuff we consultants do for clients – downsizing, restructuring, mergers and acquisitions, reorganizations, improving product development, implementing IT systems and so on – we were given a whole host of new things to sell, thanks to the outpourings of a string of management gurus, many of whom had probably never run a real organization in their lives. These were the golden years of management fashions, fads and quick fixes. The tendency for organizations to leap at the latest instant solution from self-proclaimed gurus eager to make a name for themselves became widespread. In fact, this was such common practice among management that one respected author, an ex-McKinsey consultant, wrote a book called *Fad Surfing in the Boardroom: reclaiming the courage to manage in the age of instant answers* attacking this trend. Criticizing managers for jumping from one fad to the other without looking for the fundamental causes of their problems, the author was brutally clear in her criticism of both management and their pet consultants when she defined Fad Surfing as 'the practice of riding the crest of the latest management wave and then paddling out again just in time to ride the next one; always absorbing for managers and lucrative for consultants; frequently disastrous for organizations'.[4] The biggest fad was called Business Process Re-engineering (BPR), which created billions of dollars', euros' and pounds' worth of work for consultants. The author of *Fad Surfing* called BPR 'The Consultants' Full Employment Act'.

BPR made billions for consultancies. The global head of consulting at Capgemini neatly summed up how easy it was to sell consulting at this time: 'During the 1990s, you could win good consulting engagements without much effort . . . you could be credible just by reading the right magazines.'[5]

The predator goes hungry
The bursting of the technology bubble, subsequent stock market crash and quasi-recession hit consulting badly. There were suddenly major changes in the consulting business. In the words of one commentator, 'the game is up for the old model because clients can't afford it any more. The days are gone when a client could afford to bring in his golfing chum, outline a problem and then wait for it to be solved at any cost.'[6] Several well-known consultancies went to the wall.

Around this time (2002–4), many consultancies went through difficult times and many also shed staff – in eighteen months, for example, one consultancy fired over ten thousand people. Some idea of the pressure consultancies felt can be seen in the levels of fees they were able to charge their clients. Average fees for a consultant in Britain were £326,000 per annum in 2002. In 2003 they fell about 30 per cent to around £230,000. Then in 2004 they fell about another 10 per cent to £207,000. With their profits and bonuses threatened, consultancy partners focused on what interested them most – themselves. The reaction to this fall in fees seems to have been for consultancy partners to look after their own pockets at the expense of their staff. They did this in two ways – by firing about half their non-fee-earning staff and by reducing the number of consultants allowed to advance to partner level. As the Management Consultancies Association reported, 'an axe has clearly been taken to administrative/non fee-earning costs' and 'partners now share the spoils with a smaller circle of partners offsetting any decline in their earnings brought about by falling margins.'[7] Not much place for loyalty and solidarity here.

However, although consultancy publications talked about 'tough' market conditions, moving from being able to sell a consultant's time in 2002 at eight times what you paid to the 2004 level of around five times would not be seen by most other commercial companies as extreme hardship. Yet for consultants, just making a fortune rather than a mega fortune seemed like a life-threatening crisis and some wondered whether the good times would ever come back. One consultant said, 'when the phones stopped ringing in 2001, I suddenly had a nightmare that they might never start again, that clients might just stop using consultants.'

Feeding time again
As their business declined, the consultants looked around hungrily for sustenance. However, the consultants need not have worried – a new and apparently inexhaustible food source was becoming available. New Labour was opening up the British public sector to any consultancies looking for a meal. In 2004, for example, consulting in the public sector rose 46 per cent. The turnaround in the British consulting market was extraordinary. After preaching doom and gloom, the headlines in consulting magazines suddenly started talking about the glut of work that was being thrown consultancies' way. Headlines in 2005 like 'Buoyancy confirmed – consulting market on a roll',[8] 'Consultancy fees have risen to their highest ever'[9] and 'Consultants toast feast of work from Whitehall'[10] were typical proof that in New Labour's third term business was better than it ever had been before. The problem for consultancies now was to find sufficient warm bodies to put on all their new public-sector projects. 'No shortage of new consulting assignments on the horizon within the UK public sector – but perhaps an acute shortage of consultants,' one journal wrote.[11] Another warned, 'IT skills shortage due to bite next year'.[12]

Quickly the consultancies assembled whoever they could find and pushed hordes of consultants with no experience at all of public-sector work on to projects for British government departments. So great was the consulting feeding frenzy in Britain that some consultancies couldn't even find sufficient people in this country and so had to fly large numbers in from their businesses in other European countries. But pulling in whoever they could find and putting them on public sector projects was not necessarily going to be without its problems. One specialist consultants' recruitment company explained the problem: 'The public sector has always insisted on using consulting firms that have worked in the area before. While this policy remains unchanged, the recent explosion of government consultancy projects means demand for consultants with public-sector experience now significantly outstrips supply. Consultants who have only ever worked for private companies are now reforming the Civil Service and the NHS. They are untouched by the public-sector culture and, compared to those traditionally involved, are inclined to take a much more commercial and often radical approach to introducing new processes, management structures and ways of working. Whether this will lead to rapid gains in efficiency and service quality or increased internal resistance to change remains to be seen.'[13]

Nevertheless, in the last few years British consultants have prospered as never before. In 2005 KPMG handed out £59m in bonuses to its British staff – nearly twice the level of the previous year. Likewise, Accenture posted record revenues and profits, E&Y achieved double-digit growth and Deloitte saw staff pay rising 11 per cent due to shortages and became one of the largest recruiters of graduates in the UK.

The Land of Missed Opportunity

With New Labour, we unknowingly voted in a government that was totally under the spell of its consulting friends. New Labour swallowed hook, line and sinker the new mantra that British public services were huge bloated bureaucracies that could only be modernized through competition, private-sector management and massive investment in IT systems. Moreover, the government, like most jargon-spouting managers today, had a natural inclination to prefer the easy option of presenting the image of progress rather than the harder task of actually effecting lasting change. This led to a series of headline-grabbing initiatives that were passed on to docile civil servants for implementation. Out of their depth and largely under the control of a few powerful consultancies, civil servants failed to exercise proper buying and project management, preferring instead to hand all responsibility over to just a few massive consultancies with a vested interest in ensuring that their projects were as large and as profitable as possible. Smaller suppliers with relevant products were excluded from the feast and eleven large suppliers made billions from building what was unnecessary or re-building what already existed.

Perhaps the saddest aspect of this whole sorry story is that it didn't need to be like this. The management and IT systems consultants have managed to play the oldest trick in the book on New Labour. When a management consultancy goes into a new client, they can propose to get results either by improving the way the client currently works or by fundamentally changing the whole way a client's organization is structured and operates. Projects to improve existing work processes are usually both small and difficult. However, massive organizational changes will probably mean a much larger project for the consultant. There is no perfect organizational form. This is something that clients seem not to understand. So the easiest thing to do as a consultant is to point out the weaknesses of a client's current structure and to promise that tremendous results will inevitably follow from doing the opposite of what the client is currently doing. If a client runs a highly centralized operation, you can justifiably claim that they are inflexible, unable to react to market changes or customer needs and are not developing their people's entrepreneurial skills. So decentralizing to become more adaptive, more entrepreneurial, more responsive can sound very appealing to top executives who should know better. Conversely, if an organization is highly decentralized, you can usually convince a client of the benefits of greater centralization – reducing duplication, spreading 'best practices', presenting a consistent image to the outside world and so on. In the case of New Labour, the story put about by the consultants was effortlessly simple – the old-fashioned public sector was heavy, bureaucratic, sclerotic and therefore wasteful. So the answer had to be the opposite – competition, free markets, targets and therefore efficiency.

Similarly, when an IT consultancy is asked for advice on what kind of system a client should use, they can either propose the low-cost tactical solution of upgrading something that already exists or they can try to convince the client that a whole new expensive system must be built. Naturally, new and different (and expensive) is always 'better' than just improving what is in place. Moreover, IT suppliers will always prefer hugely inflexible and costly 'big bang' developments rather than much more flexible and cheaper iterative prototyping.

As is the case with most client organizations, what really needed to be changed in departments like the NHS was actually not that complicated. Moreover, many of the necessary IT systems could have been realized either by adapting existing technology or by being built in a much more economical way. Real change could have been achieved by working with the public services rather than treating them as enemies to be defeated. When the history of the New Labour era is written, the overriding sense will be one of lost opportunities as a potentially constructive reform process was handed over to the consultancies to serve their purely commercial interests.

CHAPTER 13

What Do We Do Now?

Lessons from America

Although New Labour seem awfully keen to follow America's lead in foreign policy, they have been less assiduous in learning from the US government's experiences in how to manage big public-sector consulting and IT systems programmes. I have tried to document the way in which New Labour and its consultants seem disinclined to learn anything from the long series of consulting and IT catastrophes in Britain and to suggest that this refusal to pause and reflect could have horrendously expensive and disruptive consequences with the *Connecting for Health* programme. What is worse than New Labour's refusal ever to admit and learn from its mistakes, is that it has also abjectly failed to learn from the mistakes of others. In the 1970s and 1980s the US government experienced a similar series of hugely over-ambitious, poorly planned and abominably implemented public-sector consulting and IT systems programmes. Just as we are seeing in Britain, catastrophe followed catastrophe as the consultants became vastly wealthy in spite of (or maybe because of) their failure to deliver. The unscrupulous greed of some consultancies was so excessive that Congress realized so-called 'self-regulation' and 'codes of best practice' were laughably ineffective. Only the law could protect public funds from the consultancies' feeding frenzy. This led to an important piece of legislation being passed by the US lawmakers: the Information Technology Reform Act.

This Act is more commonly known as the Clinger–Cohen Act of 1996. The backers of the Act were two Republicans, senators William Clinger and William Cohen. The Republicans are not normally the party one would expect to be out to control the excesses of big business; indeed the fact that even the usually business-friendly Republicans felt the need to take action to curb the consultancies' greed shows how serious the issue of the plundering of US public-sector funds by consultancies had become. As one commentator wrote, 'The Act sought to remedy mounting deficiencies in the federal IT world. These included systems overruns, poor accountability and a notorious lack of attention to the business processes that should be the basis for IT investments.' These words might sound horribly familiar to anyone who has watched the unfolding farce in the British public sector. The commentator went on: 'When President Clinton signed the legislation on February 10 1996, the signal was sent that the Wild West days of federal IT were over.'[1]

The Act changed the way IT systems were bought and implemented in the US public sector, forcing departments to take responsibility for and report to Congress on the results achieved. It was hailed as 'a triumph of bipartisanship'. So much money had been siphoned off by the consultancies for so many years for so few results that the politicians understood they could no longer allow IT systems to be used as narrow party political weapons – major issues of public interest were at stake. Since the passing of the Act, the performance of IT systems consultancies in the US has been judged to have radically improved and government expenditure on IT has begun to fall.

In Britain, on the other hand, we have voluntary codes of practice and committees. The Management Consultancies Association (MCA) and Institute of Management Consultancy (IMC) have worked with the Office of Government Commerce (OGC) to draw up a so-called 'Statement of Best Practice' – a document that fails to mention the legal obligations of consultants to deliver what they have promised. The OGC has also been working with Intellect, an IT industry body, to produce guidelines and best practice advice. Again, there is no reference to the legal duties of IT suppliers. And we have an e-Government Unit and a Chief Information Officer Committee. But we have no legislation to help control the profiteering and fraud that was once so rife in the US and is now damaging our public services.

The Clinger–Cohen Act was specifically aimed at improving the value the US government gets from its IT. There is one other feature of US law that can also be used to control the behaviour of consultancies working for government. The False Claims Act, a Civil War-era law rejuvenated by Congress in 1986, was not specifically aimed at consultancies. In fact, recently the main offenders have been drugs companies and medical care providers. But the Act has also helped expose activities by the US divisions of such British government suppliers as Ernst & Young, PwC and Oracle. In particular, it was used to expose the travel expense rebate fraud practised by many consultancies and led to PwC repaying $41.9m to the US government in 2005. While the Act only leads to the recovery of about $1.4bn a year from suppliers, it is generally accepted that it dissuades companies from trying to defraud the US government of many hundreds of billions more. A great strength of the Act is that it contains *qui tam*, or whistleblower, provisions. 'This is a mechanism that allows citizens with evidence of fraud against government contracts and programmes to sue, on behalf of the Government, in order to recover the stolen funds. In compensation for the risk and effort of filing a *qui tam* case, the citizen whistleblower or "relator" may be awarded a portion of the funds recovered, typically between 15 and 25 percent.'[2] An ex-partner from PwC was reportedly in line for an award of up to $10m for filing a *qui tam* against PwC over travel expense rebate retention.[3] Clearly, the *qui tam* provision is a pretty powerful incentive for companies to be careful about how they extract money from government as, if they stray too far from the path of righteousness, they run the risk of either an honest or a disgruntled employee filing a *qui tam* and earning millions in the process. As two US senators noted when reviewing the positive results of the Act: 'Studies estimate the fraud deterred thus far by the *qui tam* provisions runs into the hundreds of billions of dollars. Instead of encouraging or rewarding a culture of deceit, corporations now spend substantial sums on sophisticated and meaningful compliance programmes.'[4]

In the UK we do theoretically have a 'whistleblower act'. However, a person revealing any alleged misdeeds has to take enormous personal risk. Naturally, in the UK we have nothing like the *qui tam* provision of the False Claims Act that rewards people who act in the public interest, so there is little to no disincentive for consultancies to take the New Labour government for every penny they can get.

What We Should Do but Won't

Across All of Government

Under New Labour, the whole process of democratic accountability has broken down and been replaced by cronyism, profiteering, spin and outright lies. If we are to save our public services, we must act to restore some semblance of democratic accountability. There are many measures that should be implemented in Britain to try and control the rapacious plundering of public funds by the consultancies. Unfortunately, none of these measures will happen because we have a government that is determined to protect its own reputation for infallibility, in which only it still believes. The fact that this means New Labour have put the interests of profit-maximizing consultancies above the interests of those who pay taxes and use public services is, after the Iraq War, the greatest betrayal of the electorate that had once had such high hopes of the Blair and Brown administration.

On the legal front, New Labour could take a lead from the US and pass two pieces of legislation. It could admit the need to treat the £70bn plus being given to consultants as a cross-party issue of public interest and could propose a law similar to the

Clinger–Cohen Act. Additionally, if the government passed a False Claims Act with a *qui tam* provision, as they have in the US, this would probably result in a flood of actions from consultants angry at the morally unacceptable practices of their employers and would lead to the almost immediate recovery of many hundreds of millions and probably billions of pounds. This money could then be more usefully invested in front-line services than in consultancy partners' offshore bank accounts and holiday homes abroad.

In the area of public administration, we need a new Chancellor of the Exchequer – one who actually believes the Treasury exists to safeguard value for money for the taxpayer. The government could then pass legislation making the finance directors in government departments responsible directly to a reinvigorated Treasury rather than have them reporting to their bosses, the department heads (accounting officers). In this way, department heads would know that it might be more difficult to cover up their own spending misdemeanours. The Treasury should accept that they have a duty of 'care and attention' to manage value for money for taxpayers' funds and should by law be automatically informed of any management or IT systems consulting projects costing more than, say, £1m. Moreover, the Treasury should receive monthly progress reports from all such projects and have the power to intervene if any project appears to be falling behind schedule or delivering less than was promised. In addition, the Treasury should have a legal obligation to enforce taxpayers' legal rights that consultancies receiving public money deliver according to their contractual obligations. Any consultancy failing to deliver what it has contracted to provide should be sued by the Treasury. Additionally, a windfall tax on the main consultancies and PFI/PPP companies could get back just a few of the many tens of billions they are draining from the taxpayer.

As for the Office of Government Commerce, we preferably should at least change the management of – or just abolish – the OGC as it seems to have become an ineffectual, self-serving bureaucracy that has aligned itself too closely with the consultancies and has failed to represent the best interests of the taxpayer. If the OGC were abolished tomorrow, I doubt anybody in Britain would either notice or suffer from its disappearance and this would release at least £30m that could go back into front-line public services.

The Public Accounts Committee should be put on prime time TV so that senior civil servants can earn their keep as comic entertainers of the highest order. Or, if the PAC is to become effective, we need to radically strengthen its powers. For example, it should be able to instruct the NAO as to which areas of government it wishes to see investigated instead of having to wait in vain (often for years) as the NAO deftly avoids any contentious issues until it is too late for meaningful action to be taken. There should be no requirement for the NAO to agree to details of its audits with the departments being audited. This might make them start to look more like real audits rather than 'gentleman's agreements'. Moreover, the PAC should have the power to demand quarterly progress reports from relevant departments to see whether its proposals are being acted on or not. If the PAC finds that department heads are continually ignoring its recommendations, it should have the power to formally reprimand them. Two reprimands should automatically result in immediate dismissal with loss of pension rights. This might help department heads understand they are paid by the taxpayer to serve the taxpayer (as represented by the MPs on the PAC) and are not owed a generous living because they happen to be part of a self-supporting, self-perpetuating old boys' (and girls') network.

As for Identity Cards – drop the scheme as soon as possible. Identity Cards may or may not be a good idea. They may or may not help protect us from our enemies. They may or may not contribute to reducing fraud and other forms of criminality. I wouldn't know. However, what I do know is that any Identity Cards programme run by a thoroughly dishonest New Labour government, managed by demonstrably incompetent civil servants and implemented by unaccountable consultants will be an unbelievably expensive disaster. With clear goals and effective management, using small specialist suppliers and the right low key, low cost iterative development approach,

Identity Cards could probably be successfully deployed for quite a modest budget – but this would not be possible with the current New Labour administration and its ever hungry consulting friends in charge.

PFI should be dropped. Why pay £700m for a PFI hospital when a publicly commissioned one could be built for £500m saving £200m by cutting expensive consulting and finance as well as massive profits for the PFI companies? As for using PFI and PPP techniques in education, defence, prisons and policing – these should be abandoned immediately and responsibility for improving these essential services should be given back to those with a public service, rather than a profit, motivation.

Push Out the Pen-Pushers

It is an unfortunate fact of life that organizations with highly effective, visionary leadership tend to make limited use of consultants, whereas organizations with management that are weak, divided among themselves or out of their depth use large amounts of consulting and often seem to become dependent on their consultants.

Perhaps one of the biggest mistakes made by New Labour was to allow government departments to spend vast sums of our money on consultants while the government made no effort at all to improve the quality of leadership in those departments. You can spend as much as you want on consulting, but if an organization is hopelessly led by over-promoted, incompetent, time-serving, back-covering bureaucrats, most of it will be wasted. There is a small group of business leaders in Britain who have demonstrated throughout their careers an ability to turn failing organizations around by providing clear direction, leadership, motivation and a sense of purpose. Had the government installed some of these real leaders at the head of its major spending departments before it began its £70bn consultancy spending spree, we might not have seen the catastrophic waste of money that we are now witnessing. Until we have real leaders taking over the management of government departments, billions more will be carried off by consultants while providing precious little in return.

Managing Consultants

Fees rates for all consultants working for government should be cut by 30 per cent with immediate effect. In addition, at least a third of all consultancy projects should be cancelled. The contracts of all remaining consultancy projects should be reviewed to ensure that the full legal obligations of the consultants are clearly identified, agreed and enforced. Notification of breaches of contract by consultants should be formally issued to any consultancy found not to be delivering on its initial promises. In particular, all outsourcing contracts and proposals should be reviewed centrally to establish whether they really are in the public interest. It is far too easy for consultants to fool naïve and inexperienced government departments and local councils into signing up to multi-year outsourcing contracts that place few real performance obligations on the suppliers and can only be broken off at huge expense to the taxpayer. As I recommend above, the Treasury under a new Chancellor should probably take responsibility for implementing these measures.

Of course, the consultancies will claim that reductions in their fees and cancellation of some projects represent blatant breach of contract and they will threaten the government with legal action at these attacks on the industry's integrity and profitability. The prospect of Serious Fraud Squad investigations of consultancies' charging practices and expense billing should take a little wind out of the threats of some of the consultancies. Moreover, the government should offer whistleblowing rewards to any consultant who provides evidence of dishonest or fraudulent business practices by any consultancy. At the same time, the government should establish a criminal offence of 'complicity to defraud public funds' which can be used against any consultant found either participating in or trying to cover up the abuse of public funds. The prospect of fines and prison sentences should help build consultants' awareness of the personal risks of acquiescing too readily to their employers' unscrupulous practices.

Consultancy partners and consultants need to understand very clearly that there are moral and legal differences between siphoning off money from private-sector companies and taking billions from public services. Only by the draconian application of measures such as those I propose here will consultancy partners get the message that the public-sector feeding frenzy is over – and that it may even be time to pay back some of the billions they have misappropriated. After a lot of heat and energy has been expended in outraged protestations of innocence as the consultants try to bluff their way out of the mess of their own making, these actions should produce a consultancy industry that is more interested in finding new cooperative ways of working with government and is less inclined to try and fight its way out of the corner into which its own amoral business practices have driven it.

New committees and parliamentary enquiries, and a more active Treasury under a new Chancellor, may have a limited role to play in curbing the plundering of public funds by the consultancies. But of all the possible measures to control the excesses of the consultancies, the most effective would be the whistleblowers' Act with *qui tam* provisions. As events in the US have indicated, the consultancies' greed can only be tamed by their fear of exposure by their own staff and their fear of the consequences of that exposure.

Connecting for Health (CfH)

If *Choose and Book* is still not working, it should be put on hold for a few years and the money from the programme fed back into front-line patient care. An investigation should be conducted into the suppliers, Atos Origin, to understand if they are in any way responsible for either the delays or cost increases. If they are, the government should seek full compensation, which should also go straight back into patient care.

We should probably stop the CfH programme in its present form and cancel all the contracts with the Local Service

Providers as they are against the public interest. Here, of course, there will also be much bluff and bluster from the consultancies and threats of legal action for breach of contract. But measures like whistleblowing rewards and the threat of investigations into whether they have defrauded public funds or have been complicit in doing so, and the possibility of subsequent prosecutions should help some of the consultancies understand that their longer-term interests lie in cooperation with government rather than confrontation. The only CfH consultancy contracts that should be kept should be those for routine maintenance of existing systems.

The board of CfH should all be removed and replaced – they have too much personal capital invested in the way the programme is currently being run to accept that it should be radically changed. CfH is so critical for the country that it should be treated as an issue of national importance rather than risking becoming a massive profiteering opportunity for just four huge companies. In the same way as we create a government of national unity in times of emergency, we need to transcend the interests of one party and four big companies and run CfH for the public and not for a few New Labour politicians and their consultants. A cross-party programme board of MPs should be set up. They should be allocated a sum of money – say £5bn. They should then invite the smaller and medium-sized specialist medical systems suppliers to form a consortium to propose how the useful elements of CfH can be implemented in a tactical, low cost way rather than the current high cost juggernaut approach. Re-use of existing technology, interoperability, distributed databases and market competition should be the guiding principles rather than unnecessary reinvention, monolithic uniformity, centralized databases and monopolistic market control. The elements that should be implemented are electronic patient records, electronic prescriptions, electronic imaging and cost and management information.

We should set up a project management board made up mainly of clinicians representing the main groups of hospitals. Moreover, the useful systems should be developed at just a couple of test locations using an iterative prototyping development approach. Once the project management board was satisfied with the systems' effectiveness and robustness, they could be rolled out to other locations. We will probably find that this approach will give us a fully implemented CfH in a greatly accelerated time-frame for less than £5bn for the whole NHS, rather than the over £30bn that the existing approach will cost. This will get us back to the kind of figures that were mooted when the programme was originally launched. Moreover, rather than just enriching four already massive IT consultancies, this encouragement of many smaller companies to create a competitive market for medical IT systems will probably result in Britain developing a world-beating medical systems industry with massive export potential as other countries also inevitably move to improve the use of technology in their health services over the next few years.

An axe should be taken to NHS administration. The government should pass a law requiring non-medical and non-cleaning staff expenses in hospitals not to exceed say 10 per cent of overall staff costs by the end of 2006, 8 per cent by the end of 2007 and 7 per cent by the end of 2008. Any hospital breaching these targets should be found to be committing an offence of wasting public funds and the chief executive should be barred from any form of employment in the public sector for five years. Any employee reporting management fiddling the figures should be rewarded with a percentage of the savings made after the employee's reporting of the incident and the hospital chief executive should be automatically dismissed with loss of pension rights. Moreover, any communication departments or marketing departments should be closed, the people fired and the budgets returned to front-line care. If hospitals have something important to say, the clinical staff are probably quite capable of saying it.

Hospital cleaning should be brought back in-house with cleaning staff employed by the NHS and made to feel they are an important and integral part of a team providing safe medical and care services for the sick, rather than being easily disposable low cost labour for profit-maximizing outsourcing companies. This measure alone will probably lead to a halving of the annual 600,000 plus hospital-acquired infections and of the 5,000 plus deaths from hospital-acquired infections. The money to pay for the employment of hospital cleaners as NHS employees could come from the money saved from reducing hospital administration costs to the levels proposed above and from the savings from an almost immediate reduction in levels of hospital acquired infections. This new policy could be piloted in four or five hospitals and, when it is found to be at least self-funding (and probably generating a cash surplus that could go back into patient care), rapidly rolled out across the whole NHS.

A Lesson for Other Countries

Through their dogmatism, dishonesty, naivety, self-interest and incompetence, New Labour have created a national emergency that is costing more money and ruining more lives than other more headline-grabbing disasters like the Iraq War. To treat the possible waste of £70bn of taxpayers' money, the desecration of our public services, the plundering of a cash-starved NHS as anything but a national emergency is to fail to understand the scale of what is happening in this country. Moreover, New Labour and their consultants are not yet finished with bringing the 'benefits of competition' to the public sector. After health, education is the next lucrative target for the 'modernizers' with their ideas of competition, private-sector management and massive IT systems.

The unfolding tragedy could theoretically be stopped. But that would require the Labour Party to do a *mea culpa*, accept that major errors have been made, change its leadership and work with the other political parties to salvage what can be saved from the wreckage by implementing some of the measures proposed in this chapter. It would require the recognition that, despite all the faults of the British public services, there is such a thing as a 'public service work ethic' and that this is quite different from the private-sector profit motive. We must understand that health, education, defence, policing, prisons and social services are too important in a modern democratic society to be handed over to organizations that only have a goal of profit maximization regardless of human costs. Of course the public sector can and should learn better management techniques from private-sector companies. But they should learn from, not be taken over by, the private sector. By introducing so-called 'competition' into essential public services, New Labour has destabilized the workforce, vastly increased administration and given their consultancy friends free rein for the wholesale plundering of taxpayers' money. Irreparable damage is being done as the already wealthy become even wealthier. If we are to get off this road to hell, we must give public services back to those with a public service ethic and take them away from those whose only interests are their own profits and bonuses.

Above all, we need the New Labour government to confront its current consultancy bedfellows and put the interests of the electorate over those of the unelected. I think we all know the likelihood of that ever happening.

All the proposals I have made in this chapter have been enjoyable speculation. But they are mere daydreaming – too much of our money has been squandered on worthless and incompetently managed political posturing for the government to be able turn back or even slightly course correct. What happened under Lord Birt and McKinsey at the BBC and under PwC and McKinsey at the MoD is now being replicated across the public sector. The results have been thoroughly harmful so far – they will be disastrous by the time the consultants have finished their feeding frenzy.

But maybe this book can serve as a warning to governments in other countries and particularly in the developing countries, where the massive plundering of public funds on the scale of what is happening in Britain would have an even more catastrophic effect on the lives of hundreds of millions. When the consultancies have fed on the British public sector and most of the meat has been torn from the carcass and devoured, work in the British public sector will inevitably decline and the consultancies will be looking for new opportunities. Already consultants are moving into the Third World to sell ideas that are now well past their sell-by date here. As one consultant commented in a recent book, 'if you look under the cover today, you'll see western consulting firms selling more services in the developing world where ideas that have peaked here are still new.'[5] And there have been several instances of New Labour politicians making presentations to government departments in countries like Turkey and South Africa in support of British consultancies' efforts to move into managing these countries' public services, using the type of 'partnerships' that have become so disastrously widespread in Britain under New Labour.

If they are to avoid a similar fate to Britain's, other European countries and developing countries should learn the lessons from Britain and they should learn them well. The relationship between public services delivery and private-sector profit-focused companies needs to be much more tightly controlled than it has been here. And the controls put on the behaviour of the profit-maximizing consultants need to be well established before the consultancies are allowed into public services. Moreover, these controls need to backed up by the legal threat of fines and imprisonment for any individuals found to be profiteering and fraudulently abusing public funds. So when the consultants come calling with their promises of 'modernization' and 'partnerships' and 'choice', other governments will have the safeguards in place to curb the consultants' predatory behaviour. Other governments must understand the huge differences between what the consultancies say they will do and what they actually do. And when the consultants talk of achieving clearly measurable benefits for a fixed price, other countries should review the British experience to try and find out whether the promised benefits were ever achieved and why there are always such enormous differences between the prices quoted by the consultancies and the huge sums they managed to extract from their naïve public-sector clients. The message for other countries is, 'please, *caveat emptor* [buyer beware!] – for the sake of your public services do not be taken in as easily and as thoroughly as Blair's and Brown's New Labour have been.'

Notes

1 The Government Goes Consulting Crazy

1 PAC report: *Improving the Delivery of Government IT Projects*
2 www.theregister.co.uk 31 May 2005
3 www.top-consultant.com 29 April 2005
4 Management Consultancies Association 2005 quoted in *The Times* 10 May 2005
5 The Business Column Seven 15 January 2006
6 *Daily Mail* 17 January 2006
7 www.theregister.co.uk 22 June 2004
8 *Sunday Times* 15 May 2005
9 www.theregister.co.uk 26 April 2004
10 *Child Support Reform: The views and experiences of CSA staff and new clients*, Bristol University
11 www.theregister.co.uk 12 April 2005
12 Work and Pension Committee press notice 26 January 2005
13 www.scotlibdems.org.uk/press/404141.htm
14 *Guardian* 18 November 2004
15 BBC Radio 4 *Inside Money* 28 July 2003
16 Treasury Select Committee 23 July 2003
17 Yahoo news 22 June 2005
18 www.theregister.co.uk 22 June 2005
19 *The Times* 24 June 2005
20 NAO Report on Inland Revenue Accounts 10 October 2005
21 Citizens Advice Bureau Press Release 24 January 2005
22 Yahoo news 22 June 2005 and *The Times* 23 June 2005
23 *The Times* 24 June 2005
24 ibid.
25 *The Times* 18 January 2006
26 *Sunday Times* 29 January 2006 and BBC News 2 February 2006

27 www.theregister.co.uk 19 October 2005
28 Toppin and Czerniawska, *Business Consulting*, Economist Books 2005
29 ibid.
30 www.amazon.co.uk 6 February 2006 about *Business Consulting* by Toppin and Czerniawska
31 Treasury press release 12 July 2004
32 ibid.
33 *The Times* 21 June 2005
34 *Evening Standard* 23 May 2005
35 ibid.
36 ibid.
37 *Computing* 27 April 2005
38 House of Lords Committee on Science and Technology 13 March 2003
39 *Sunday Telegraph* 31 July 2005
40 Answer to question from the author November 2005
41 PAC oral evidence *Improving Patient Care by Reducing the Risk of Hospital Acquired Infection*
42 *The Times* 19 January 2006

2 The Takeover

1 Paul Foot, 'Medes and Persians', *London Review of Books* 2 November 2000
2 Tom Bower, *Gordon Brown*, Harper Collins 2004
3 *Sunday Times* 24 November 1996
4 ibid.
5 ibid.
6 BBC News website 13 March 2001
7 *Accountancy Age* 21 November 1997
8 *Accountancy Age* 12 March 1998
9 NAO report NIRS2
10 Hansard written answers for 15 March 2000
11 Management Consultancies Association annual reports
12 Hansard 9 June 2005 Column 681W
13 MCA surveys
14 Hansard 20 January 1994 column 1118
15 In a telephone conversation with the author
16 *Guardian* 12 July 2004.
17 *The Times* 26 September 2005
18 'Accounting in Crisis', *Business Week* online 29 January 2002
19 Brand Media plc survey 2000
20 See, for example, *Private Eye* 1138 August 2005
21 *Private Eye* 1106 May 2004
22 Press Association 23 March 2000
23 *Guardian* 1 July 2002
24 'Race to the bottom' Jim Cousins, Austin Mitchell, Prem Sikka (2004) citing Joseph Stiglitz

25 *The Sink*, Jeffrey Robinson, Constable and Robinson, 2004
26 *Sunday Times* 4 September 2005
27 Parliamentary Treasury sub-committee 11 December 2002
28 FSA press release 28 January 2004
29 *Private Eye* 1100 March 2004
30 National Audit Office Report *Were they good deals?* 14 June 2004
31 PAC report 31 March 2005
32 Defence Analytical Services Agency report 2002
33 PAC Major Defence Projects report 13 October 2005
34 Hansard 17 November 2005 column 1399W
35 *Private Eye* 1045 January 2002
36 PAC press notice 28 October 2004
37 www.capitaconsulting.co.uk/clientcasestudies/NetRai.html
38 Unison, 'The business of education' July 2005
39 'Prisoner Undercover – the Real Story', BBC1 9 March 2005
40 Howard League for Penal Reform report 22 August 2002
41 *The Times* 19 September 2005
42 *The Times* 26 September 2005
43 *Private Eye* 1136 July 2005
44 *Consulting Times* April 2005
45 Hansard 20 July 2005 column 1806W
46 BBC News website 26 November 2004
47 *Daily Record* 27 November 2004
48 *Guardian* 24 August 2005
49 Reply to request under the Freedom of Information Act by the author
50 ibid.
51 Response to Freedom of Information requests by author, January 2006
52 Hansard 12 September 2005
53 *Daily Mail* 30 January 2002
54 Cabinet Office website
55 *Sunday Times Magazine* 17 April 2005
56 *The Independent* 11 February 2005
57 *The Times* 11 June 2005
58 *Guardian* 18 March 2005
59 *Sunday Times* 15 May 2005
60 David Hencke, *Guardian* 13 June 2005
61 Hansard, 21 July 2005 column WA294
62 ibid.
63 *Private Eye* 1137 July 2005
64 *Guardian* 14 July 2005
65 *Private Eye* 23 December 2005–5 January 2006

3 Defending the Indefensible

1 *Private Eye* 19 August–1 September 2005
2 PwC website 2005
3 McKinsey website 2005

4 MoD Annual Report and Accounts 2003/4
5 Oral evidence PAC 26th Report of session 2004–5
6 PAC MoD: Major Projects Report 2004
7 ibid.
8 NAO MoD Major Projects Report 2004
9 PAC MoD Major Projects Report 2004
10 ibid.
11 ibid.
12 Uncorrected transcript of oral evidence MoD Major Projects Report 2004
13 *Lions, Donkeys and Dinosaurs*, Lewis Page, Heinemann 2006
14 Defence Committee *Future Carrier and Joint Combat Aircraft* December 2005
15 *Management Consultancy* 11 February 1999
16 Uncorrected transcript of oral evidence MoD Major Projects Report 2004
17 ibid.
18 ibid.
19 ibid.
20 ibid.
21 MoD Annual Report 2003/2004
22 ibid.
23 PAC MoD Major Projects Report 2004
24 PAC 26th report of session 2004–5
25 News.yahoo.com 13 October 2005 and *Lions, Donkeys and Dinosaurs*
26 Uncorrected transcript of oral evidence MoD Major Projects Report 2004
27 *Lions, Donkeys and Dinosaurs*, page 47
28 *Sunday Times* 23 October 2005
29 ibid.
30 *Sunday Times* 23 October 2005 and 30 October 2005
31 *Sunday Times* 30 October 2005
32 ibid.
33 *Metro* 9 November 2005
34 See *Management Consultancy* 11 February 1999 and PwC website
35 PAC 13th report *MoD Progress in Reducing Stocks* June 2002
36 Uncorrected transcript of oral evidence MoD Major Projects Report 2004
37 ibid.
38 ibid.
39 ibid.
40 ibid.

4   Is Anybody Responsible?

1 PAC *Impact of the Office of Government Commerce's initiative on the delivery of major IT-enabled projects* 26th report of the session 2004–5
2 www.e-health-insider 26 January 2006

3 ibid.
4 *Impact of the Office of Government Commerce's Initiative on the Delivery of Major IT-Enabled Projects*, PAC 26th report of the session 2004–5
5 ibid.
6 ibid.
7 ibid.
8 PAC report *GCHQ: New Accommodation Programme* 2003–4.
9 ibid.
10 ibid.
11 PAC report Criminal Records Bureau 2002
12 ibid.
13 PAC report MRSA 2004
14 ibid.
15 ibid.
16 ibid.
17 ibid.
18 ibid.
19 PAC *Impact of the Office of Government Commerce's Initiative on the Delivery of Major IT-Enabled Projects*: 26th report of the session 2004–5
20 ibid.
21 ibid.
22 ibid.
23 ibid.
24 www.ogc.gov.uk/index.asp?id=1004312
25 Letter from David Varney to Select Committee chairmen 22 November 2005 House of Lords Library
26 *The Times* 26 September 2005
27 PAC report Criminal Records Bureau
28 Answer to parliamentary question from Austin Mitchell MP
29 MCA 2004/5 survey
30 *Private Eye* 1144 October 2005
31 PAC 3 December 2003

5   The Money Machine

1 *Accountancy Age* 8 July 2005
2 PAC *NIRS2 Contract Extension* December 2001
3 *Sunday Times* 22 January 2006
4 *Washington Post* 27 September 2003
5 *Wall Street Journal* 26 September 2003
6 *Washington Post* 4 January 2006
7 TSCPA and Accounting Web 8 March 2004
8 'Fraud Updates' www.trinity.edu 30 September 2003
9 *Washington Post* 4 January 2006
10 Email 19 September 2003 www.thevault.com
11 Email May 2005, details passed to the SFO

12 Memo to all staff 14 May 1993
13 *The Health Service Journal*
14 www.deloitte-ouch.com
15 Community www.thevault.com
16 Management Consultancies Association Report 2004/5
17 *The Times* 7 August 2002
18 www.theregister.co.uk 27 August 2005
19 'Masters of the Universe' ITV
20 *Guardian* 24 November 2005
21 *The Times* 23 January 2006
22 Datamonitor 14 April 2004
23 www.theregister.co.uk 14 April 2005
24 *Rip-Off!* David Craig, Original Book Company 2005
25 Community www.thevault.com
26 *The Times* 26 April 2005

6   Adding Value or Cost?

1 Tom Bower, *Gordon Brown*, p.445, Harper Collins 2004
2 MCA Surveys 1996/7 and 2003/4
3 *The Times* 25 May 2005
4 *Sunday Times* 13 November 2005
5 *The Times* 17 November 2005
6 *The Times* 20 January 2006
7 *The Times* 17 January 2005
8 *Sunday Times* 6 December 1998
9 PAC GCHQ *New Accommodation Programme* 2003/4
10 *Fast Company*, 58, May 2002
11 Community www.thevault.com
12 ibid.
13 www.theregister.co.uk 30 October 2005
14 *Punch* 16–19 June 2001
15 *Business Age* June 1995
16 *Mail on Sunday* 4 November 2001
17 *Sunday Times* 22 January 2006
18 The Standish Group Chaos Report 2001
19 *The Times* 9 November 2005
20 Client interview (contact author for details)
21 Anthony Sampson, *Who runs this place?*, John Murray 2005
22 community www.thevault.com
23 PAC *Improving the of Delivery of Government* IT Projects
24 www.top-consultant.com 13 April 2005
25 Management Consultancies Association awards 2005
26 *Evening Standard* 4 July 2005
27 *Private Eye* August 2005

7 PFI Paradise

1 'P.F.Eye', *Private Eye* special report by Paul Foot March 2004
2 The Private Finance Initiative, House of Commons research paper 01/117
3 www.hm-treasury.gov.uk/media/D90/70/PFI_signed projects_dec04.xls
4 Pre-Budget Report November 1997
5 *Financial Times* 11 January 1997
6 Hansard 12 March 1996, column 827
7 HM Treasury pre-budget report December 2005 table B25
8 www.dh.gov.uk/Root/04/12/35/73/04123573.pdf
9 MoD press release 12 December 2005
10 see Building Schools for the Future website
11 Public Private Finance website league tables
12 www-unison.org.uk/pfi/caseagainst.asp
13 Major Contractors' Group press release 9 September 2005
14 HM Treasury press release 22 September 1997
15 ibid.
16 Treasury Taskforce technical note 5 'How to construct a public sector comparator'
17 Treasury Taskforce technical note 3 'How to appoint and manage advisers to PFI projects'
18 Treasury PFI statistics, table of signed deals
19 Unison, 'How the big 5 accountancy firms influence and profit from privatization policy', June 2002
20 Declan Gaffney and Allyson Pollock, 'Pump-priming the PFI: why are privately financed hospital schemes being subsidized?' *Public Money and Management* January–March 1999
21 Department of Health memorandum to Health Committee 2000
22 House of Commons research paper 01/117 *The private finance initiative* December 2001
23 PAC hearing
24 Unison 'A web of private interest: how the big 5 accountancy firms influence and profit from privatization policy', July 2002
25 Edwards, Shaoul, Stafford & Arblaster for the ACCA 2004
26 *Guardian* 22 January 2003
27 George Monbiot, 'Our very own Enron?', *Guardian* 28 June 2005
28 National Audit Office report November 2002
29 ibid.
30 *Observer* 24 July 2004
31 BBC News website 30 July 2001
32 BBC News website 3 September 2001
33 P.F.Eye - a *Private Eye* special report, 1102 March 2004
34 Letter to *Guardian* from Richard Taylor MP 19 November 2005
35 Audit Commission report 'PFI in Schools' 16 January 2003
36 NAO report June 2003
37 'Paying the cost? PPP and the public service workforce', Sanjiv Sachdev, June 2004
38 Arthur Andersen and Enterprise LSE, 'Value for money drivers in PFI',

17 January 2000
39 Centre for Public Services, 'What future for public services?'; Unison 'A web of private interest'; Dr Chris Edwards, University of East Anglia 'The private finance initiative and value for money'
40 Treasury speeches index 2003
41 *Public Service Magazine,* Winter 2001 issue
42 Hansard 30 January 2002 column 286
43 Department of Health statistics 14 December 2005
44 ibid.
45 Pollock and Gaffney, 'Pump-priming the PFI, Public Money and Management' Jan–March 1999
46 *Guardian* 16 December 2005
47 Monitor press release 16 December 2005
48 Anthony Sampson, *Who runs this place?,* John Murray 2005
49 www.healthdirect.co.uk 28 October 2005
50 Chartered Institute of Management Accountants NHS conference 1 June 2005
51 *Private Eye* 1147, December 2005 and *Financial Times* 19 January 2006
52 *Financial Times* 27 January 2006
53 www.hm-treasury.gov.uk/media/D90/70/PFI_signedprojects_dec04.xls
54 HM Treasury pre-budget report December 2005 table B25
55 HM Treasury pre-budget report December 2005 table B24
56 *Private Eye* 1150 January 2006
57 *Private Eye* 1148 December 2005
58 BBC *Today* programme 1 October 2002, quoted in 'How the big four firms have PFI under their thumbs' Unison January 2003
59 *Guardian* 4 February 2002

8   Revolving Doors

1 Prime Minister's speech to CBI 11 November 1997, quoted in George Monbiot's *Captive State*
2 Hansard 7 May 2003 column 723W
3 Speech to Lib Dem party conference reported in *Guardian Unlimited* 25 September 2002
4 www.hm-treasury.gov.uk/about/about_secondee.cfm and Hansard 21 July 2005, column WA272
5 Hansard 12 May 2003 column 45W
6 Treasury press notice 8 August 1999, announcements 17 April, 17 May, 15 September 2000
7 *The Times,* 26 June 2005
8 *Private Eye* 1133 May 2005
9 www.number-10.gov.uk Prime Minister's speeches 24 February 2004
10 *Public Service Magazine* FDA July 2005
11 www.networks.nhs.uk/uploads/2005_Aug/Creating_Patient_Led_NHS_Commissioning.ppt#4
12 Cabinet Office spokesman quoted in *Financial Times* 26 November

2005
13 BBC News Online 15 December 2005

9   We've Seen it All Before

1 PAC report on Libra
2 PAC report *Improving the Delivery of Government IT Projects*
3 *Computer Weekly* September to November 2004
4 PAC report *The Passport Delays of Summer 1999*
5 PAC report *Criminal Records Bureau* May 2002

10   Welcome to *Connecting for Health*

1 *Daily Telegraph* 30 October 2004, *Accountancy Age* 17 November 2004, www.theregister.co.uk 12 October 2004
2 www.top-consultant.com 16 June 2004 quoting British Computer Society estimates
3 House of Lords Committee on Science and Technology 13 March 2003
4 *The Times* 8 February 2006
5 *Computer Weekly* as reported on www.theregister.co.uk 12 October 2004
6 *Independent* 21 November 2005
7 *The Times* 2 December 2005
8 *The Times* 23 November 2005
9 *Computer Weekly* 17 January 2005
10 www.e-health-insider.com 26 January 2006
11 *Sunday Times* 13 November 2005
12 ibid
13 PAC report *The 1992 and 1998 Information Management and Technology Strategies of the NHS Executive*
14 PAC report *Improving the Delivery of Government IT Projects*
15 *The Times* 14 October 2005
16 www.e-health-insider.com 14 October 2005
17 Society for Computers and Law 5th Annual Conference November 2005

11   Heading for Meltdown?

1 *Sunday Times* 6 November 2005
2 *The Times* 26 January 2006
3 *Computing* 26 March 2003
4 www.e-health-insider.com 8 November 2005
5 www.e-health-insider.com 26 April 2005
6 PAC report *Improving the Delivery of Government IT Projects*

7 *Connecting for Health* Business Plan 2005/6
8 House of Lords Select Committee on Science and Technology
9 *Guardian* 13 June 2005
10 *Health Reform in England*, Department of Health 13 December 2005
11 NHS *Connecting for Health* website 22 December 2005
12 www.e-health-insider.com 19 January 2006
13 PAC report *Patient Choice at the Point of GP Referral* October 2005
14 www.e-health-insider.com 1 November 2005
15 www.e-health-insider.com 1 December 2005
16 ibid.
17 *Private Eye* 16–19 September 2005
18 www.e-health-insider.com, 44, 30 November 2005
19 *Evening Standard* 15 November 2005
20 www.e-health-insider.com 19 January 2006
21 *The Times* 3 October 2005
22 www.ureader.co.uk 29 July 2005

12   The Unholy Trinity

1 House of Lords Select Committee on Science and Technology 13 March 2003
2 *The Times* 1 November 2005
3 *Management Consultancy* 24 August 2005
4 Eileen Shapiro, *Fad Surfing in the Boardroom*, Capstone 1996
5 Toppin and Czerniawska, *Business Consulting*, Economist 2005
6 www.top-consultant.com 5 July 2002
7 www.top-consultant.com 6 June 2005
8 www.top-consultant.com 10 October 2005
9 *Management Consultancy* 24 June 2005
10 www.telegraph.co.uk 2 May 2005
11 www.top-consultant.com 3 November 2005
12 www.e-health-insider.com, 186, 5 August 2005
13 *Executive Suite* 12 December 2005

13   What Do We Do Now?

1 www.taf.org 13 December 2005
2 ibid.
3 www.govexec.com 25 July 2005
4 ibid.
5 www.top-consultant.com 30 June 2005